Zero-sum Economics

$\Sigma\varnothing$

How to Fix Economics, Solve Poverty and Save the World! 2022

Steven McAtee

October 2022

<Copyright message>

Published by: Splat Concepts Australia 2022

All rights reserved

Cover Art by Agata Broncel
Bukovero - Book Cover Designer
bukovero.com
bukovero@gmail.com

"On my world, there are books, thousands of pages, about the power of one mind to change the Universe. But none say it as clearly as this."

Delenn (re: Japanese stone garden) in Babylon 5, played by Mira Furlan.

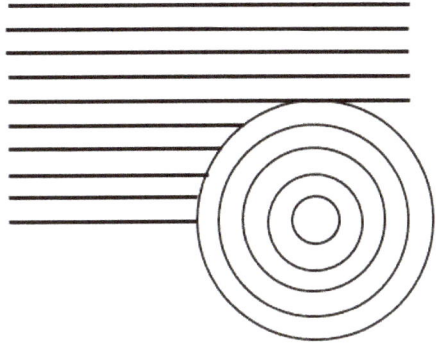

Cover art Description:
I wanted to have something funny. This is kind of a serious book, which is depressing.
I found an image of "Fortuna" a Greek goddess of fate. The wheel of fortune image which is from "The Noble Men's Book of Cases" or "des Cas des nobles hommes et femmes" by Jehan Boccace or Giovanni Boccaccio, (1313-1375) … I think!
https://gallica.bnf.fr/ark:/12148/btv1b10532640k/f7.item#
The wheel of fortune has broken and crushed Fortuna, along with other cartoon figures either crushed by the wheel or running from it. One other figure is on top of the wheel running away with the money. The idea is that a few people have broken the wheel and is attempting to run off with the money, while ignoring the damage done by the process.
The other features in the picture are the arrow chart representing "growth", green because "growth is good" even if it crushes everyone else.
Finally, the Sigma symbol is the symbol for sum in math and the broken wheel (a zero) represent "Zero sum".

Contents

Contents

Contents

Contents

Contents

Contents

Contents

Contents

1. Figures

Contents

Contents

Contents

Contents

Contents

Tables

Contents

Preface

Initially, as an Engineer, I was interested in developing a game like SimCity™ (Electronic Arts) and playing around with economics. It was fun, but not exactly a world-changing project. Then I started looking into economic theory. After a few months, I came to one conclusion: economics is incomplete and therefore ineffective at explaining what happens in the real world.

I have a Master's degree in engineering. What I am good at, as an engineer, is developing simulations. So, naturally, that's how I approached economics. The same mathematical techniques that are used for simulating the current and voltage in an electronic device, or the mechanics of a machine, were used in the research for this book.

The key constraint I followed was that money behaves in a zero-sum fashion throughout its flow through an economy, much in the way that energy and momentum are conserved in physics. This meant that money in an economy should behave like a physical entity within a physics or engineering simulation, and that I could create similar simulations for economics. With the zero-sum constraint, the simulations demonstrated phenomena occurring in the real world that economists find difficult to explain!

I had hoped to do a PhD on Zero-sum Economic Theory, but after speaking with economics professors at several major universities, I quickly concluded that the academic community would not accept a PhD thesis (or even a research paper) on this topic. I thought they might be interested in the idea itself, especially as the way I was doing this research actually included a method for stabilising the economy, and a method for getting prices to deflate … in theory at least. It was extremely disappointing, but not surprising. Professors are busy people, and radical change is not going to happen overnight.

Many said: "This is not how we look at economics. Go study economics, and then you can do it our way." While in general I agree with this idea, I see a problem with the way economics is taught and practised. Starting with the same body of data, economists frequently arrive at varied conclusions, which suggests there is a need to look at the subject in a new way—hence, this book!

On to plan B̶ C̶ D!

Write a book on the topic—it's not as formal an approach as a PhD thesis, and doesn't claim the same credibility, but it's a first step towards getting the idea into the public arena so people can start thinking along these lines. This book is somewhat like a thesis, having an academic style of writing supported by many references, calculations, formulae and diagrams. While it is not officially a university thesis, I have sought to maintain the quality of research required by a thesis.

As I commence writing, I have been looking at 'Zero-sum Economics' for over 2 years—collecting statistics, developing the theory, and writing software, i.e. conducting the dogged and potentially mind-numbing research that now allows my ideas to be presented formally.

I encourage the reader to persevere on the journey through the landscape of diagrams and mathematical formulae to be found within. Wherever possible, I have included complete mathematical derivations of the final formulae. It was important that I demonstrated that solid mathematics underpinned the major features of the theory, but if you don't have a maths background, you may prefer to skip the derivations and focus on the significance of the formulae in terms of the theory.

The book does not have to be read from front cover to back, but I recommend reading the Introduction first, as it explains the premise of the theory. Then, if you want to skip to the end and see how to stabilise the economy and solve poverty, go straight to Part III. I note that in doing so you would miss all the arguments supporting Zero-sum Economic Theory and the methodology of its applications, but if you do skip ahead, you can always refer back when necessary.

So why am I writing a book instead of doing an economics degree in the traditional way? It's very simple: this book concerns a theory that shows mathematically that it *is* possible to solve poverty and economic instability. This is not what mainstream economics teaches, but this book is for the broader community. In this arena, I can write a book without being restricted by what other people believe is relevant to economics. So far, the academic economics community has not come up with a theory that can solve poverty. I believe this theory does.

The main point of making a book is to get my idea out and have other people 'review' it. A PhD involves having your work 'peer reviewed', which is why a thesis has more credibility than a general literary book. If nothing else, I hope this book will create enough interest in the topic so that I (or someone else) can do a PhD and write some research papers on the subject. The outcome I hope for is that the ideas presented here will be formally introduced to the broader community. Peer review and acceptance by the academic community can come later.

It doesn't hurt me in any way to introduce these ideas to the public. The work I have done here is mathematically rigorous and should be able to stand up to scrutiny. Even if Zero-sum Theory is disproven, in the words of Edison, "I have not failed. I've just found 10,000 ways that won't work." All we need is one way that does solve poverty, and two to three billion people will have happier lives. If this book gives economists a few new ideas to work with in this quest, I'll be fine with that.

Best of luck!

Steve

Acknowledgements

Thanks to my Master's degree supervisors, Romesh and Michelle, who with patience and encouragement, guided me to completion of my thesis. They gave me the confidence to start this book.

Many thanks to Tonghua for assistance with the differential equations.

Thanks also to my awesome editor, Jeanette, for making the thousands of edits required to get this into print.

Acknowledgements

Overview

The purpose of this book is to present a new economic theory—a theory not currently used by economists, but one which I hope can be used to improve our understanding of how economic systems operate. For many economists, I suspect, a leap of faith will be required to be able to accept this theory.

My key observation is that the entire economy is limited by the zero-sum nature of monetary transactions. Many economic theories suggest that money is 'exogenous', i.e. the amount of money in the economy is determined by factors external to that economy. This creates the impression that money is not a determining factor in the general operation of an economy, and as a result, many economic theories entirely avoid examining the flow of money in an economy. In contrast, the Zero-sum Theory presented in this book is mainly concerned with the movement and distribution of money.

The main premise of a zero-sum system is that for any profit made by one entity in the system, there must be a corresponding loss somewhere else in the system. Many economists disagree with this idea. I have concluded, from my research, that most economists believe everyone should be able to have a reasonable standard of living as long as they are willing to work hard. Zero-sum Economics shows that even if everyone works hard, some or even most of the people involved will lose money and thus will not have the same opportunities and standard of living as those who profit from their enterprises.

It is something of an uphill battle to get this theory out in the world, simply because of the way economics is taught. Economists prefer to teach the theories that they already understand, and they generally attempt to avoid the use of complex calculus. Zero-sum Theory uses engineering-based analysis to examine the flow of money through an economy.

Part I of this book reviews historical and current economic theories, both microeconomic and macroeconomic, and compares them with the new Zero-sum Economic Theory. This provides a justification for the theoretical basis of the techniques used to explain the behaviour of economies.

Part II presents the mathematical theory for creating Zero-sum Economics simulations. These simulations are run with statistics collected from real-world economies (particularly those of the USA, Australia and Europe) and the results are analysed.

Part III demonstrates how to use the simulations to show how to stabilise the economy. Stabilising the economy would mean that the oscillations in economic performance caused by business cycles were minimised or eliminated. As a result, poverty could be eliminated or at least minimised, and it would also be possible for governments to fund any programs they found necessary.

Zero-sum Economic Theory highlights particular problems in economics. It is possible to show how these problems can be either addressed entirely or limited in effect. Previous economic theories have not been able to demonstrate a practical method for stabilising an economy or eliminating poverty. Although 'Zero-sum Economics' is at this stage a theory that requires further testing, I believe it represents a step forward for everyone.

Overview

PART I

Part I of this book introduces Zero-sum Economic Theory and compares it with historical economic theories, both microeconomic and macroeconomic. It then examines how these economic theories are used to explain various economic phenomena.

1   Introduction

Economics has been studied since the 1700s. We have made significant progress in our understanding of how money moves around an economy, and why people buy goods in the way they do. However, current economic theories have not explained important phenomena, including business cycles, some aspects of inflation, or the causes of wealth inequality. Furthermore, economists still do not understand how to effectively control an economy to enable 100% employment and to avoid poverty.

'Zero-sum Economic Theory', as developed in this book, focuses on the movement of money around an economy. It is easily shown that a single transaction of money is a zero-sum event. This means that, in the wider economy, any gain or profit made must be balanced by a corresponding loss of money elsewhere in the economy.

The overall purpose of this theory is to develop simulations consistent with existing measurements of economies. These simulations have been developed to show that various economic phenomena can be generated by assuming zero-sum conditions, and that in some cases the phenomena are actually caused by the zero-sum conditions. The objective is not necessarily to be able to make 'accurate' predictions, but to be able to generate system outputs consistent with the phenomena measured in the current economies. The simulations will not be able to make predictions about the stock market or individual companies. However, they can show how Zero-sum Theory can be used to predict various economic phenomena, using real economic statistics. These predictions can be compared with those obtained using other economic theories, thus showing where Zero-sum Theory is consistent with current theories and where it differs. The phenomena examined here include inflation, business cycles, wealth distribution, and global labour.

Introduction

The 'Circular Flow of Money Theory' is a current economic theory that shows how money flows internally in an economy. This is used as the basis for the Zero-sum Economic Models. The Circular Flow of Money Theory divides the economy into three main types of entities: 'Consumers', 'Producers' and 'Governments'. In Zero-sum Models, these entities interact with one another in specific ways that can be modelled mathematically. By directly analysing the Consumer–Producer (CP) Model, a mathematical function for inflation can be derived that is consistent with real-life data. From the relationship between Consumers and Producers, business cycles can be predicted and examined: by considering the profits made by Producers, and creating a model for investment, it is possible to demonstrate how a Zero-sum Model can produce regularly occurring business cycles.

The distribution of money directly influences what is called 'aggregate demand' in economics. Consumers can be thought of collectively, i.e. as an aggregate, and the amount of money they have is a limit on what they are able to spend (their demand). By considering a range of Consumers (with differing income levels) and Producers, it is shown here how wealth distributions occur. Finally, by considering the differences in the cost of living between countries, it is possible to explain how global labour markets occur.

What I am finding is that we have two systems that operate together but have different properties. The Production trade side in "Non-Zero-Sum" but the underlying monetary system is "Zero-Sum" as shown in Figure 1.

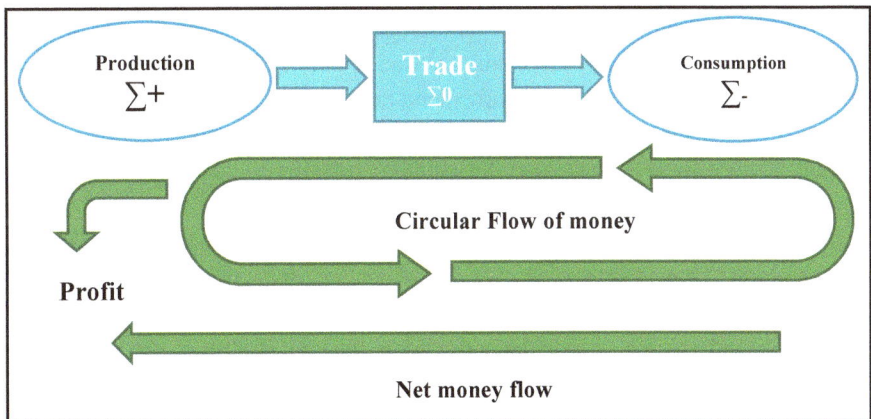

Figure 1: Inherent problem in the Economy

What happens is the money system since it is zero sum builds up money leaving less available to cycle through the system. **The conflict in the inherent nature of the two systems results in recessions that are artificially induced by a lack of money directly not a lack of productivity.**

A range of Zero-sum Models are further developed and analysed in Part II of this book. They are then employed to numerically demonstrate the various phenomena, using real historical data from the USA and Australia. Through this process, it has emerged that the predictions generated by these models (i.e. Zero-sum Economics Models) are consistent with observations of real-world economies.

Part III of this book describes how to modify the economy to create the potential for negative inflation, maximised employment and minimised poverty.

1.1   What is a 'Zero-sum Economy'?

What is a zero-sum game? A zero-sum game is

"A game in which the sum of the winnings and losses of the various players is always zero, the losses being counted negatively."

(Collins English Dictionary – Complete & Unabridged 10th Edition) [1]

The most basic component of Zero-sum Economic Theory is the idea of a zero-sum game. In such a game, involving a closed group of people ('the Players'), the winnings of one Player must correspond to the total losses of all the other Players. This is apparently a very difficult concept for some economists to accept, as they do not believe that the economy operates as a zero-sum game.

Poker is a game with which most people are familiar. All the players put money into the 'pot'. They draw a set of five cards each, and the winner is whoever has the set of cards with the highest value. Let's say everyone puts in $100 at the beginning, and one player gets the entire pot at the end. With four players, the pot is worth $400. This means that four players lose $100 at the start (–$400) and one player wins $400 at the end (+$400). All up … –$400 initially, +$400 at the end. Hence, the changes in states 'sum to zero'. Poker is just one example of a 'zero-sum game'.

Introduction

People don't usually like to think of their entire lives as a game, so I describe the economy as a 'zero-sum system' rather than a game. The difference between a system and a game is really just a matter of perception. Systems have components; games have players. In a game, the 'final decision' about who wins is the important part. In a system, the important thing is usually the work that gets done.

The way a system operates can be zero sum, especially if it is a 'closed system'. An 'open system' has external inputs and/or outputs through which the control variable (money in an economy) can be generated or lost. A car that uses fuel is an example of an open system. Fuel from the fuel tank is pumped into the engine, which explosively combines it with air to produce torque in the engine. Waste products (carbon dioxide and water) are expelled from the exhaust. Fuel is consumed and is ultimately removed from the system by the operation of the engine, and it takes manual operation to add fuel back into the car so that it keeps working. In an open system, something needs to be continually added to the system; in keeping with conservation of energy and mass, something will always be output. In the car example, the input is the fuel. The outputs include both the carbon dioxide and the torque.

A 'closed system' is something that does not have any external inputs or outputs. Returning to the analogy of the car, the oil is effectively in a closed system. Oil is pumped around the car's engine to reduce friction inside the engine, then gathers in the sump. You still need to refill the oil and replace the filter occasionally, but on a day-to-day basis a well-maintained car should use significantly less oil than it does fuel.

Back to economics! It was said by Carl Sagan, when looking at images of earth from the Voyager probes,

Look again at that dot. That's here. That's home. That's us. <u>On it everyone you love, everyone you know, everyone you ever heard of, every human being who ever was, lived out their lives</u>. The aggregate of our joy and suffering, thousands of confident religions, ideologies, and <u>economic doctrines</u>, every hunter and forager, every hero and coward, every creator and destroyer of civilization, every king and peasant, every young couple in love, every mother and father, hopeful child, inventor and explorer, every teacher of morals, every corrupt politician, every 'superstar,' every 'supreme leader,' every saint and sinner in the history of our species lived there—on a mote of dust suspended in a sunbeam.

C. Sagan and A. Druyan, *Pale Blue Dot: A Vision of the Human Future in Space.* [2]

[I wanted to include Sagan's 'pale blue dot' quote. It's cool! And I like space exploration.]

Sagan's view of earth would suggest that the global economy is a closed system: all economic activity occurs in a single space, i.e. on Earth; therefore, whatever is happening in the economy must be happening in a closed system. A complete proof, however, requires us to think about how an economy operates. There are aspects of economies, of course, that are not zero-sum limited. Nevertheless, a definition of what a Zero-sum Economy is would be:

A Zero-sum Economy is an economy in which the flow of goods is limited by zero-sum conditions.

The flow of goods in all of the current world economy is limited by money. In this book it is demonstrated that money does indeed operate under the limitation of zero sum—this can be observed simply by looking at what happens in a single transaction. Many economists, however, do not believe economies are zero sum, because the *value of commodities* can change arbitrarily.

1.2 Theories of Value

One problem I have with this is the idea of value itself. Even economists have several different theories of value including: Subjective, Cost, and Inherent value theories, among others. The more modern Marshallian value system was created to explain the problem of water vs diamonds. Water is a cheap product that is common and needed by all people for their survival. Diamonds are expensive and not needed for anyone's survival. Marshal explained that the more of a product we have the less we value it or conversely the more rare something is the more expensive it will become, in many cases irrespective of other even inherent value systems. This value system creates the basis for Supply vs Demand analysis, which interestingly enough, seems to work.

So, let's take a look at this in detail. We can consider a few different products and what happens when they become rare or more common.

- When Food becomes more common people can only eat so much of it so after a point it becomes wasteful, so it makes sense that the value would decrease. When food becomes rare people need it so it can become extremely expensive.
- Cars when common can become more of a burden as they have significant maintenance costs (fuel, insurance etc.)
- Land becomes more valuable the more one person has as it can become more productive. When land becomes rare to purchase the price and hence the value goes up.
- Shares Are similar to land in that the more one person owns the more they own of a company, hence the more valuable they become. Also the less shares that are available for trade the more expensive they become.

So Many products become cheaper the more they have due to inherent reasons, food that can't be eaten goes off, maintenance costs increase with cars. However, some products such as shares or land increase in value when a person own more of them. Conversely, most products become more expensive when rare.

The idea that available resources (money can be used) to generate demand is explored in section 4.6. This shows that income or savings distribution can be used to generate a demand curve that is very similar to the behaviour of Marshallian demand. The point being that there may be several ways of getting to an inverse relationship between quantity and price that we see in the economy, not simply that the value of the product itself.

1.3   Money and value

The main difference between Zero-sum Economics and earlier economic theories is that the previous theories assume that trade is non-zero sum (because the value of the products traded is perceived to increase when they are traded). Take, for example, a farmer who sells his crop for money. When the farmer has excess crop (i.e. he doesn't want to eat it all himself), the standard economic theory says that he values the crop lower than someone else might value it (for example, a baker who could use the crop to make bread to sell on to his customers). Alternatively, the baker can determine the value of the crop by considering how much he would have to sell his baked goods for in order to make a profit.

The problem with the first pricing system is that *value is perceived.* There is no guarantee that the baker will be willing to pay the price that the farmer wants. The second pricing system is essentially determined on a cost basis. Either way, the total 'value' in the system increases down the supply chain. This is ultimately the way the economy motivates people to produce goods and sell them to people who 'want' them.

Table 1: Traditional economic analysis

	Initial state		Final state	
	Farmer	**Baker**	**Farmer**	**Baker**
Crop	100	0	0	100
Crop value	100	150	100	150
Money	0	150	150	0
Total value	100	150	150	150
Sum of total value	250		300	

One of the main functions of microeconomics is that it is supposed to be able to determine the 'value' of products. Despite 200 years of research, there are no economic theories that reliably explain what the monetary value of a product or service should be. The idea that value is not inherent is not new. Carl Menger [3], among others, discussed the concept of the 'Subjective Theory of Value'. When we examine the Farmer–Baker situation purely in terms of what exchanges hands, rather than the 'value' of what exchanges hands, Table 2 is generated.

Table 2: Zero-sum Economic analysis

	Initial state		Final state		Sum of changes
	Farmer	Baker	Farmer	Baker	

Crop	100	0	0	100	
Money	0	150	150	0	
Change in crop	−100		+100		0
Change in money	+150		−150		0

Examining the transaction mathematically, by simply looking at what was actually traded, not at the value of what was traded, the changes add up to zero. In this example, neither the amount of money nor the amount of crop change. Both crop and money transactions are zero sum! However, if you look at the value transferred in an economic system, as opposed to the actual exchange of goods, you will get a different result.

A single transaction is a zero-sum event;
therefore, all transactions are zero-sum events;
therefore, in terms of trade, the entire economy must operate as a zero-sum system.

This is the core of Zero-sum Economics.

The problem with zero-sum systems is that whenever someone makes a profit, someone else must make a corresponding loss. Obviously, poverty is caused by a lack of money, and if businesses don't have enough money to hire people, they don't, which leads to unemployment. Hence, money is the root of all evil, not 'value'!

When the amount of money in the economy is constant, the exchange of money in the economy becomes a limiting factor. In many ways, this concept is similar to the ideas of conservation of matter in chemistry, or conservation of energy and momentum in physics. Matter is never changed by chemical reactions. Therefore, the same elements are found on either side of the equation. In physics, the conservation of energy is a fundamental property of physics. No

11

physical actions can take place without a transfer in energy; overall, however, energy is never gained or lost. Even in nuclear processes involving a change in mass, energy is conserved, because mass is a form of energy.

For the entire system, all transactions must be zero sum; even the creation and destruction of money should be able to be tracked to individual events. A single transaction can be defined as shown in Table 3.

Table 3 Any transaction in which a quantity is transferred and none of the quantity is created or destroyed is a zero-sum event. The first important thing to note here is that there are no units given for the quantity, which means that it can refer to anything—money, crops, bread, cars, nuclear warships, etc. The second point to note is that the amount transferred ('T') can take any numerical value. Hence, if one transaction is zero-sum, they all are.

Table 3: General transactions

	Initial state		Final state	
Entity	A	B	A	B
Quantity	0	T	T	0
Change in A		$+T$		
Change in B		$-T$		
Sum of changes		0		

Much of the difficulty economists have with the logical argument for Zero-sum Economics is in the second step. They argue, "In the aggregate, money can be created."

An aggregate simply means a collection—in terms of this argument, the entire collection of transactions and entities. However, there are only two places where money is created:

1. in banks, through what I think (if I understand it correctly) is an incidental effect of creating debt or using credit; and
2. in a Mint, which creates physical currency under governmental control. (If regular people do it, it's called counterfeiting!)

Introduction

Governments control the release of physical currency; hence, there is minimal benefit directly for Consumers. Producers (mainly banks and potentially other Producers) control credit and loans. The whole point of Producers is that they make a profit, so even when they 'create' money in this way, the Producers are the ones who receive the profits (interest on debt). Consumers never receive the benefits.

Most of the simulations presented in Section 5 use a fixed amount of money and do not use any money creation. These include the CP Model in Section 5.1.1, the CPG Model in Section 5.1.2, the Business Cycle Models in Section 5.1.3, the Cash Distribution Model in Section 5.1.5 and the Global Labour Model in Section 5.1.6. The real-world economic models in Section 5.1.7 for both the USA and Australia do use money creation. However, this is only done by the Government and uses real data from the corresponding government treasury departments. The reason for using real data is that currently there is no good model that can be used to predict when money should be created. However, what you will find in Section 5.1.7 is that the method used still produces a realistic interaction that is consistent with statistics collected from the real world.

In the following sections, I examine some of the theories of economics, indicating where zero-sum limitations occur. Existing economic theories are not completely wrong—for the most part they are correct. Zero-sum limitations, however, can be used to explain some economic phenomena that are not 'well understood' using the current theories as they stand.

In the Zero-sum Models that have been created for this research, the population comprises two main groups: 'Producers' and 'Consumers'. Producers create goods or services that are traded for money. Consumers consume those goods. Consumers also work for Producers to create the goods that are sold, and in return are given a wage (money). Consumers then pay for the goods with the money they have earned. The whole point of being a Producer is to make a profit, which means that Producers must give less money in wages than they receive for the goods. 'Governments' are a third type of entity used in the models. They manage tax and welfare, but for the most part do not interfere with the exchange of goods between Consumers and Producers.

1.4   What *is* zero-sum in economics?

There are many aspects of economics that can clearly be shown to be zero-sum limited. If any 'event' or transaction in an economy can be examined mathematically to show that the changes that occur add up to zero, this means the event is zero sum (see Table 2).

1.4.1   Money

The whole point of money is that it can be swapped for products and services. When money is traded, no money is lost or destroyed or created. This shows that money is zero sum.

1.4.2   Trade

The whole point of trade is to move goods from one owner to another. Trading does not create or destroy the goods. As such, it must be zero sum.

1.4.3   Time

Economics usually considers goods and 'services'. Time is related to services. A service is essentially time spent on a task for someone else (either a customer or a client). Every person chooses what they do with their time, and whether they work for someone else or work for themselves.

Table 4: Zero-sum time analysis

Daily activity in 24 h	Initial state (h)	Final state(h)	Change in state (h)
Sleep	8	8	
Work	8	10	+2
Recreation	8	6	−2
Total	24	24	
Sum of changes			<u>0 h</u>

The budget itself may not be zero-sum—but any *changes* to the budget are. As there is finite input, changes can only be made to the allocation of spending within the budget. An increase in one expense has to be offset by an associated decrease in one or more of the other expenses, i.e. the situation is zero sum.

Table 5 shows a few of the activities that a person has performed. In the initial state, that person spent 8 hours on each of the three activities. However, in the final state we see that this person has done 2 hours' overtime. Hence, the work time has increased, in this case to 10 hours. There are a finite 24 hours in a day, which means that some other activity has had to be reduced to compensate— recreation has been reduced by 2 hours. As always, add up the changes—if they equal zero, we have a zero-sum system. Here is the reason for everyone's lament: "I need more time!"

1.4.4   Budgets

A budget is essentially the allocation of a fixed amount of resources across various activities. The budget itself may not be zero-sum—but any *changes* to the budget are. As there is finite input, changes can only be made to the allocation of spending within the budget. An increase in one expense has to be offset by an associated decrease in one or more of the other expenses, i.e. the situation is zero sum.

Table 5: Zero-sum budget analysis

Budget	Initial state ($)	Final state ($)	Change in state ($)
Income	1000	1000	
Expenses			
Savings	100	0	−100
Bills	500	700	+200
Food	200	200	
Recreation	200	100	−100
Sum of changes			**0**

1.4.5   Markets - Work

As with budgets, a market for the most part has a fixed number of Consumers. Typically, a business will operate in a city or a country with a limited number of people. Even if businesses become large enough to become global, there is still a limit of around 7.3 billion people on earth. So, there is always an upper limit to the number of Consumers. Producers attempt to get these Consumers to buy their products. Any increase in market share by one Producer means a corresponding loss for another Producer.

Table 6: Zero-sum market analysis

Budget	Initial state ($)	Final state ($)	Change in state ($)
Consumers	1000	1000	0
Producers			
A	300	100	−200
B	400	500	+100
C	300	300	0
D	0	100	+100
Sum of changes			<u>0</u>

The same problem occurs with work. If you have a burst pipe you might get three quotes from plumbers, but only one plumber will be hired. If one is unavailable, that one loses the work and another gains the work. So, the work is zero sum between the plumbers. One comment that frequently occurs in the current economy is that people just need to "work harder". Given the Zero sum nature of work and markets in general this statement is, put simply: wrong. Even if an individual increases the amount of work they accomplish, due to the zero sum nature of work, this will result in someone else losing out in a market.

1.5   What is *not* zero-sum in economics?

Many economists will argue that the entire economy cannot be zero sum because there are aspects of the economy that are not zero-sum. The latter is not in dispute. If everything was zero-sum, no changes would have occurred over the last 200 years. Skyscrapers weren't around 200 years ago, so clearly something must have changed. The same technique used for zero-sum components can be used to check for non-zero-sum components. We examine the initial and final states and see if the changes add up to zero. If not, the system being examined is not zero sum.

1.5.1   Production

Production is a net positive activity. Initially, goods do not exist; after production occurs, goods do exist.

1.5.2   Consumption

Consumption is a net negative activity. Things that are produced are consumed. Food and water are the most common products thought of as being consumed.

1.5.3   Value

Value is one of the core concepts economics attempts to unravel. How much is something worth? The value of a product is ultimately up to whoever buys the product—which means it is entirely subjective. In mathematical terms, subjectivity can be expressed as the amount of money a person is willing to pay, with the ultimate limit being the amount of money they have. This represents the most a person can pay for a product. This idea is called the 'Subjective Theory of Value' and is discussed further in Sections 1.8.3 and 4.6.

The value of a product can change rapidly without any trade occurring. Think of the stock market crash headlines: "Billions of dollars lost in a day!" Actually, no money has disappeared at all. In an economy, money doesn't often disappear. What changes is simply the amount that people are willing to pay for a particular stock. The stock price does not change anything about how the company operates; nor does it change the amount of money the company collects. If a company has 100 million shares, and suddenly the price of a single share drops from $100 to $80, this effectively changes the total value of the company by $2 billion. The point here is that the value of the company has changed, but no money has changed hands.

1.5.4   Knowledge

Giving someone else knowledge does not remove that knowledge from your own mind. The same knowledge can be given to any number of people without any negative effects. Incidentally, having knowledge does not mean there will be an opportunity to apply that knowledge.

1.6   Zero-sum and Non-zero-sum Economics

One of the most common arguments people make against a zero-sum explanation of the economy is that if you examine value and production, 'clearly' they are not zero sum. Goods are produced every day and these goods are worth something.

Let's say we have a group of people. The first person has $100 and everyone else has $0.

Value	$0	$0	$0	$0	$0	$0		$0
	⚇	⚇	⚇	⚇	⚇	⚇	...	⚇
Money	$100	$0	$0	$0	$0	$0	...	$0

The first person hires the second person to help them build a house, and the second person ends up with the $100.

Value	$100	$0	$0	$0	$0	$0		
	🏠	⚇	⚇	⚇	⚇	⚇	...	⚇

Money	$0	$100	$0	$0	$0	$0	...	$0

The next day the second person hires the third person to build another house.

Value	$100	$0	$0	$0	$0	$0		
	🏠	🏠	🧍	🧍	🧍	🧍	...	🧍
Money	$0	$0	$100	$0	$0	$0	...	$0

And so on.

Value	$100	$100	$100	$0	$0	$0		
	🏠	🏠	🏠	🧍	🧍	🧍	...	🧍
Money	$0	$0	$0	$100	$0	$0	...	$0

...

Value	$100	$100	$100	$100	$100	$100		
	🏠	🏠	🏠	🏠	🏠	🏠	...	🧍

M on ey	$ 0	$ 0	$ 0	$ 0	$ 0	$ 0	...	$ 1 0 0

Note that the total amount of money in the system is always $100. It is simply being transferred between the people. With every transaction, the value in the system increases; hence, the total value in the system is non–zero sum.

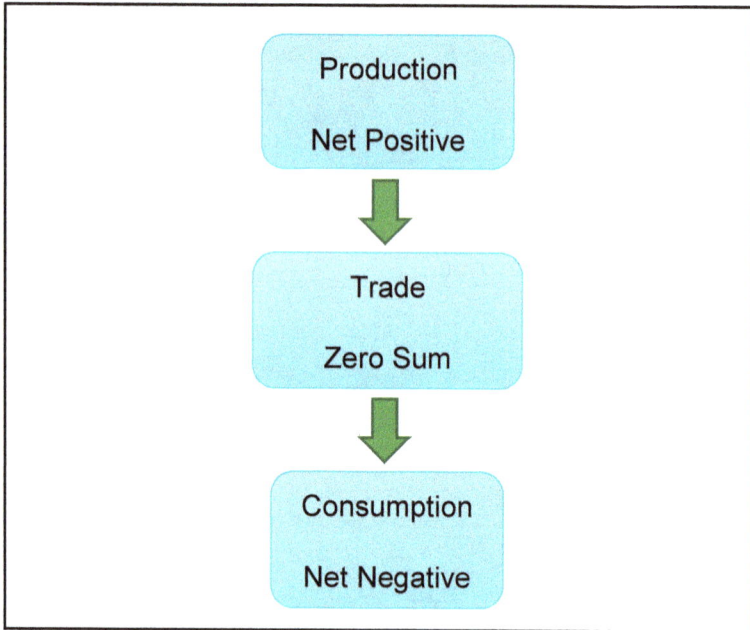

Figure 2: Economy System Design

From this description, a system design can be developed as shown in Figure 2. This shows that in an economy Production is a net positive operation, and that eventually products are transferred to Consumers, which are net negative operation. In between these two operations is trade which is zero sum.

This experiment demonstrates that a zero-sum limited system (a group of people trading labour for money) can produce net non–zero-sum results (value), and that it is possible to have both zero-sum and non–zero-sum effects operating in the same system. Complications arise when further effects are considered, such as inflation and reselling a house, but this is a good starting point.

1.7 Barter versus money

Many economists consider that a workable economy could take the form of a very complex barter system. The general argument is that everyone can produce something or provide a service. In practice, for every person to receive every service that they require would be quite difficult under such a system. A great many transactions would need to occur for everyone to acquire their goods and services.

Another difficulty with a barter system is that it is difficult to identify whether you are making a profit. In a barter system, many of the losses are hidden, because there is no way of determining whether the value of your assets has increased or decreased. In contrast, when using a standardised system of money, it is easy to tell whether you have made a profit: at the end of the day you have more money than you started with. In a barter system, the hidden nature of the losses can result in a more equitable distribution of wealth around an economy. I am not, however, suggesting a return to barter. It is far simpler and more productive to use a monetary system; however, the monetary system has the problem of having a zero-sum nature.

1.8 Economics and psychology

I like to split the study of economic theory into two parts: the psychology of economics (what people value and how much they are willing to pay) and the mechanics of economics (money, trade, supply and demand, etc.). Money, the main mechanical tool of economies, is a centrally defined tradable item that we can swap for any other product or service.

The mechanical tools of economics are associated with particular behaviours that are inherent in the larger economic system. People have choices, and the way in which they make choices is the subject matter of psychology. 'Freedom of choice', however, doesn't necessarily mean that people can do anything they want; they are limited by the 'system' within which they live—often what appears to be a choice may be reducible to just one viable option. Although in any given situation it cannot be guaranteed that a person will behave in a particular way, in a 'large' population it is often possible to see patterns of behaviour emerging.

'Value' is the primary psychological concept in economics. What do people value, and why do they value it? In economic terms, the main thing people have control over is how they spend their money, i.e. spending is the main way in which they exercise economic choice. The amount of income they receive is not a choice; it is ultimately someone else's decision. A client makes a decision about whether to purchase a product or service; an employer decides to give someone a job and pay a salary. The choice made is by the person who pays the money, not the receiver.

The mechanical tools and processes involved in economics can be measured (money, income, taxes, production, etc.). Psychology, on the other hand, is very difficult to model directly. I do not claim to have any training in or significant knowledge of psychology; however, what I can show mathematically and numerically are the effects behaviours have on the mechanics (the flow of money and products through an economy) and the requirements that those mechanics place on the economy. For example, with business cycles, the economy does not recover until people who have money spend it on people who don't. In terms of requirements: the people who have money are required to spend it on the poor for the economy to recover. Often, what may appear to be a psychological behaviour involving free choice is actually behaviour constrained by the system itself—i.e. it is a 'systemic behaviour'.

1.8.1   Survival

From human psychology, we know that the will to survive is a strong motivation for human behaviour. Thus, our minds have evolved to help us find food and water, reproduce, and form families and communities. We have also created belief systems, which in turn help us to form cultures. Cultures exist because they can help people survive. The variety of cultures around the world show that there are many ways of surviving. A rule or belief that is accepted in one culture may be completely ignored or even considered reprehensible in another. Hence the term 'culture clash'.

Challenging ideas can annoy those who are invested in maintaining a particular belief system. I suspect this book will annoy a lot of people—especially business people, economists and (possibly) economics students. Why do people get annoyed about ideas like mine? They are, after all, just ideas that can be either ignored or examined more closely to see if they hold merit. The answer is that, to a certain extent, these ideas undermine some people's beliefs about how they can survive.

When people get annoyed to the point where they issue death threats, they are feeling that their survival is being threatened. They have specific beliefs about what enables them to survive. If an idea is promoted that questions their survival strategies, this can be interpreted as a threat to their survival. The quickest way to annoy someone and get them to act aggressively is to threaten their survival. From such interactions come religious wars, racism, etc.—that fun stuff where people end up dead—all caused, at least to some extent, by a group of people feeling threatened by 'new ideas'.

If you are facing death, economic arguments become irrelevant. This is why when catastrophes occur; people are often killed if they attempt to 'hoard' food and water. People who don't have the essentials are facing death, so they have a choice to either kill the person who is hoarding and take their food and water— or die.

An example used in economics textbooks [4] describes a situation in which a shopkeeper increases the price of water after a catastrophic event that shuts down the water supply. It is suggested that in this event, raising the price of water is a sensible strategy to allow the water to be distributed effectively. Such reasoning, however, does not take into account survival instincts. According to game theory, the possible scenarios are shown in Table 7.

Table 7: Game theory of a water shortage

	Leave without water	Kill shopkeeper
Consumer	Die	Live
Shopkeeper	Live	Die

This is why, during such catastrophes, economic systems are suspended and rationing occurs. Rationing is an attempt by authorities to reduce the stress caused by limited necessities (and to reduce deaths!). At the broader level of an entire country, consider the case of a famine, as shown in Table 8.

Table 8: Game theory of a famine leading to revolution

Game strategy	Famine	Revolution

23

Poor people	Starve to death	Live
Rich people	Keep all the food and live	Heads on pikes

Whether at the local level or at the broader level, no-one wants to play live-or-die games. The only way to avoid these issues is not to get into the situations in the first place.

This pattern of response to new ideas can be seen among business people and economists, although mostly with fewer dead people. Many of these people work their entire lives at businesses or on economic theories, doing good work, in most cases! However, if you suggest that businesses can actually cause problems, business owners become very angry. Such an idea can be interpreted as a threat to survival. Business isn't just something that people 'do'; it is a means by which many people 'survive'.

Another reason that this book will annoy people, especially economics students, is that Zero-sum Theory will require them to learn calculus … no one wants to do that much work!

Finally, most people only have local knowledge and can only act locally. Very few people have access to global information; also, it takes a long time to acquire such information; hence, people have to use the local information they have available in order to make decisions in a reasonable amount of time.

1.8.2   Local optimisation: the fog of war

The 'fog of war' is a military term used when commanders in the field have limited knowledge about their enemy, and even about their own troops. The difficulty in earlier eras was that commanders often did not know where their enemy was, or much about the terrain. To acquire such knowledge required the use of scouts, who could take days to report back (if they weren't killed in the process). This situation often led to commanders of armies operating without a good understanding of the surrounding environment.

The same thing occurs in economics. Businesses do not know how much money their clients have, and they do not know how their competitors operate their businesses. This can lead to particular thought processes. Many opinions people hold about others rest on a patent lack of global knowledge.

For example, rich people and poor people tend to find fault with one another.

- Rich people sometimes think poor people are lazy.
- Poor people sometimes think rich people are jerks.

Why do these opinions occur? Because each side is preoccupied with their own problems (local information). They assume that the other side lives within the same restrictions. Hence, it is common for people to believe that different behaviours are a result of psychological issues rather than due to differences in 'local' environment. We live in an interconnected society, and money is a shared resource that cycles (rather unevenly) throughout the system. Ultimately, businesses decide how many jobs exist, who gets them, and how much their products cost. When Consumers run out of money, they stop spending and businesses lose income.

Businesses perceive the loss in income and assume that either their workers aren't working hard enough, or that poor people aren't working hard enough to afford their products. Hence, "Poor people are lazy."

Poor people only see that they don't get the jobs they want, and hence that they can't afford to buy the products. Hence, "Rich people are jerks."

Neither opinion is based on the whole picture. To really understand a situation, you have to look at all of the components together.

1.8.3   Value

Psychology is all about what people think. The psychology of economics focuses on what people value and thus are willing to put effort into. There are many theories that discuss value in economics, including the Theory of Marginal Value, the Intrinsic Theory of Value, the Labour Theory of Value, the Power Theory of Value and the Subjective Theory of Value.

Marginal Value Theory is based on the idea that for a rare product, the more a person has, the less the product will be valued. Intrinsic Value Theories suggest that the value of a product is determined by its inherent properties. The Labour Theory of Value uses a concept of intrinsic value, in which the value of a product equals the labour cost to produce the product.

Part of the problem with Classical Economic Theories is that they attempt to combine the studies of the mechanical and psychological components of economics. This creates a lot of confusion. The price of a product is not the same as its value. Price, is usually based on how much it costs to make the product (plus a profit margin). The price is always determined by the person selling it. Whoever is selling the product must value the product less than the buyer values it, and more than the cost; otherwise, there is no one to buy the product and no way to make a profit. The buyer must value the product more than its price, otherwise he/she would not purchase the product. This means that there is no inherent numerical 'value' for a product, but that the value is based on perception. This is the 'Subjective Theory of Value' again (Sections 1.5.3 and 4.6.

Consider an auction. An item is put up for sale, sometimes with an estimated value, sometimes not. Over the course of the auction, buyers progressively increase their bids. Does this mean that the value of the item is increasing over the duration of the auction? Is the value of the item its initial value, or is it the final bid? Either way, an auction demonstrates that the value of an item can change and is different for different people.

1.8.4   *Free choice and systemic behaviour*

A choice is where people have multiple options and decide to take one option over another, based on their own internal values and on what occurs in the world around them (the 'system'). A systemic behaviour occurs when, irrespective of the apparent options available, people will generally all make the same choice in a given set of circumstances.

Systemic behaviours are common, but they usually occur under very specific conditions. A system operates in particular ways and produces specific responses to stimuli or disturbances. If people are involved in the system, they tend make similar decisions in response to the same stimulus.

For example, a roundabout forces drivers to drive around a central island, so traffic accidents can be eliminated without slowing drivers down. The roundabout is the system and the behaviour is the way people drive around the roundabout, typically according to a keep-left or keep-right law (depending on the country).

Introduction

A stock market crash can occur when everyone starts selling stocks at lower prices. Once the stock prices start falling, more people panic and the behaviour reinforces itself.

Operating a business requires the making of a profit; hence, business owners must make decisions to allow the business to make a profit; if not enough money is coming in, business owners have to cut costs. Hence, business management decisions must be made to keep the business running, rather than for the benefit of employees or customers.

In many ways crime can be considered a systemic behaviour. When people run out of money and there are no jobs available, they have the choice either to starve or to do something illegal to get money. As shown in later chapters, the typical operation of an economy drains people of their money. As a result, when people become unemployed and need money for basic necessities, choosing the option to do something illegal becomes more likely.

In more general terms, why do people behave badly? I suggest it could be because they have limited choices.

When resources become scarce, prices increase, which according to economic theory reduces demand. The downside is that some people miss out—to the point of starving to death when food or water is scarce, such as when large disasters occur. People become desperate. Since we don't want to be running around killing each other, governments restrict or eliminate the trading of essential commodities in times of crisis (e.g. through rationing during wartime). What does that teach us about economics and behaviour? It teaches us that economics does not provide an adequate account of what occurs in the real world. To predict what will occur, you need to think beyond money and economics to the system that people are operating in.

Current economic theories don't consider behaviours as systemic. As a result, economic analysis often cannot explain what people end up doing in the real world. The rules of economics are useful for making businesses more profitable. The problem is that if businesses are collecting money according to zero-sum conditions, Consumers must be losing. As economics does not acknowledge zero-sum conditions in the economy, it draws the focus away from this impact.

1.8.5   Changing Behaviours or changing the system

The problem with free will is it is very difficult to change the way people behave. If people want to do something they will find a way to do it. The only way to really change people comes down to pharmaceuticals, imprisonment or just shooting people ... most of which are ,especially for an entire country, against international human rights law or just plain war crimes. So they are difficult to implement.

Table 9: Game theory of a famine leading to revolution

Free Will	Systemic Behaviors
Anything is Possible.	Behaviors are restricted by the system itself
People control all actions	Restricted, but not necessarily dictated
People are independent	People are interdependent
Blame People	Blame the system

Changing the system might take a bit of effort, but it happens all the time. Governments exist specifically so that laws can be changed. New Businesses are created every day. New technologies are developed every day that effect how we all work and live.

My research focuses on systemic behaviours. I examine how money and business create systemic rules that limit the choices people make. The reason is: it is relatively easy to change a/the system. It is really difficult to change the way people think and the choices they make given the situation they are in. My overarching strategy for examining economics and poverty is to find out ways we can change the way the system works so that people can make choices that result in making the world a better place for everyone.

1.8.6   Corporate momentum

Corporate momentum refers to a tendency for corporations, and despite the name cultures, governments or any organisations to refrain from changing how they perform tasks. There are a few reasons for this, which include the fact that it takes time to get the information required to make informed decisions, but it also includes a general inability or desire for people to avoid making changes as changes can be scary.

One way these problems are addressed in engineering is called continuous improvement. Continuous improvement requires tasks to be monitored and adjusted over time. The adjustments to engineering processes are validated by experiments before being implemented completely. This is why large corporations employ researchers to both find better ways to make their products as well as make new products.

This can and is done by businesses and governments but rarely by cultures. As such, cultures have a tendency to stay the same over much longer periods of time, decades or even hundreds of years. The problem is there is generally no central authority that enforces the culture; the entire population simply follows the cultural rules. This allows cultures to evolve, but if the environment the culture finds itself in changes the culture may not keep up with the changes and disappear.

The point of bringing this up is to show that cultures need to be able to change as much as a government or business, but this requires everyone in the culture to be both aware of the problems we all have and be willing to make changes.

1.8.7 Summary

Psychology is about what people think and value, which is what determines their actions in the real world. As a general rule, people think and behave the way they do to help themselves survive. This applies to their adoption of religions, cultures, gangs, and even business practices. When there are limited resources, there is competition, and people can feel that their survival is threatened. Compounding this, people tend to have limited information; they view their situation from a limited perspective. Limited information, combined with a perceived threat and strong survival instincts, can result in people acting aggressively, and even violently. We should try to avoid inciting such behaviour through economic practices, but this will require better understanding of how economic systems operate (i.e. education), access to accurate media reports and government statistics, and (most importantly) significant changes in the way the economy operates (see Chapter 6).

1.9 Mechanical economics

The mechanical components of economics are purely concerned with money: where it is, who owns it, and where it is going. Economics and trade are not 'natural'; they have been created by humanity to assist in survival. 'We', the human race, could have complete control of how the economy operates—provided we can get everyone to agree to operate in a particular way!

1.9.1 Money

Money is the main component that makes an economy a Zero-sum Economy. It is the primary unit of measurement in an economy. Money is used to track how much profit is being made and the value of the items traded.

1.9.2 Income

Income is money that is received by an entity in a Zero-sum Model. It can come in the form of wages paid to Consumers, or of sales by Producers (i.e. from purchases made by Consumers).

1.9.3 Tax

Taxation is at present used as Government income. The main difference between an income and taxation is that taxation is not voluntary; it is required by law.

1.9.4 Technology

Advances in technology allow Producers to produce more product per person than in previous incarnations of the production process. [Say that five times really fast!] What this means is that fewer workers are required to satisfy the market. The advancement of technology can be classified as a mechanical process. Technology determines the factor relating 'the number of people employed at a business' to 'the number of products produced'. The better the technology, the smaller the number people who are needed to produce the product. The problem with this is that the fewer people you are paying to produce the product, the fewer people can actually afford the product.

1.9.5   Summary

In summary, Zero-sum Economics applies primarily to the mechanical components of economics, the three biggest of which are money, income and tax. The fact that these three are zero-sum allows money to be transferred, which means that if anyone in the economy makes a profit, someone else in the economy must make a loss. Assets can be accumulated in a manner that is not zero sum; however, there is a tendency for the people who have money to accumulate more assets.

1.10 Microeconomics

Microeconomics is the study of the economic behaviour of the most basic components of an economy—individual and aggregate 'Consumers' (individuals seeking to purchase products) and 'Producers' (individuals and businesses with a product to sell). Consumers are also defined as the workers employed by Producers. Investors can belong to either of these groups, but they are defined as the people who have extra money. Microeconomics is concerned with how all of these people make decisions. Such decisions include when, where and whether to make a purchase, and how to 'collect' money (e.g. how many workers to hire). I say 'collect' money, rather than 'make' money, which is what a Mint does. Microeconomics is responsible for determining the basic rules for operating businesses and making a profit.

There is no conflict between the vast majority of microeconomic theories and Zero-sum Economics, because zero-sum systems are mainly concerned with the global picture, i.e. macroeconomics. Microeconomics is mainly concerned with individual businesses and products. In Section 3.1, however, I have identified some limitations of the current microeconomic theories.

1.11 Macroeconomics

The individual components in an economy can be grouped together as markets and industries, which can then be examined collectively. Zero-sum Economics is mainly concerned with the economy as a whole. Hence, the basis of Zero-sum Theory comes from macroeconomic theory. Macroeconomics commonly refers to the economics of a nation, and is used to inform Governments on how they should develop economic policies for entire countries. It is concerned with measuring the total input and operation of a country or an entire economy—as opposed to microeconomics, which seeks to explain the financial interactions between the individual components within an economy. Macroeconomics can be defined as the economic factors that are external to individuals.

It is difficult to examine every entity in an economy, so macroeconomics often uses regression analysis to simplify and extract rules or trends from data. Regression analysis is a technique for fitting mathematical functions to input datasets. Sometimes this works well. However, if the underlying mechanics of the system are not well understood, regression analysis can fit well to the wrong function. This is the old problem of correlation versus causation, confusion about which can lead to the drawing of false conclusions.

The main macroeconomics concepts relevant to Zero-sum Economics are: the Circular Flow of Money, gross domestic product (GDP), business cycles, inflation and interest rates, wealth distribution, global labour, and aggregate supply and demand. In the following chapters, these phenomena are examined in detail to show why they are not well understood in current economic theory. Furthermore, it is shown that Zero-sum Economic Theory can be used to explain such phenomena.

1.11.1   The Circular Flow of Money Model

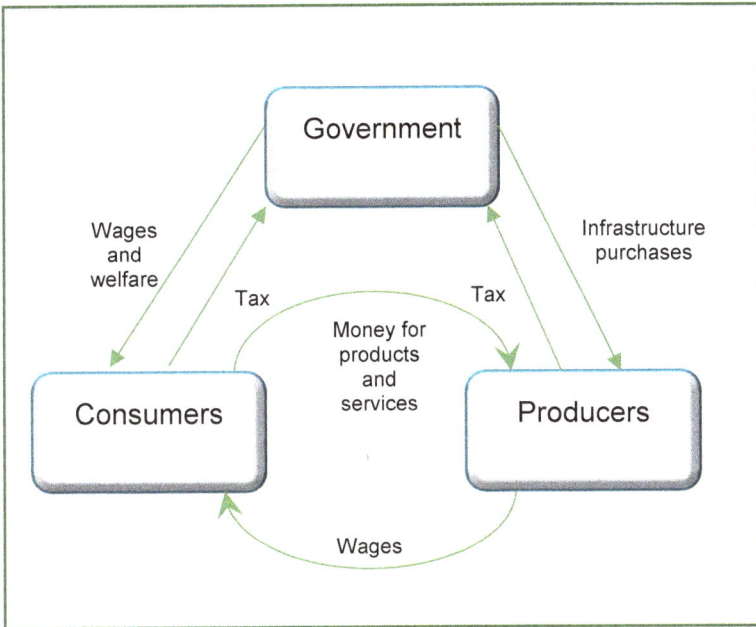

Figure 3: Circular Flow of Money Model

The 'Circular Flow of Money Model', as shown in Figure 3, is a basic model of how an economy operates. It shows the flow of goods and money between the various entities present in an economy. The simplest form involves Producers and Consumers, who trade goods and services for labour. More complicated versions of this model incorporate Governments and divide Producers further into resource development and other business industries.

The basic Consumer–Producer (CP) Model is used as the starting point for all Zero-sum Models. These models are then examined in the context of other economic phenomena that have been observed in the real world.

1.11.2   Gross Domestic Product

GDP is a measure of an entire country's productivity. It is often used as a measure of the country's aggregate supply in macroeconomics. Aggregate supply and demand are simply the total supply and demand of a group of Producers and Consumers, respectively.

1.11.3   Business cycles

Business cycles have long been observed in economies. These cycles are described as periods of declining economic output followed by periods of investment and recovery. Despite the fact that business cycles appear in economic data reaching as far back as 1840 (presented in Section 5.1.3), many economists admit that this phenomena is still not well understood.

With the use of Zero-sum Economic Theory and the CP Model, an explanation is presented for how money distribution causes this cyclic behaviour. In Part III of this book, I demonstrate how to eliminate these oscillations from an economy, using the CP Model and other Zero-sum Models.

1.11.4   Inflation and interest rates

Inflation is a tendency for prices to increase over time. In most macroeconomic systems, inflation is simply measured, and there is no attempt to identify the source of the occurrence. Prices do not change magically. It is always a business person's decision to increase prices. I have examined the causes of inflation, taking into account local knowledge of Consumers and Producers and the systemic behaviours described in Sections 1.8.2 and 1.8.4.

A relationship has long been observed between employment and inflation: when the unemployment rate increases, inflation decreases. There is said to be an inverse relationship between inflation and unemployment, and this is portrayed in the 'Phillips curve'. The Phillips curve was first discovered in 1958 by A.W Phillips [5] and has since been investigated by many others [6–12]. Using Zero-sum Theory, we can analyse the performance of a simple CP Model and derive an equation for inflation that is consistent with the Philips curve.

1.11.5   Wealth distribution

The top 1% of the population own 50% of the wealth in the world [13]. Despite this, current economic theories do not have a model that explains how this situation can have occurred. To expand the Theory of Zero-sum Economics, the current statistics on wealth distribution are reviewed, along with various theories proposed to explain it. I show (in Part III of this book) that it is possible to change wealth distribution by modifying the flow of money in the economy. ['Perish the thought!' say the rich.]

1.11.6   Global labour

Globalisation has caused (and allowed) companies to offshore jobs to countries where labour is cheaper than in the original host countries. The decision to offshore is typically made because managers are looking solely at the cost of hiring labour, rather than considering the flow of money in the world. Again, this is an optimisation decision based on local information only.

Using Zero-sum Modelling, it is possible to show why this phenomena occurs and how the relationship between the cost of living and the global labour market affects the global economy.

1.12 Zero-sum Economics

Zero-sum Economics differs from previous economic theories in separating the mechanical and psychological components. One of the distinguishing features involves the understanding of 'value'. In Zero-sum Economics, value is always considered to be a psychological concept. For simplicity of modelling, it can be assumed that there is no inherent monetary value in any product: the important thing to look at is the distribution of money. Previous theories have often assumed that value is the only part of an economy that is important, going so far as to label money as 'exogenic', i.e. created externally. This I suspect gives economists the impression that money is not important. I venture to propose that money is *endogenic*, i.e. internally produced, from which I take the next logical step.

With Zero-sum Economics, the following rule is true for money in the economy:

If a gain occurs in any part of a system, there must be a corresponding loss somewhere else in the system.

The Zero-sum Models illustrate that by tracking the flow of money in a system, many of the economic phenomena that are not well understood can be explained.

Products cost money, but the amount of money is not the value of the product. Cost is independent of the psychological effects and decisions that determine a product's value. Psychology, however, is difficult to model accurately, so it is very difficult to establish the inherent value of any product. Thus, Zero-sum Economics focuses on the mechanical effects. As previously discussed, many of the phenomena present in economics can be attributed to systemic behaviours that are directly related to the mechanical aspects of economics.

In this research, I have focused on four main phenomena—all frequently described in current economic theory as 'not well understood': business cycles, inflation, wealth distribution, and global labour.

1.12.1   CP Model of an economy

The most basic model of an economy is the CP Model, which simply examines the flow of money between the two entities: Consumers and Producers. Consumers purchase goods from a Producer. Producers pay Consumers for their work. Simple enough.

The limitations on the operation of the entities are as follows:

- There is a fixed amount of money distributed between the two entities. Money already exists and is not created or made by either the Producers or the Consumers.
- The whole point of being a Producer is to 'collect money'. As a result, the Producers attempt to pay less for wages than they charge for their products. The difference between the cost of the product and the wage is the profit margin.
- Consumers work for Producers and are paid a corresponding wage.
- If not all of the Consumers can afford to buy the products, the Producer does not produce for them, and will as a result cut costs by reducing employment.

Using these rules, the maximum output is considered to be the amount of money that each entity has. Think of it as the collective bank balance. The CP Model shows that as long as the Consumers have enough money, their balance will be reduced at a constant rate. When the Consumers run out of money, the income of the Producers will be decreased, and some Consumers will become unemployed, with a decay rate equivalent to the profit margin the Producers have set. In mathematical terms, the decay rate is represented by

$$e^{-Mt},$$

where M is the profit margin and t is time.

This model does not show what happens to the money distribution in the real world, but it does show that the inherent nature of an economy is for productivity to decay over time. This is the first part of a business cycle.

1.12.2 Business cycles

Business cycles are about patterns of spending and investment. The mechanical component is the spending of what needs to be paid for the products needed. This outlay is balanced against investment. An investment can be many things: money spent on research, advertising, building new infrastructure—anything, as long as the money spent makes its way back to Consumers. The choices people make concerning how much to invest and where to invest are actually quite difficult to predict, even though there has been a large amount of research into the subject [13–22].

It is, however, still possible to examine the effects of investment on business cycles. The Zero-sum Models can be adapted to include investment and to show that economic output only improves once investors have spent sufficient money for it to get back to Consumers. Technically, investors can be either Consumers, Producers or even a Government; the main function of investors is to spend money so that it is received by another entity in the system. To reach full productivity, Producers must invest enough money in Consumers such that all of the Consumers have enough money to purchase their goods.

In Section 5.1.3 it is shown that under the right investment conditions, cyclic behaviours occur, and that under some conditions this behaviour becomes sinusoidal.

1.12.3 Inflation

As mentioned previously, inflation is caused by a choice made by business people concerning what action should be taken to improve the income of a business when that income is reduced. Typically, business managers attempt to increase revenue by increasing the price of their products. The decision to increase prices is usually based on local information. It is assumed that the income is decreasing due to the internal issues of the business. As managers do not have access to global information about their customers, they cannot take into account the general state of Consumer wealth. Also, managers are only capable of taking local actions within their businesses.

In terms of Zero-sum Economics, a mathematical expression for inflation is derived from the CP Model. This expression incorporates cost-push and demand-pull inflation, along with a modifier consistent with the Phillips curve.

To examine the inflation phenomenon, historical financial data are examined. The data show that peak inflation actually coincides with recession. This indicates that business managers decide to increase their prices when their income falls. As discussed in Section 5.1.4, the CP Model can be used to demonstrate cyclic behaviour in an economy. To model inflation, all one needs to do is relate the increase in price to the decrease in income.

1.12.4   Wealth distribution

It has already been observed that currently the top 1% of the population own 50% of the wealth in the world [13]. Current economic theories do not account for this phenomenon. Economists often assume that the extreme wealth discrepancy indicates exceptional motivation and effort on the part of a gifted minority. In Section 5.1.5, it is shown that Zero-sum Theory can be used to predict the wealth distribution of a set of Consumers and Producers.

1.12.5   Global labour

One of the 'recent' economic phenomena is the rise in offshoring of labour to countries where it can be obtained more cheaply. It can be shown that the cost of living is the main factor determining labour costs, and that the cost of living, when influenced by inflation, causes a shift in employment between countries.

By modelling two Governments with two sets of Consumers with different living costs, it is possible to show how Producers favour the Consumers with the lowest living costs and will offshore jobs to the cheapest supply of labour. Under these conditions, the cash distribution is examined to see which county benefits.

This phenomenon is examined with respect to current data concerning the cost of living and the cash distribution between a number of countries. This shows that much of the motivation for offshoring is related to the cost of living in the source country, and that the country with the lowest labour rate ends up with the majority of the cash.

1.13 Summary

In this chapter, I have sought to introduce the basic concepts of economics, and of Zero-sum Economics in particular. I have attempted to highlight the differences between previous economic theories and Zero-sum Theory by differentiating between real psychological choices and 'mechanical' systemic behaviours. It was noted that people's opinions and decision-making can be based on a lack of global knowledge.

The main feature of Zero-sum Economics is that money distribution in the economy is limited by zero-sum mechanics: in any zero-sum system, any gain must have a corresponding loss somewhere else in the system.

Chapters 2 and 3 review the historical and current theories of micro- and macroeconomics. The strengths and weaknesses of the various theories are highlighted.

In Chapter 4, Zero-sum Economic Theory is presented in more detail and compared with previous theories. The operation of Zero-sum Economic Models is reviewed in detail, and I describe how the models provide useful explanations of economic phenomena that are not well explained by existing theory.

Chapter 5 presents the full operation of various Zero-sum Models and examines their responses to various phenomena, including business cycles, inflation, wealth distribution, and global labour.

The CP Model is used initially, and then the Consumer–Producer–Government (CPG) Model is introduced. Finally, the models are demonstrated using actual economic data, and the outcomes are compared with the situation in the world today.

Chapter 6 shows how it is possible to use these models to eliminate business cycles, and to provide a stable economy that operates at maximum productivity. It turns out that this would ensure that everyone has enough money to survive, i.e. it would eliminate poverty!

Chapter 7 and 8 reviews the research presented and draws conclusions from the models.

2 A brief history of economic theories

The second chapter in a PhD thesis would typically be a literature review—an investigation of previous and current research relevant to the topic. Such an investigation seeks to establish that the PhD topic being researched is a new concept. Here, in Chapters 2 and 3, I review the major economic theories from earliest to current, and show that the idea of zero-sum systems as applied to economics has not previously been explored in the academic literature.

There are more individual observations and theories that could be covered here, but I have focused on the major advances in the field of economics that are relevant to the development of Zero-sum Economics. I have provided the background of knowledge required for understanding this topic, and shown that there is an area of knowledge that is missing in the current literature, a 'knowledge gap' in academic terms.

Today's economic theories were initially developed in the 18th to 20th centuries, and include Classical [23], Neoclassical [3, 24], Marxian [25], Socialist [26–29], Keynesian [30], Evolutionary and Current Capitalist Economic Theories [4, 31–38]. These theories, extended in various ways, now provide the basis for the majority of the economics theories discussed in current economics textbooks [4, 31–38]. They set out the rules within which the various economies operate, describe the techniques for measuring the economic phenomena, and predict the effects of the rules on the outputs of the economies. Many of these rules have been influenced by the moral motivations of the researchers.

2.1 Classical Economics

The earliest economic theories are referred to as Classical Economics. They introduce the most fundamental concepts related to supply and demand, and to how people make economic decisions.

The earliest ideas influencing economic theory can be traced back to David Hume's *A Treatise of Human Nature* [39], in which he discussed the motivations inherent in human nature, and the outcomes of such motivations. The three books making up this work cover such topics as understanding, passions and morals. Hume described the human passion for owning property and the joy of ownership, and he examined the principles of morality and motivation as they pertain to governments and people in general; he did not, however, establish any mathematical relationships to indicate how these principles can be applied to economics.

In *The Wealth of Nations* [23], Adam Smith further discussed the motivation for commerce, noting that the main driver is self-interest. He demonstrated how a free marketplace enhances economic exchange between self-interested traders, that supply and demand regulates market prices, and that government regulation of such phenomena does not improve the availability of a product.

David Ricardo, in *On the Principles of Political Economy and Taxation* [40], discussed supply and demand of products, and recommended strategies for income tax. He also presented evaluations of the effects of the rules for taxation on the economy.

The works of John Stuart Mill include *The Principles of Political Economy* [41], *On Liberty* [42] and *Utilitarianism* [43]. In *The Principles of Political Economy* [41], he discussed the difference between what economics measures and what human beings really value. Mill argued that we should sacrifice economic growth for the sake of the environment, limit population to ensure that people have space to live, and prevent starvation by matching food production with population; finally, he made a case for providing welfare to the poor. In *On Liberty* [42], he discussed the use of law to coerce people into performing particular tasks, and ultimately argued that force should only be used in self-defence. In *Utilitarianism* [43], he argued that economics should aim to benefit (and reduce suffering for) all people.

Concepts established by Classical Economics and still in use include the principle of supply and demand [23], [40], Cost-of-production Theories of Value [23, 40], income tax [40] and welfare [41, 43]. In connection with these concepts, particular actions are recommended (on philosophical and moral grounds), at both government and individual levels. Mathematical formulae have rarely been provided for their justification.

2.2   Neoclassical Economics

Neoclassical Economic Theories expanded and refined the earlier Classical Economic Theories. Many of these theories were quantified in mathematical formulae and examined in real-world situations. These theories included the Theory of Marginal Utility, Theories of 'Value', and the Quantity Theory of Money, among others.

Walras' Law refers to the mathematical notion that excess market demands (or, inversely, excess market supplies) must sum to zero. The Theory of Marginal Utility attempts to explain why different goods have different values. Adam Smith [23] was one of the first people to notice the 'diamond–water paradox', and the Theory of Marginal Utility [24, 31, 44] was used to explain why items that were not essential for survival, such as diamonds, tended to have a higher price than products required by the larger population. This theory showed that the more the value of a product diminished, the more each person had of it. The Marshallian Partial Equilibrium Theory, sometimes called the Marshallian Theory of Supply and Demand, claims that when people have more than enough access to, e.g. water, the loss or gain of a small amount of water will have a limited effect on them; the loss or gain of a small number of diamonds, which have a much more restricted supply, will be much more significant to them. Marshallian Partial Equilibrium considers a single commodity, and attempts to find the equilibrium point for supply and demand. The equilibrium point is the crossover point between supply and demand, as shown in Figure 4.

Basic supply-versus-demand curve

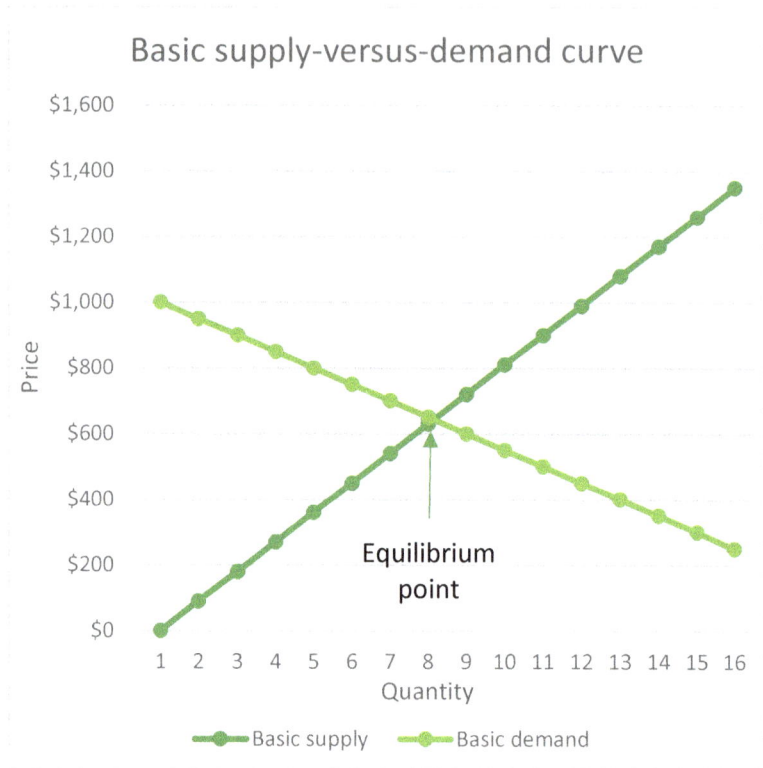

Figure 4: Zero-sum supply-versus-demand curve

An extension of this idea is the General Equilibrium Theory, which was developed by Leon Walras [45–47]. General Equilibrium theory expands on Marshallian equilibrium by considering all products and markets in an economy (as opposed to the Marshallian theory, which considers a single product). It attempts to explain the function of economic markets as a whole, as opposed to the market dynamics of individual products. General Equilibrium Theory tries to show how and why all free markets tend towards equilibrium in the long run. Walras notes that individual markets don't necessarily reach equilibrium—only that they approach it.

The Quantity Theory of Money (QTM) [24, 31, 48] was developed to explain inflation. In its transactions version, the QTM states that the total value of all sales of goods must necessarily equal the total value of all purchases.

The QTM is based on the following hypotheses:

- Inflation is fundamentally derived from the growth rate of the money supply.
- The supply of money is exogenous.
- The demand for money, as reflected in its velocity, is a stable function of nominal income, interest rates, etc.
- The mechanism for injecting money into the economy is not that important in the long run.
- The real interest rate is determined by non-monetary factors (such as productivity of capital, and time preference, explained below).

The money supply is literally the amount of currency existing in the economy. This includes physical currency as well as currency represented in bank accounts. Growth in the money supply at present occurs as a coincidental aspect of loaning by banks. The QTM suggests that the way that money is created is not particularly important in terms of the economy, but that the growth of the money supply is important.

One widely discussed concept is 'demand for money'. Theories for the demand for money include Fisher's Transactions Approach [49], Keynes' Theory [30], the Tobin Portfolio Approach [50], Boumol's Inventory Approach [51] and Friedman's Theory [52]. These theories incorporate such ideas as the need for currency to be able to make purchases, desire for investment returns, and speculation on the change in value of money. In general terms, these theories discuss and examine various motivations for people to hold onto cash, versus investing or simply spending their income. However, it does not consider the distribution of money among people in an economy.

Money velocity is literally the amount of money spent over a given period of time. It is assumed in the QTM that when the availability of money is restricted, the velocity of money will increase to compensate, thus ensuring that everyone is capable of purchasing the products they require.

The productivity of capital refers to the amount of money that a piece of manufacturing equipment (capital) can generate. For example, a modern printer can print tens of thousands of pages for less than a cent per page, and the printer itself may cost five to ten thousand dollars. The productivity of the printer is determined by the relationship between the amount of capital outlaid and the value of what it can produce.

The real interest rate is the interest rate after taking into account the rate of inflation, i.e. the difference between the inflation rate and the rate or interest rate on loans or savings.

Time preference is the relative value of a product, or even of money itself, when compared with that of the same item at a different time.

The QTM can be summarised in the following formula:

$$M \times V = P \times T,$$

where:
M is the money supply,
V is the velocity of money,
P is the average price of all products and
T represents the total transactions occurring in the economy.

Pigou [16, 48] examined the impact of unemployment on the value of money. He also proposed the Pigovian tax, which is a tax levied on an activity that has an external cost, such as environmental pollution (e.g. the recent 'carbon tax').

Weintraub [53] explained that Neoclassical Economics rests on three assumptions:

1. People have rational preferences for particular outcomes, and these preferences can be associated with values.
2. Individuals value maximum utility, whereas firms value maximum profits.
3. People can only act independently when in the possession of full and relevant information.

Utility is a measure of how much a person will value one product over another. This means that Consumers attempt to maximise their satisfaction with the products they buy, while minimising the cost of these products.

Although the various branches of Neoclassical Theory employ different lines of reasoning, they all use the same assumptions.

Marxist political writer and social revolutionary Paul Mattick in *Economics, Politics and The Age of Inflation* [54] argued that the Subjective Theory of

Value leads to circular reasoning. He claimed that prices are supposed to measure the 'marginal utility' of the commodity. However, prices are required by Consumers in order to evaluate how best to maximise their satisfaction. Hence, subjective value 'obviously rested on circular reasoning'. As utility represents the comparative value of products, marginal utility represents the change in utility the more a product is available. This means that the more of a product people have, the less people will want that product. Despite the use of marginal value as an economic concept, there is still much discussion over the idea.

An alternative to Marginalism is the Subjective Theory of Value [24, 31, 44, 55]. This theory suggests that the value is determined by the individual and the desired purpose of the good, instead of by any inherent property of the good or any resource or requirement for the good's production. Again this theory has its detractors.

In summary, Neoclassical Economic Theories expanded and refined the previous Classical Economic Theories, using mathematical relationships to express their theories and attempting to describe various economic phenomena on the basis of the logic and rules developed from Classical Theory. Despite the fact that the Neoclassical rules are currently the most widely accepted for operating economic systems, there are still criticisms that these theories do not fully reflect real-world economic situations [19, 56, 57].

2.3   Capitalist Economics

Technically, Capitalism is a compilation of those Classical and Neoclassical Theories that are 'not' Marxist or Socialist. There are, however, particular features that distinguish Capitalist societies around the world.

These include:

- preference for private enterprise over government regulation
- free markets
- user pays systems.

One of the guiding principles of modern Capitalist Economics is the idea of 'laissez-faire'. This principle suggests that the economy operates at an optimum level by itself: any Government or external pressure to change the way it operates will produce an economy that operates at a suboptimal level; Governments should not interfere with the operation of free enterprise; free markets are a good idea.

Ultimately, what occurs in a Capitalist Economy is that whoever wants to use a product or service has to pay for it, essentially without Government support. As a result, Capitalism has a tendency to create large income and wealth disparity [19, 26, 30], and on this account it receives significant criticism.

2.4 Marxian Economics

During the era of Classical and Neoclassical Economics, many people noted abuse of power by Capitalists in the pursuit of wealth. This led to reactionary comment by many people, most notably by Karl Marx. Marx's *Das Kapital* [25] examined in detail the general operation of 'Capitalist' industries. He discussed the nature of commodities and money, then he argued that commodities are valuable if they have utility, and that for an item to be a commodity it must be transferred to another owner.

The idea of surplus value was introduced. Surplus value is effectively the profit made by selling a product above the cost of making the product, taking into account the costs of the labour, the tool wear and the initial resources for making the product. Marx demonstrated that Capitalists require the value of a product to be larger than the cost of producing it in order for there to be motivation to create the product.

He reviewed the employment conditions of the 1800s, when there were many cases of employers overworking employees (considered illegal at the time), the use of child labour, and atrocious working conditions in manufacturing facilities. The working conditions were examined economically. The economic value of labour was described as the amount of work possible during a day. The working conditions often caused or exacerbated the employees' health problems and left little time for activities outside work. This demonstrated that the working conditions 'robbed' employees of their ability to enjoy their lives and, as a result, of the majority of the value of their labour. He felt that the overwork reduced the employee's ability to utilise their incomes for their own benefit outside of work.

Marx compared hourly wages with per-piece wages. He studied the final price of products and the amount of profit made in relation to fully paid versus exploitative labour. The differences in wages, productivity and cost of living between countries was also discussed. Throughout Marx's work, Capitalism and Capitalists are repeatedly described as using labour exploitatively, purely for the purpose of gaining wealth.

Later researchers [58–61] have reviewed Marx's work and 'Post-Marxian' Economic Theory and highlighted some limitations, detailed below.

Bowles [58] compared Marxian with Post-Marxian Theory. Both are based on the idea of using labour as the basis for determining value. He noted that many Post-Marxian researchers prefer to use mathematical tools (such as Thermodynamics and Chaos Theory) to explain economic phenomena.

Stiglitz [59] discussed recent changes in economic theory and compared these new ideas with those of Marxian, Walrasian and even Keynesian concepts. His review established a set of properties found in information economics.

These conditions included:

- Markets are not Pareto efficient.
- Markets may not clear.
- Markets may be zero or very small.
- Rents are pervasive; reputation rents are necessary for ensuring product quality.
- Competition may be highly imperfect, even when there are many participants in the market.
- The distribution of income matters for economic efficiency.

Information economics examines the effect of information on economic decisions. It suggests that there is a cost to the use of information, which has implications for contracts and contract enforcement.

Jefferson and King [60] focused on the treatment of domestic labour. They noted that the economic value of the vast majority of domestic labour has been discounted in both Marxian and Neoclassical Theory. Such labour, it was suggested, would account for as much as 64% of GDP.

Much of Marxian Theory is developed from the idea that products should be valued in terms of the labour required to produce them; hence, the labourers should be able to receive the benefits of their labour directly. The majority of Marxian Economics consists of verbal descriptions, and there is a lack of robust mathematics for demonstrating the mechanics of the operation of an economy. Hence, it has been used more politically than for determining how economies operate. Post-Marxian Economics incorporates more mathematical models than Marxian Economics, but it is still based on the value of labour. The mathematical description of these theories is often considered redundant because they often produce the same results as Neoclassical Economics.

2.5   Socialist Economics

The ideals of Socialism are based on Marxist ideology, i.e. that workers should receive an equal share of profits. State Socialist redistributive economies are characterized by the allocation and distribution of goods through central planning. The most notable implementations of these theories are by countries such as Russia and China, neither of which have faithfully followed the original precepts. Unfortunately, implementation of Socialist Economics usually results in the Government controlling the vast majority of the wealth, but not addressing the issues of the working class.

Schumpeter's, *Capitalism, Socialism and Democracy* [26] was considered one of the greatest works of social theory of the 20th century. In it, he compared the economic processes of Socialism and Capitalism, and argued that Capitalism will fail and Socialism will supersede it. Schumpeter reviewed events leading up to his location in history to discuss the operation of Socialism and Capitalism in various countries. He concluded:

Marx was wrong in his diagnosis of the manner in which capitalist society would break down; he was not wrong in the prediction that it would break down eventually. The Stagnationists are wrong in their diagnosis of the reasons why the capitalist process should stagnate; they may still turn out to be right in their prognosis that it will stagnate—with sufficient help from the public sector.

J. A. Schumpeter, *Capitalism, Socialism and Democracy*. London, UK: Routledge, 2013. [26]

Despite this conclusion, neither prediction has yet occurred. Also, Socialism, despite its good intentions, did not end up providing the working class with an equal distribution of wealth or the prosperity that was hoped for. In fact, in modern times, most of the countries that used socialist strategies to operate have since abandoned the idea of total socialism in favour of partial or even completely capitalist strategies.

In *What Was Socialism, and What Comes Next?* [27], Verdery reviewed the nature of Socialism and some of the changes that occurred in the economies of the countries of Eastern Europe as Socialism came to an end there. There were changes in the ownership of property and its redistribution throughout the states. The process that occurred in Romania was examined in detail. The decomposition of the Communist state was compared with a transition to feudalism, and the consequences of the break-up were explored. He noted that many of the Governments have transitioned from Socialist ideals to military dictatorships, i.e. to more authoritarian Governments, rather than to purely democratic Capitalist styles of Government.

In *A Theory of Market Transition: from Redistribution to Markets in State Socialism* [62], Nee discussed some of the changes that occurred when Socialist Economies reformed into more Capitalist Economies. He discussed a theory that predicts the changes that occur in household income and wealth distribution, based on measurements made before and after the dissolution of Socialism. This theory showed that by switching from a centralised planning–based economy to privatised Producers, political power and privilege shifts to the Producers.

The fact remains that most countries that based their economic strategies on Socialist Economics failed economically, and they have since converted to Capitalism in some form. Whether these failures were the result of inadequate understanding and application of economic theory, internal political problems, or external competition with Capitalism remains a point of contention.

2.6 Keynesian economics

Keynes [30] in his book *General Theory of Employment, Interest and Money* gives a detailed discussion of Classical Economic Theory, interest rates and the effects of these on employment.

He examines Classical economics in detail with respect to employment, interest rates, investment, savings and the general operation of the economy. He goes on to establish the theories that:

- The wage is equal to the marginal product of labour.
- The utility of the wage when a given volume of labour is employed is equal to the marginal disutility of that amount of employment.

Several categories of unemployment are defined:

- frictional
- voluntary
- involuntary.

These states of unemployment are then discussed in detail; Keynes investigates both how they occur and potential strategies for solving the various types of unemployment. The idea of 'employment function' is developed by considering the elasticity in labour, and he examines the operation of this function. Professor Pigou's *Theory of Unemployment* [16] is referred to heavily in the sections on unemployment—Pigou's theories of unemployment are examined and his strategies for managing unemployment and wages are compared with Keynes' employment function.

He goes on to discuss the Theory of Prices, which involves how prices are set by demand, resource distribution and wages, and then to consider how the money supply affects pricing.

Finally, he concludes that Capitalist–Neoclassical systems of economics have failed to provide full employment, and have created or maintained a disparity in wealth and income.

Keynes has written on many other topics, including business cycles, inflation, laissez-faire economics, and the future of economics. His work has been considered so influential that a school of economics has been developed based on his theories.

However, there are criticisms of his work, for example by Mankiw [22], who argues against the Post-Keynesian reliance on technological change as the primary source of business cycles. He also argues that various other phenomena (labour supply, monetary policy, inflation, government spending and market equilibrium) described by Keynes as being potential influences on business cycles have been discredited.

2.7 Modern research

Modern research has expanded to consider almost every aspect of life and society. Starting with the original topics of business, trade and inflation, research has expanded to include global issues such as international trade, climate change, and even the economic effects of personal issues such as aging, marriage and education. There are far too many topics to give a complete exploration of the topics, let alone cover the entire spectrum of research. The vast majority of economics research is undertaken with genuine good intentions to improve the lives of everyone.

Many general theories about the general operation of economies have been developed. Some take inspiration from ideas originating in other branches of science, including the concepts of Uncertainty, Chaos Theory and Evolution. As an overview, Keen [56] identifies key features of the following schools of economics, as quoted below:

Austrian Economics, which shares many of the features of Neoclassical Economics, has a slavish devotion to the concept of equilibrium.

Post-Keynesian Economics, which is highly critical of Neoclassical Economics, emphasizes the fundamental importance of Uncertainty, and bases itself upon the theories of Keynes and Kalecki.

Sraffian Economics is based on Sraffa's concept of the production of commodities by means of commodities.

Complexity Theory and Econophysics apply concepts from non-linear dynamics, Chaos Theory and physics to economic issues.

Evolutionary Economics treats the economy as an evolving system along the lines of Darwin's Theory of Evolution.

S. Keen, "Debunking macroeconomics," *Econ. Anal. Policy*, vol. 41, no. 3, pp. 147–167, 2011. [56]

Ultimately, none of the current theories for economics have been globally accepted, and most are open to criticism. Keen's *Debunking Economics* 2011 [56] examined the bulk of economic theory and argued that the vast majority of the theories fail to explain actual real-world economic phenomena.

In *Capital in the Twenty-First Century* (2014) [19], Piketty reviewed the current state of economic wealth worldwide and attempted to find possible explanations. He also proposed a possible solution to inequality in wealth distribution: a wealth tax that would encourage those with the most wealth to redistribute it to others less fortunate.

In general terms, the majority of economics-based problems that we see in the world do not seem to have changed over the years. We still see the effects of regular recessions, large wealth disparity, and poverty. Further research is required in order to determine solutions for these problems.

2.8   Summary of economic theories

The justification for most economic theory is of two types:

- moral
- functional.

Morality- or ethics-based theories, such as Marxism and Socialism, attempt to define what the economy should be trying to achieve. Typically, they include ideas such as: "Wealth should be shared equally!" or "Economics should take into account environmental and social factors."

Functional economic theories are related to what actually occurs in an economy. They usually make measurements of economic performance, and attempt to create mathematical models of the various phenomena in an attempt to understand why they occur.

What is lacking is a fundamental model that can be used to establish the mathematical relationships as expressed in an economy. There is very little use of or reference to systems analysis models that could be used to determine the nature of the interactions between the groups of entities in an economy. Also, while zero-sum concepts are occasionally mentioned in economic theories, none of the literature reviewed has considered the idea that the entire economy has zero-sum limitations. In fact, some economists reject the idea that the economy has zero-sum limitations [63].

From this review of the literature, a pattern emerges: the vast majority of economic theories are more political ideologies than mathematical descriptions of relationships between the entities. Neoclassical Economics comes the nearest to using mathematical analysis to make predictions about pricing. This may explain its continued popularity, notwithstanding its limitations.

Despite the variety and depth of the research being conducted in all of the schools of economics, a theory is yet to emerge that can conclusively explain a number of economic phenomena, or address the difficulties caused by poverty and by the disparity in wealth between the various individuals and nations.

3   Economic theory

The economic theories reviewed in the previous chapter have been used to develop the present-day microeconomic and macroeconomic theories. Microeconomics is concerned with the operation and decision-making processes of individuals within an economy, whereas macroeconomics looks at the operation of the overall economy.

3.1   Microeconomics

Microeconomics is the study of the most basic components of an economy—Consumers (or workers), Producers (or businesses) and Governments—and how these individual components make economic decisions. Such decisions include whether to purchase, how many people to hire … everything that businesses or individuals do to 'collect' or to move money from one entity to another. These are the basic rules of operating businesses and making a profit.

Microeconomic theory is about optimising individual businesses for maximum profits, rather than for maximum production (creating enough of a product for everyone). Who gets to have products when there is a limited supply? Obviously, whoever has the most money. When Producers do not or cannot make enough of a product, prices increase until only the Consumers who can afford the product buy it.

The main tool used in microeconomics to maximise profits is the relationship between supply costs and demand. Supply costs include production costs, which are affected by how much of a product is produced. Demand can be a need or want. Many factors affect supply costs and demand, and these in turn affect the profits made by a business and the number of Consumers who can afford or who want to purchase their products.

3.1.1   Supply

Supply costs are defined by the relationship between the cost of producing a single item of a product and the quantity of a product being supplied. In general terms, the more of a product that needs to be produced, the more expensive the production system will become. To convey this concept, economists usually simplify this relationship to a linear equation showing that, on average, the more of a product that is produced, the higher the cost of production, and thus the higher the price, as shown in Figure 5. As a general rule, the higher the price of a product, the more the Producers are willing to produce it.

Basic supply curve

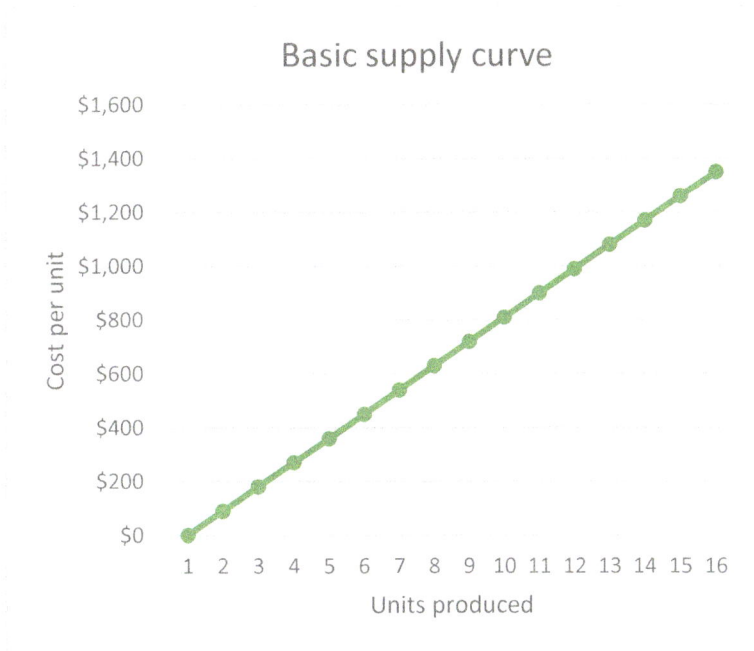

Figure 5: Example of a basic supply curve

The price of the product incorporates both the cost of production and the profit made. As a result, when costs decrease, more profit is made. In such a situation, economists are able to show that this causes the supply 'curve' to shift to the right, allowing more products to be produced.

3.1.2   Demand

Demand in economics is expressed as the amount of money a Consumer is willing to pay for a product or service. The basic assumption is that demand will decrease the more available a particular product is; thus, the price will be lower for more common products or services. Demand is usually simplified to a linear relationship between price and quantity, as shown in Figure 6.

Basic demand curve

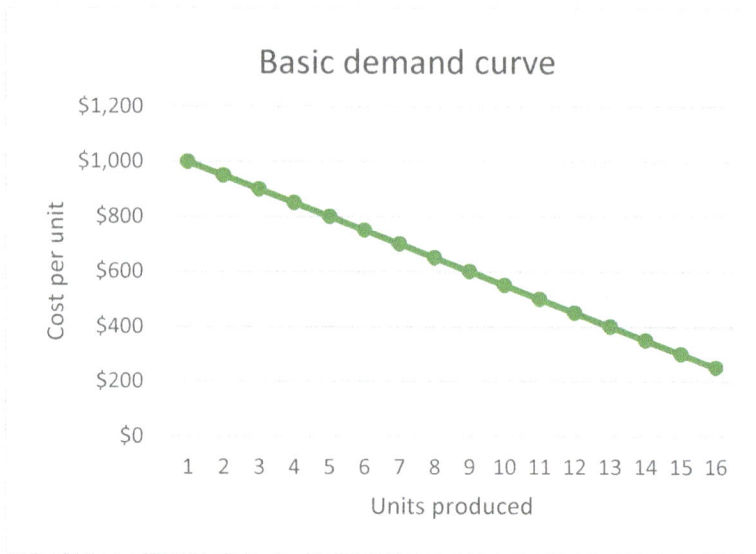

Figure 6: Example of a basic demand curve

3.1.3   Supply versus demand

Supply-versus-demand curves are the main tool that economists use to determine the 'optimum price' and 'optimum production level' (which is said to occur at the 'equilibrium point'). The optimum price is the price at which the maximum profit can be obtained. Figure 7 shows a basic supply-versus-demand curve. The optimum price and number of products is indicated by where the supply curve meets the demand curve. From Figure 7, the production of eight units at a price of $600 each would be optimal and would produce a total income of $4800.

What is noteworthy is that when a product is priced according to the equilibrium point, all of the products being created are sold. The general principle in microeconomics is that businesses will adjust a price until it reaches the equilibrium point.

Basic supply-versus-demand curve

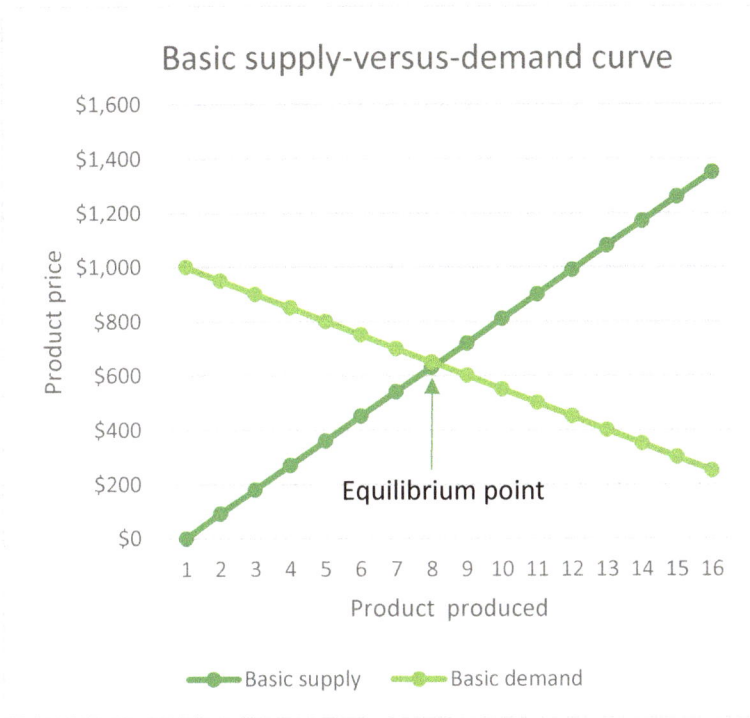

Figure 7: Example of a basic supply-versus-demand curve

A number of other features of the supply-versus-demand curve are used by economists to estimate the various phenomena, including:

- elasticity
- marginal utility
- product substitutions
- Consumer surplus
- the 'bandwagon' effect
- the 'snob' effect
- monopolies
- profit maximisation
- market equilibrium
- Government interventions (e.g. price controls).

3.1.4 Elasticity

Elasticity is a measurement of the sensitivity of a product's sales or production to changes in price. Essentially, it is the slope of the supply curve. This measurement is useful when choosing between products. Consumers generally prefer cheaper products. If only part of the market can be supplied at one price, a second product can supply the rest of the market. Exactly how much of the market can be supplied by each product can be predicted by the supply-versus-demand curve.

3.1.5 Marginal utility

The utility of a product is the amount of satisfaction a Consumer receives from consuming a single unit of a product or service. The marginal utility is defined as the additional satisfaction a Consumer gains from purchasing an additional unit of a product or service.

3.1.6 Product substitutions

Pindyck and Rubinfeld (2009) have formulated the following definitions.

Substitute goods are goods which, as a result of changed conditions, may replace each other in use (or consumption). A complementary good, in contrast to a substitute good, is a good with a negative cross elasticity of demand. This means a good's demand is increased when the price of another good is increased.

R. S. Pindyck and D. Rubinfeld, *Microeconomics* 6th edn. Upper Saddle River, NJ: Pearson Prentice Hall, 2009. [64]

Essentially, people prefer cheaper products and will buy a substitute, even if it is not an equivalent product!

3.1.7 Consumer surplus

A Consumer surplus occurs when some Consumers can afford to pay more for a product than it is currently priced at.

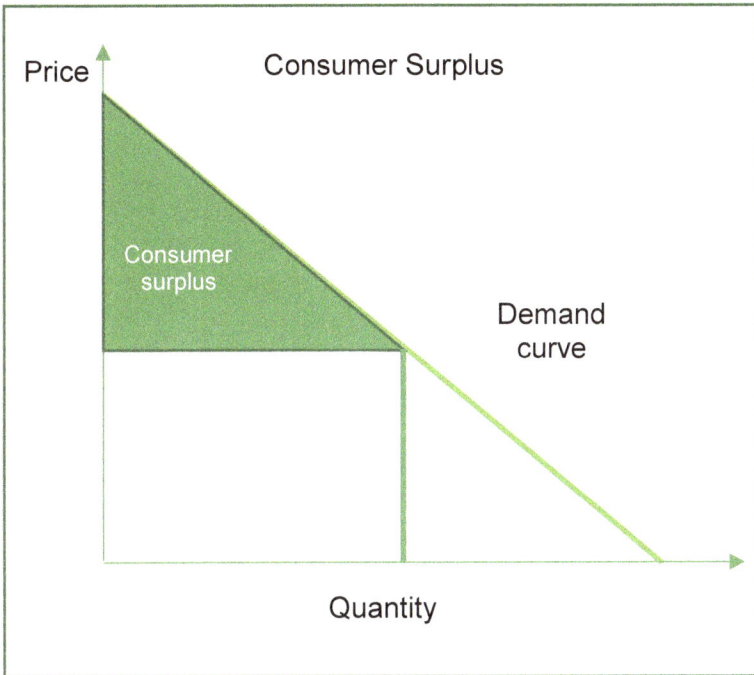

Figure 8: Consumer surplus

3.1.8   The 'bandwagon effect'

Everyone wants the same thing! In other words, as the popularity of a product increases, it may mean that more people want the same product or at least a similar product.

3.1.9   The 'snob effect'

Some people want something special! This is in many ways the opposite of the bandwagon effect. People sometimes want something unique, so they may want to have a special item custom made, or to buy a 'prestige' product.

3.1.10   Monopolies

When there is only a single supplier of a product, the supplier can arbitrarily increase the price of its products. Businesses often like the idea of a monopoly as it gives them far greater control over pricing and allows them to maximise their profits.

3.1.11   Profit maximisation

Ultimately, the purpose of microeconomics is to optimise the performance of an individual business—which means that it attempts to maximise income, minimise costs and maximise profit. In most economic theory, it seems there is no limit to how much profit can be made.

3.1.12   Market equilibrium

The general theory for market equilibrium suggests that when all market Producers and Consumers are connected by trade, an equilibrium price for all products will eventually be established. The idea is that by finding the equilibrium price, the market will autonomously optimise for the maximum profits possible, as shown in Figure 9.

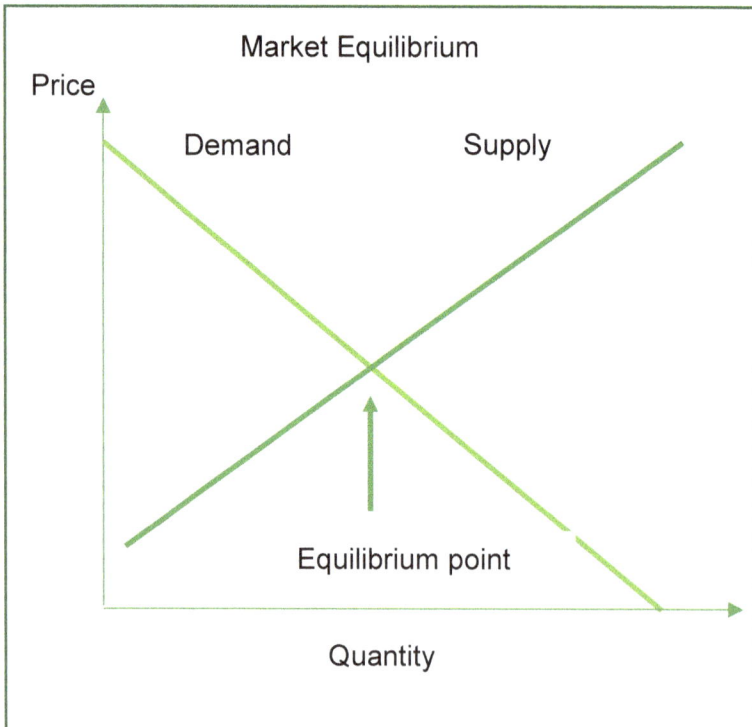

Figure 9: Market equilibrium

General dynamic equilibrium (GDE) is a method for computing the equilibrium prices of a set of products, using supply and demand calculations. It was initially developed by Léon Walras [24], and several variations have been developed by other researchers. This technique is promoted by the school of Austrian Economics, among others.

3.1.13   Market Saturation

All products follow a pattern of sales. Initially few people buy the product. Sales increase as people become more aware of the product and potentially as the product itself improves. Eventually sales peak as the majority of people acquire the product. The product itself will decay and need to be replaced. Sales then continue to fall until the sales rate falls back to the decay rate as shown in Figure 10.

The decay rate depends on the product itself. Some products such as food have nearly a 100% decay rate. Others such as Housing have a very low decay rate.

Market Saturation

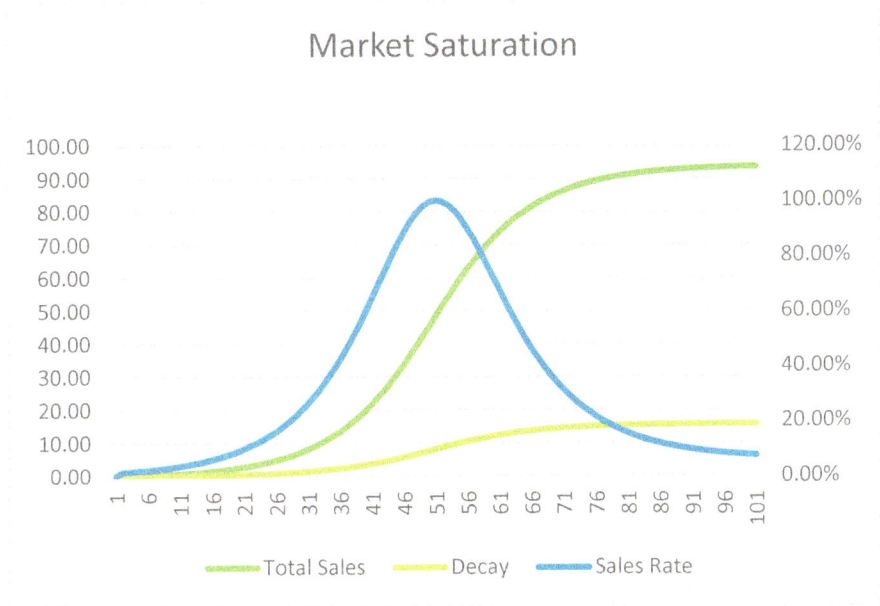

Figure 10: Market Saturation

3.1.14   Government interventions: price controls

The effects of government policies such as providing subsidies or placing trade tariffs on particular goods can be examined. Government price controls can either increase or decrease the cost of goods in order to decrease or increase product purchases, respectively.

3.1.15   Summary of microeconomics

Microeconomics is about local optimisation. It asks: how do I make my business more efficient at collecting money? Microeconomic theories generally predict economic phenomena for individual businesses over short time periods quite well. The predictions start to fail when many businesses and Consumers operate together in the one market and the situation becomes more complex. This is where macroeconomics is required.

3.2   Macroeconomics

Whereas microeconomic theory considers individual behaviours in an economy, macroeconomics measures the operation of economies as a whole. The individuals in an economy can form groups, such as markets and industries, that can be examined collectively. Many macroeconomic phenomena that are observed in the global economy are not well understood.

3.2.1   Circular Flow of Money

We can analyse an economy in terms of the Consumers, Producers and Governments, and it can be shown that money continuously cycles between the three entities, as shown in Figure 11.

Economic theory

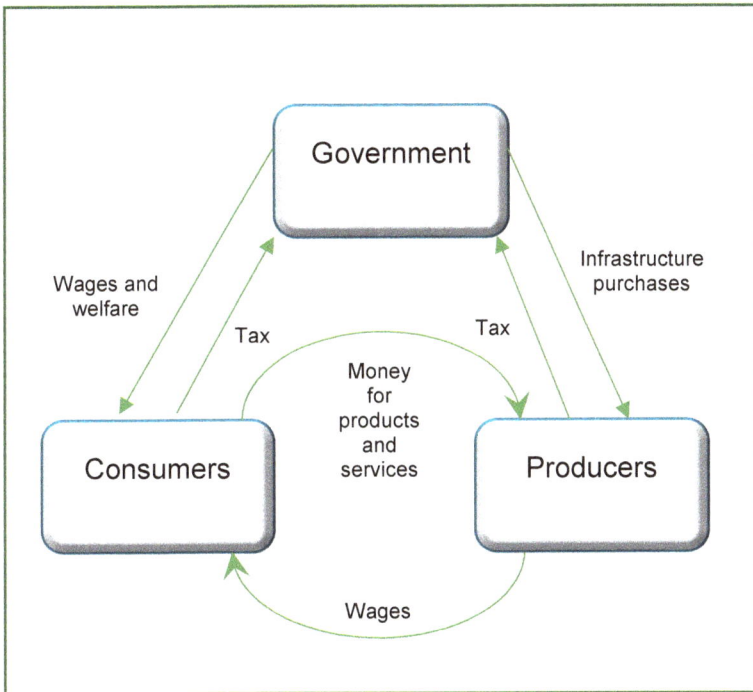

Figure 11: Circular Flow of Money Model

A more detailed version of this model also incorporates investments and resources.

Other portrayals of the Circular Flow of Money break Producers down into resource providers, and show investment flow in order to examine the relationships between industries and Governments. This can be extended to show the relationships between most industries involved in the economy.

3.2.2   Shocks

Producers typically have a supplier, and these suppliers have their own suppliers, and this repeats itself until the entire economy is linked together. Also, in the opposite direction, Producers have clients and their clients have clients, who eventually become the Consumers. When a Producer decides to increase or decrease prices, their suppliers and or clients will have extra money or less money. This excess or shortage is then transmitted to the clients or suppliers and flows through to the rest of the economy.

65

There are many types of shocks. A productivity shock is a form of shock that allows more or less productivity. A technology shock occurs when a new technology is implemented in an economy. The new technology can cause a productivity shock; it may also make other technologies redundant; these effects will be transmitted through to the rest of the economy.

3.2.3   Business cycles

Every 4–10 years, the wider economy sees a reduction in GDP. The reduction in output is called a recession if it lasts long enough. Historically, this has always been followed by a period of 'investment', in which the economy recovers. Business cycles are characterised by a decrease in economic output, followed by a corresponding increase. Typically, the decrease in economic output is distinguished by a financial crisis of some description. Despite the fact that business cycles have been observed since as far back as 1857 (in the USA), macroeconomic theory has not yet found a way to explain it that is universally accepted. In 1817, Robert Owen [65, 66] presented the argument that business cycles were caused by underproduction and overconsumption as a consequence of wealth inequality. In *Nouveaux principes d'économie politique* [67], Jean Charles Léonard de Sismondi argued that business cycles, or 'periodic economic crises', were not caused by external events such as wars. The idea of periodic crises was further developed and examined by Keynes [30] and many others, including Schumpter [26, 68, 69], Charles Dunoyer [70], Johann Karl Rodbertus [71], Karl Marx [25] and Henry George [72].

Not even the latest research [73–75] has fully explained why these events occur. The difficulty with researching this phenomenon is that there is such a volume of discussion about and so many models for business cycles that it is impossible to give a complete review of all the literature. I have focused here on the major developments in our understanding, and also examined some of the more recent ideas published in the peer-reviewed literature.

King and Rebelo [75] reviewed many of the early attempts to explain business cycles, and the Real Business Cycle (RBC) Model in particular. They examined some of the potential causes of business cycles, such as the effects of labour supply, technological development, and welfare. They concluded that business cycles are primarily caused by 'real' factors, which ultimately cause changes in aggregate productivity. This model has been expressed mathematically and shown to be able to simulate business cycles. The modelling showed that the productivity shocks require a highly elastic labour supply and variable capital utilisation, and demonstrated that technological shocks must be sufficiently large before they will affect the economy at large.

Smet and Wouters [74] examined shocks and frictions in US business cycles, using Bayesian methods and dynamic stochastic general equilibrium modelling. The methodology used was based on the New Keynesian or New Neoclassical Synthesis (NNS) models. This research attempted to model the US economy from 1966 to 2000. It was found that 'demand shocks' (such as risk premium, exogenous spending and investment-specific technology shocks) can explain a significant fraction of the short-run variances. It was concluded that this methodology is flexible enough to fit the majority of US macroeconomic data from 1966 to 2000.

Iacoviello [73] examined the causes of specifically financial business cycles, again using Bayesian methods and dynamic stochastic general equilibrium modelling. The modelling showed that the losses incurred by banks can trigger a recession, which is then exacerbated by credit restrictions. Using the model, he estimated that as much as two-thirds of the 1927 Great Recession was caused by financial shocks.

In summary, despite the volume of work on the subject of business cycles, there is little consensus between theories about causes. So far, no one theory to explain business cycles has been completely accepted by all schools of research.

3.2.4   Inflation

Previous models of inflation from Classical and Neoclassical Economics show that an insufficient supply of goods drives up prices. This type of inflation is typically referred to as cost-push or demand-pull inflation. Cost-push inflation is related to the cost of labour, raw materials and other production expenses. Demand-pull inflation occurs when Consumers demand more of a resource than is available. The Consumers with the most money are the ones who end up getting the resource as they drive up the price till it is out of reach of the poorer individuals.

In their early work [76], Samuelson and Solow (1960) stated that inflation was not well understood. They examined the theories proposed to explain the inflation in post-war USA—chiefly demand-pull– and cost-push–based theories, which were the most prevalent at the time. They also examined the QTM, which suggests that Governments printing too much money cause businesses to increase their prices. The example given is typically based upon the observed inflation rate in Germany after World War I. The QTM and the Velocity of Money concept were accepted as the main reasons for post-war German inflation, but Samuelson and Solow noted that other researchers still disagree with this theory.

Both the UK and US economies were examined and compared with respect to the Phillips curve, which shows the relationship between inflation and unemployment: higher unemployment leads to lower inflation. Samuelson and Solow [76] showed that this relationship is true, i.e. as unemployment is reduced, inflation increased. They concluded that there have not been any 'feasible institutional reforms' that could solve both inflation and unemployment.

Inflation is typically described in terms of supply shocks or demand shocks, where either supply is suddenly restricted or demand is suddenly increased. These effects are regularly seen in economies, but economists disagree as to whether or not these cause continuous inflation.

Researchers have often focused their inquiries on particular countries. The following reviews present investigations into the inflation scenarios in the UK, Italy, Turkey, China, Pakistan and Ghana.

Willett and Laney [77] discussed Keynesian and Monetarist Theories of Inflation. In reviewing these theories, they stated that cost-push and demand-pull causes of inflation are essentially the same thing. They suggested that Keynesian Theories focus on short-term inflation, whereas Monetarist Theories focus on long-term inflation. They also discussed the relationship between unemployment and inflation with reference to the Phillips curve. They noted that there is little agreement about medium-term causes of inflation. They examined wages, Government debt and money supply in both the UK and Italy, and observed that there was a general increase in all three measurements in both countries, but little correlation over short periods of time. They concluded that cost-push and demand-pull theories could not be relied upon to explain inflation, but they did not present any alternative method.

Kibritçioğlu [78] discussed and compared many of the main economic theories of inflation, including the Classical, Monetarist, Structuralist and Keynesian

Theories, as well as their modern versions. Some of the Monetarist Theories have complex mathematical models encompassing the entire economy. These models typically describe the Velocity of Money in an economy. Kibritçioğlu [78] examined the case of Turkey from the years 1950 to 2000 in terms of the contemporary political policies, noting increases in the price of oil over this period. A review of other research was included to show how inflation had been explained by previous researchers. Many researchers considered that one-off incidents (typically supply shocks) could explain the inflation. Kibritçioğlu, however, argued that such incidents could not explain the persistent high inflation experienced in Turkey.

Chand [79] examined food inflation in India over the years 1980–2010. During 2009, a major drought was experienced that reduced local food production. Despite the fact that there had been excess food production in previous years, the excess in production did not protect against the reduction in production during the drought. Chand concluded that the main reason for the food inflation of 2010 was a supply shock due to the drought, exacerbated by a lack of effective storage. Grains can only be stored for three months before they become inedible. This reduced the supply of food and hence increased inflation. Chand suggested that an improvement in appropriate storage technology, especially in rural areas, and redirecting some of the food destined for export to storage could overcome this type of problem. In economic terms, Chand demonstrated the real impact of supply shocks on inflation (specifically, the effect of drought on food prices).

Ha et al. [80] examined the historic levels of inflation in mainland China. The theories of inflation were reviewed, including the conventional Phillips curve and the new Phillips curve. They suggested that the conventional Phillips curve attempts to relate the 'output gap' or output shortfall of a country to expected price rises, and explained that the difficulty with this approach was indirectly estimating the output gap, especially for countries experiencing significant structural changes. In contrast, the new Phillips curve uses the 'real marginal cost' instead of the output gap. They concluded that the new Phillips curve characterises mainland China's inflation better than the conventional method does. The main causes of inflation were found to be world prices, exchange rates and labour costs.

Khan et al. [81] examined the causes of inflation in Pakistan. Several of the classical causes of inflation were examined, including excess of money, national debt, external lending, increases in labour costs, a high level of federal taxes, and Government policies in general. They concluded that to control inflation, domestic production needs to be favoured over imports (especially food and commodities required by the population), and that exchange rates need to be controlled more effectively.

Mustapha and Khalid [82] discussed Monetary and Keynesian Theories of Inflation, especially with reference to investment returns and Government debt. The social effects of high inflation were examined, and it was noted that high inflation affects poorer people disproportionately more than it does wealthy people. Several scenarios of investment were examined, and they showed that high inflation reduces lenders' effective profits. It was concluded that high inflation reduces the value of money over time, and hence reduces the value of any investment.

Harvey and Cushing [83] used a Structural Vector Auto-Regression (SVAR) Model to identify the causes of inflation in Ghana. The results of this analysis showed that neither monetary nor structural factors could explain the inflation experienced by Ghana. They concluded that there is a strong feedback relationship between inflation and exchange rate depreciation, so Ghana should attempt to reduce its reliance on imports if they wish to stabilise inflation. They noted that this confirms the findings of other researchers, and that for African countries, exchange rate depreciation is a major causal factor of inflation.

In summary, the main theories attempting to explain inflation are based on observations of economies at the macro scale. The research presented identified several types of inflation, including cost push, demand pull and exchange rate. Despite the volume of research, none of the literature reviewed has determined appropriate methods for avoiding or minimising inflation without causing other problems. Also, none of the literature reviewed has managed to derive causes of inflation from basic models or principles of economics.

3.2.5   Gross domestic product

GDP is the total value of goods produced in a country over a period of time, typically a year. This measurement is useful for determining how well the economy of an entire country is performing over time.

3.2.6   Wealth distribution

The common phrase about wealth distribution is: "The rich get richer; the poor
get poorer". This phenomenon is described in more specific terms by many
researchers. The Pareto Principle relates to the effort required to get a particular
gain. Typically, 20% of the effort is said to be responsible for 80% of the
benefit. In terms of wealth distribution, the Pareto Principle says 20% of the
population gets 80% of the wealth. The Gini Index is a measure of wealth
distribution based on the Pareto Principle. If the Gini Index is 0.0, all wealth is
distributed evenly; when the Gini index is 1.0, all wealth is 'owned' by a single
person.

Davies et al. [84] examined the world distribution of household wealth, using
economic data from a total of 34 countries. Using regression analysis to compile
missing data, an estimate for 150 countries was generated (95% of world
coverage). The distributions calculated show that the USA (34%), Europe (30%)
and Wealthy Asia (24%) own the vast majority of the wealth in the world. The
Gini index is used to show the variation in wealth distribution between the
countries studied, calculating the worldwide average Gini Index for the year
2000 to be 0.893. This is significantly higher than a previous estimate for 1998,
which calculated the worldwide Gini index at 0.795 [85].

Other statistics were discussed, including the aggregate wealth distribution of
the richest 10% and richest 1% of the population, the distribution of wealth in
individual countries, and the distribution of wealth collectively. Future trends for
wealth distribution, again both worldwide and for individual countries, were
discussed, noting that China in particular is likely to continue to distribute more
wealth to the middle class.

In their modelling methods, Davies et al. used regression analysis to show what
happened in the past, and they were able to estimate future trends. Notably, the
research presented by Davies et al. [84] did not explain 'why' the wealthy
continue to accumulate wealth, resulting in Gini Indexes approaching 1.0.

Carroll et al. [86] discussed the distribution of wealth in European households.
The Gini coefficient was discussed, and they related wealth distribution to the
Marginal Propensity to Consume (MPC). The models were developed based on
over 62,000 bank records from fifteen countries. The Gini Index for Europe was
calculated to be approximately 0.65. This study differentiated between general

wealth and liquid assets, and concluded that wealth inequality affects the ability of 'fiscal stimulus' to recover from economic downturns.

Corneo and Jeanne [87] discussed the relationship between the distribution of wealth and perceived social status. They used Romer's AK Model [20] to generate endogenous economic growth for their model. his was used to determine the effect of spending money on status, compared with the effect of reinvesting money. One conclusion was that equality enhances economic growth because it makes it easier for everyone to ascend the wealth hierarchy. They also suggested that competition in social status increases disparity in wealth, as people often overinvest in their social status.

Hoch and Mohan-Neill [88] discussed the effect of education, and looked at whether financial literacy can help alleviate wealth and income inequality in the USA. They examined the results of surveys of people who had received some education in economics. It was found that the majority of the people interviewed preferred a more even wealth distribution, but they were less supportive of wealth redistribution or even of equalizing of educational resources.

Razak [89] investigated wealth distribution, especially that between countries. Income disparity between countries was discussed with particular reference to the initial conditions in the countries (looking at whether those initial conditions determined final wealth distributions). An argument was presented that wealth distribution is caused by inequality in standard of education. Razek developed a mathematical relating investment in education to income and the inheritance of wealth from past generations. It was concluded that the initial conditions do make a difference to wealth distribution.

Despite the fact that the wealth distribution phenomenon has been remarked on for a long time, a theory has not been developed that explains its occurrence from basic principles. Most of the literature reviewed seems to assume that the major factor determining wealth accumulation is the choice and effort people put into work. Again, none of the literature reviewed has examined any influence of zero-sum systems on wealth distribution.

3.2.7   *Exchange rates*

Exchange rates are established to allow the different currencies to be exchanged between countries. They allow goods to be traded between countries, with each country using their own currency. The problem with exchange rates is that the exchange rates can fail. When money builds up in one country, the exchange rate between that country and other countries becomes extremely large.

3.2.8   Balance of trade

Trade between countries allows specialisation to occur: some countries can create particular goods more easily than others due to the favourability of climate and/or the availability of resources, and as a result there can often be an imbalance between exports and imports. Countries usually attempt to make sure that they do not import more than they export, but it is often difficult to ensure that this balance is maintained.

3.2.9   Monetary policy

The main question monetary policy attempts to answer is how much money needs to be in circulation. Answering this question is complicated due to the effects of inflation, unemployment, exchange rates and the general productivity of the economy.

There is an argument that suggests that too much money in an economy can cause excessive inflation. This occurred in Germany after World War I (1924, 1931) [90], and more recently in Zimbabwe (2009)[91]. In both places, inflation increased to such a point that it was called 'Hyperinflation'; this ultimately resulted in the associated currency being abandoned. Because of this phenomenon, most countries avoid releasing significant amounts of money into their economies. Monetary policy is usually developed so that interest rates are minimised and the general productivity of the economy is maximised.

3.2.10   Global labour

Recently, it has been noted that globalisation has significantly reduced production costs. Conversely, many of the jobs that were available in the 'Western' world have been 'offshored' to countries where labour is cheaper.

In his essay, Blinder [92] reviewed the history of the phenomenon of offshoring in relation to textile manufacturing, which initially began in the UK, was transferred to the USA and more recently moved to China. He reported that less than one million US jobs had been offshored, which is less than 1% of the entire employment market in the USA. He also looked at the rise and fall of manufacturing jobs in the USA. He considered the overall historic levels of employment and production in both agriculture and manufacturing and noted that, while the percentage of jobs in agriculture had significantly dropped, the number of jobs in total was roughly the same. To maintain the same level of employment, other areas of employment outside agriculture have increased along with the growth of the population.

The effects of education were considered, and it was noted that highly skilled workers are just as susceptible to offshoring as less skilled workers. Different types of jobs were reviewed, and it was found that the jobs that will not be offshored are those that involve personal interaction; the jobs that are offshored are typically 'impersonal'. Blinder concluded that rich countries will shift their employment focus away from impersonal services to personal services, also adding that personal services are likely to become more expensive. Large, complex, multifaceted adjustments will be necessary across many areas of government and society in general. He asserted that protectionism will not prevent offshoring, and recommended that people educate children for any new kinds of jobs that will become available. He forecast that the USA will more likely cope better than Europe, as he believes the USA is "more flexible" than Europe or Japan.

Levy [93] discussed the trend of offshoring of labour by companies to countries where employee incomes are significantly lower than in the source country. He noted that one of the major enablers of the offshoring trend is the rise in telecommunications technology. Statistics for job losses were reviewed, including associated changes in income for employees, ex-employees and business owners. He concluded that the business owners and shareholders stand to receive the vast majority of the benefit from the offshoring phenomenon. He showed that ex-employees are often only able to find re-employment at an equivalent job 69% of the time, and 55% of ex-employees move to lower-paying jobs (approximately 25% suffer pay cuts of up to 30%). In summary, "Eighty-six percent of ex-employees were worse off after displacement and 56% greatly so."

Baldwin [94] reviewed the effects of globalisation, specifically for Europe. Two generations of offshoring were discussed: the first was the wave of low-skilled, high-labour jobs being transferred to countries where labour was cheaper; the second wave of offshoring was explained as due to the advances in telecommunications technology. He noted that jobs involving individual tasks (rather than entire industries) are the most affected by offshoring.

He concluded that globalisation will continue, which will create pressures to reallocate economic resources across sectors, firms and occupations, but that the direction and nature of the changes are impossible to predict with any accuracy. From this, it was recommended that Governments attempt to be more flexible so they can adapt to the changes that will occur.

Aspray et al. [85] reviewed the effect of globalisation on software development. The types of work offshored were reviewed, along with the education required in both the source and destination countries. Patterns for offshoring were examined in various countries, particularly in relation to the operation of US and Japanese technology firms. Typical strategies involve setting up subsidiary companies or joint venture companies in the offshored country and operating these from the source country, or simply contracting out the work to existing technology companies. It was noted that many of the countries to which software development has been offshored have significant problems with software piracy and maintaining intellectual property (IP).

Liu and Trefler [96] reviewed the changes resulting from offshoring jobs, focusing on the number of jobs offshored and the change in earnings of workers. They concluded, in contrast to Levy, that there has been minimal change in the overall level of wages: workers who moved to lower-paying jobs found their income reduced by 13.9%, but workers who changed to alternative fields had their income increased by 12.1%.

Despite the evidence that offshoring is significantly detrimental for employees in source countries, most of the literature reviewed was positive about the overall effects of globalised labour markets. One of the major points that none of the literature reviewed mentioned is that offshoring also offshores knowledge. The people who perform the jobs must have the same knowledge as the displaced employees; this means that any future developments will likely come from the offshored employees. None of the literature reviewed has shown any link to zero-sum systems or to the difference in cost of living between each of the countries.

3.2.11   General Economic Theories

The following section introduces a few economic theories, especially ones related to money. A few have been accepted by academia, but some are still controversial. Other texts go into far more detail that here but these are introduced as they are relevant to a few details in chapter 8 of this book.

3.2.11.1   The Velocity of Money Theory

The Velocity of money is a measurement of the rate at which money is exchanged in an economy. It is typically calculated by taking GDP divided by the total money supply. This represents the rate at which one unit of money supply currency is being transacted for goods and services in an economy.

The Velocity of money theory suggests that as more money in an economy, the slower it will cycle. This suggests that prices will typically scale with the amount of money on an economy.

Despite this theory measurements of real economies show the velocity of money is typically higher in expanding economies and lower in contracting economies. In "The Counter-Revolution in Monetary Theory" Milton Friedman [97] wrote:

"Perhaps the simplest way for me to suggest why this was relevant is to recall that an essential element of the Keynesian doctrine was the passivity of velocity. If money rose, velocity would decline. Empirically, however, it turns out that the movements of velocity tend to reinforce those of money instead of to offset them. When the quantity of money declined by a third from 1929 to 1933 in the United States, velocity declined also. When the quantity of money rises rapidly in almost any country, velocity also rises rapidly. Far from velocity offsetting the movements of the quantity of money, it reinforces them."

It is clear that the velocity of money does change, but there is still some discussion over the factors involved.

3.2.11.2   The Value of Money Theory

The value of money theory is closely related to the quantity of money theory, and related to inflation, exchange rates. The value of money theory shows that the more money that is introduced into an economy the less valuable the money becomes.

  "The value of money is determined by the demand for it, just like the value of goods and services. There are three ways to measure the value of the dollar. The

first is how much the dollar will buy in foreign currencies. That's what the exchange rate measures. Forex traders on the foreign exchange market determine exchange rates. They take into account supply and demand, and then factor in their expectations for the future.

For this reason, the value of money fluctuates throughout the trading day. The second method is the value of Treasury notes. They can be converted easily into dollars through the secondary market for Treasuries."

There are two factors that are related to the value of money: Inflation and Exchange rates. Inflation is defined by the increase in prices over time. Exchange rates are defined by the relative amount of money when exchanging currencies. These factors are affected by the amount of money in an economy. Economists have attempted to show that the more money in the economy the higher inflation becomes.

Hyperinflation seems to occur when the effects of inflation and exchange rates combine to produce a feedback loop resulting in uncontrolled rapid inflation. Historically this has resulted in the elimination of the currency. This suggests the value of the currency becomes zero.

Historically we find that even the roman empire suffered from inflation where they needed to produce more currency especially in the last century of its existence [98]–[102]. As such, we can see that many of the problems in economics have existed as long as there have been economies.

3.2.11.3 The Trickle-down Theory

The Trickle-down economics theory claims that the benefits for the wealthy trickle down to everyone else in an economy. These benefits are tax cuts on businesses, high-income earners, capital gains, and dividends.

Trickle-down economics assumes investors, savers, and company owners are the real drivers of growth. It suggests any extra cash from tax cuts to expand businesses. Investors will buy more companies or stocks. Banks will increase lending. Owners will invest in their operations and hire workers. All of this expansion will trickle down to workers. They will spend their wages to drive demand and economic growth.

This theory has been widely criticised, despite its use by prominent political groups.

3.2.11.4   Money is exogenous to the economy

The typical explanation of the money supply is that it is controlled by a central bank, but not to stabilise the economy. As such, both definitions can apply as per the definitions below.

The "money supply" is "exogenous" if we believe that it is set directly by the central bank; private agents within the economy will set interest rates on instruments in response to the supply of money. (Exo-is the Greek root that indicates that something is external; in this case, the money supply is set externally to the model of the private sector.) [103]

The amount of money in the economy is not specified directly by any commercial or even the Reserve Bank. Many argue that money itself is not important at all to the economy, but the "Value" of products is the important part. This suggests that money is exogenous to the economy.

The "money supply" is endogenous if we believe that the central bank sets the policy rate of interest; the level of money is determined by factors within the private sector. (The root endo- implies that it is an internal property; that is, the level of the money supply is determined within the model of the private sector.) [103]

The fact is the reserve bank controls the money supply via Loans, which allegedly can be used to create cash. This should mean that the money supply is dependent on the internal demand for money, which suggests money is endogenous.

3.2.11.5   How Is Money 'Created'?

This section has been compiled from several different sources describing how money is created ion the banking system [104]–[108], This process can is discussed further in Section 4.8.

Currency comes in 2 types: Bank Notes and Coins. Banknotes are produced by Reserve Banks and account for most (about 95 per cent) of the value of currency. The rest is accounted for by coins produced by Mints. Commercial Banks purchase currency from the Reserve Bank as required to meet demand from their customers and, in turn, Reserve Banks ensures that it has enough banknotes on hand to meet that demand. Previous research points to a number of drivers of demand for currency. The most important is the size of the economy.[109] This is consistent with people holding some fraction of their income in this most liquid form of money in order to undertake transactions.[110] Some share of demand is also accounted for by the desire for a liquid store of wealth. The value of currency in circulation as a share of nominal GDP has actually increased over recent years (to around 4 per cent), which suggests that this source of demand has grown strongly. This increase has been observed in a range of countries and is consistent with the low level of interest rates, which has reduced the opportunity cost of holding money (compared with holding interest-bearing deposits).

When customers withdraw currency from an ATM or a bank branch, the value of their deposit holdings declines and the value of their currency holdings increases. The stock of broad money, however, is unchanged. (This is a zero sum transaction where the total value of broad money remains constant.)

The vast bulk of broad money consists of bank deposits. These banking liabilities are created when a household or business has funds credited to their deposit account at a bank. One way this can occur is when a business deposits currency it has earned into as bank. Such transactions add to deposits **but do not create money because the bank customer is simply exchanging one type of money (currency) for another (a deposit)**. In other words: This is a "zero-sum" transaction.

Money can be created, when financial intermediaries make loans. Accordingly, the concepts of money and credit are closely linked in a modern economy, albeit not one for one. When a bank extends a loan, it makes money available to the borrower, for example, to buy a car, a house or equipment for a business. The bank may credit the deposit account of the borrower, who withdraws the funds to make their purchase. Alternatively, the bank may directly credit the deposit account of the seller on behalf of the borrower. In either case, the loaned funds will tend to find their way into a deposit somewhere in the banking system. This process adds to the supply of money.

The process of money creation is constrained in numerous ways and depends on the behaviour of borrowers, banks and regulators, as well as the stance of monetary policy.
In the first instance, the process of money creation requires a willing borrower. That demand will depend, among other things, on prevailing interest rates as well as broader economic conditions. Other things equal, lower interest rates or stronger overall economic conditions will tend to support the demand for credit, and vice versa.
The bank then has to be willing and able to issue the loan:

It has to satisfy itself that the borrower can service the loan.

The bank must maintain a sufficient share of its assets in liquid form to meet any drawdowns relating to the new loan, as well as meeting any withdrawals from existing depositors.[111] Otherwise, the bank runs the risk of failing to meet its obligations when they fall due.

The bank's loans and other assets need to be backed by adequate capital. Capital is needed to absorb unexpected losses arising from defaults or other sources of variation in the value of assets.

The interest rates charged on loans must cover expected losses on the loan portfolio, as well as the costs of deposits and other sources of funding. Revenues from loans and other assets will also have to cover the operating costs of the bank, while allowing it to earn a profit so that shareholders can earn a reasonable return on the bank's capital.

All of these considerations imply that money creation occurs at some cost, which serves to constrain the extent of lending. These constraints are reinforced by regulatory requirements for liquidity, capital adequacy and lending standards set by the Australian Prudential Regulation Authority. Other things equal, anything that reduces the willingness or ability of banks to make loans can be expected to result in lower growth of (system-wide) money. [105]

The process of money creation is not the result of the actions of any single bank, but the banking system as a whole creates money. A single bank may make loans by drawing on its liquid assets, yet not receive the corresponding deposits created in return. Before extending further loans, that bank would need to raise funds in other ways – for example, by issuing debt or equity securities or by waiting for its deposits and liquid assets to rise via other means.[107]

This is because there are other sources of funding besides deposits – and indeed, loans are not the only assets held by banks. Other funding comes from issuance of debt and equity. The shares from different sources are in line with the actual funding behaviour of the banking system over recent years. Banks attempt to balance their own liabilities (which includes both their own loans and debts to Government) with the money available in deposits and other assets. [104]

In the modern economy, most money takes the form of bank deposits. The principal way bank deposits are created is through commercial banks making loans. Whenever a bank makes a loan, it simultaneously creates a matching deposit in the borrower's bank account, thereby creating new money. The reality of how money is created today differs from the description found in some economics textbooks:

- Rather than banks receiving deposits when households save and then lending them out, bank lending creates deposits.
- In normal times, the central bank does not fix the amount of money in circulation, nor is central bank money 'multiplied up' into more loans and deposits.

Although commercial banks create money through lending how much they can lend if they are to remain profitable in a competitive banking system. Prudential regulation also acts, as a constraint on banks' activities in order to maintain the resilience of the financial system. And the households and companies who receive the money created by new lending may take actions that affect the stock of money— they could quickly 'destroy' money by using it to repay their existing debt, for instance.

Monetary policy acts as the ultimate limit on money creation. The Bank of England aims to make sure the amount of money creation in the economy is consistent with low and stable inflation. In normal times, the Bank of. England implements monetary policy by setting the interest rate on central bank reserves. This then influences a range of interest rates in the economy, including those on bank loans.

In exceptional circumstances, when interest rates are at their effective lower bound, money creation and spending in the economy may still be too low to be consistent with the central bank's monetary policy objectives. One possible response is to undertake a series of asset purchases, or 'quantitative easing' (QE). QE is intended to boost the amount of money in the economy directly by purchasing assets, mainly from non-bank financial companies. QE initially increases the amount of bank deposits those companies hold (in place of the assets they sell). Those companies will then wish to rebalance their portfolios of assets by buying higher-yielding assets, raising the price of they cannot do so freely without limit. Banks are limited in those assets and stimulating spending in the economy. As a by-product of QE, new central bank reserves are created. But, these are not an important part of the transmission mechanism.

Changes in the stock of broad money are the result of a myriad of decisions, including those of banks, their borrowers, creditors and shareholders. These decisions take place within the framework of a range of regulatory and institutional arrangements. The Reserve Bank does not target a particular level or growth rate of money (although it has done so under a previous monetary policy regime).[108] Instead, the Reserve Bank has some influence on the money stock via the effect of its interest rate target for the overnight cash rate on other interest rates in the economy. These in turn affect the cost of borrowing and economic conditions more generally. Ultimately, borrowing and lending decisions – and thus the creation of money – are constrained by the need for prudent banking behaviour, the budget constraints of borrowers and the profitability of lenders.

Previous regulatory regimes, which had earlier required banks to hold a minimum share of their deposits as reserves with the Reserve Bank, these regimes have been replaced with modern prudential regulation and market discipline. The demand for and supply of credit is the real driver of money which can be examining the behaviour of credit and money over time. [102]

Despite the intentions of banking regulators, these systems have continually failed to provide a stable economy. The intention of the money creation system is not to stabilise the economy or even encourage growth. There are many people who are critical of these processes and many reasons to be critical. Christopher Kent noted [105] "Capital is needed to absorb unexpected losses arising from defaults or other sources of variation in the value of assets. " This highlights one of the biggest problems of the banking system, We can certainly guarantee that over time values will change, housing prices typically go up, but they can and do go down often (Property crash dates). The other problem is the debt also gets charged interest, which means the debt will always increase. A typical home load with an interest rate of 5% over 30 years results in a factor of 2.7 times (calculate out 1.05^{30}) the initial value. This means for any loan of this value the person who gets the loan will have to pay back 2.7 times more money that the money created. Ultimately, with these constraints this system is guaranteed to fail resulting in financial crises, such as the great recession.

3.2.12   Summary of macroeconomics

From the review of the literature presented here, it can be seen that many of the economic phenomena have no models to explain why they occur. Typically, their existence has been noted from real measurements of existing economies. Economics attempts to measure human choice, which tends to be illogical, erratic and inconsistent over time and between individuals. Many economists assume this is the major reason for the difficulties in measuring economic phenomena and for the phenomena themselves. The vast majority of the economic theories reviewed have used regression models based on real data from economies, but generally do not provide an underlying model from which their theories can be developed. It is notable that these phenomena have not been studied using systems analysis or in terms of zero-sum limitations.

One of the things that I think has significantly changed in the last century is the nature of economics. Economics is often described as the study of the choices made when confronted with scarcity of resources. The difference between now and a century ago is the volume of production of which the human race has become capable. We can now literally move mountains to acquire the resources we need or want. We have cities with millions of people, mostly living happily, fed and housed.

Most of the resources the human race has previously struggled to obtain are now not unlimited, but they are certainly not rare. We produce approximately 4 billion tonnes of food every year [112]. With a population nearing 7.5 billion people it should be possible for everyone to have enough to eat—approximately 1.5 kg per person per day (or approximately 0.75–1 kg/day after subtracting loss due to food spoilage). Despite this, the world still has poverty, and the wealth of the world is extremely unbalanced, with 1% of the world's population owning 50% of its wealth.

If you ask people if they want to be rich, most people say, "Yes!" If you ask people if they want to be poor, no one says, "Yes." Yet despite this, there are definitely poor people in the world … and yet people still assume that poverty exists because people want to be poor or perhaps aren't willing to make the effort to become more wealthy. The conclusion one can draw from these observations is that there is a disconnect between what we understand and what actually happens. I suggest that there is a significant misconception about how economics operates—hence, my desire to introduce the new theory of Zero-sum Economics!

4 Zero-sum Economics

In this chapter, the assumptions and rules used in Zero-sum Theory are explained, and some economic phenomena are then examined in the light of Zero-sum Theory. Chapter 5 contains experiments undertaken to numerically test the assumptions and rules presented here. These experiments seek to answer the question: "Does this theory correlate with the observations current economists have made about the operation of economies?"

Zero-sum Economics uses many of the same rules as previous economic theories, but it incorporates a few extra restrictions. The main restriction is the assumption that the economy, in terms of money, operates under zero-sum limitations. Limits on population, market size and demands are also considered.

Throughout the history of economics, many people have thought of the production cycle as 'transforming' money into products, and vice versa. This idea has been widely accepted by the population at large. However, when money is actually traced, it becomes obvious that money is never created or destroyed by trade; it is merely transferred to a new 'owner'. Thus, Zero-sum Theory does not consider that money is transformed, but instead that it flows around the economy.

The main consequence of Zero-sum Economics is that the economy is limited by money that is transferred by zero-sum transactions. The system itself is closed, and the entities interact via transactions. Money can only be added into the system by Governments. Technically money is created by banks as they create debt, but as debt is considered an asset the value of the debt is ignored for the purposes of modelling money. In Zero-sum Models, banks are simply considered to be Producers as everything they do is aimed at making a profit.

The entities in a zero-sum system can be described as Consumers, Producers and Governments. These entities can be thought of as groups of people or as aggregate collections. More detailed models split up the initial three entities into smaller groups.

The main measurement of interest is the amount of money ('balance') that each entity has. From the incomes and expenses of the various entities, it is possible to examine the operation of the entire economy, and to compare predictions based on Zero-sum Economic theories with measurements from real economies.

Control Theory is described in Section 4.3. It is an engineering theory that allows systems to be analysed and their 'natural response' to be determined mathematically. A natural response is a term from control theory. It is the response of a system to an impulse function. [Horrible mathematics, calculus, differential equations! ... But don't panic!] These system models can then be used to determine the operation of the system under various conditions. Zero-sum Theory uses Control Theory, along with the system models described by economic theory, to explain economic phenomena.

Ultimately, Zero-sum Theory can be used to identify places where people's choices are limited and to explain the reasons for the limitations. Such limitations often create systemic behaviours that can have a detrimental effect on the entire system. Bad things can happen in an economy, not because people intentionally make them happen, but because people have limited choices.

4.1 Transactions

As discussed in Section 1.2, the first restriction of Zero-sum Economics is that all transactions (for example, the act of giving someone else $20) are zero sum.

Table 10: Zero-sum transaction analysis

	Me	Them	Sum of changes
Initial state	$20	$0	
Final state	$0	$20	
Total		$20	
Change in cash	–$20	+$20	<u>0</u>

In this example, we have a fixed resource of $20. One entity loses $20 (–20) and one entity gains $20 (+20). The sum of the changes is zero. Hence, the transaction is zero sum.

This is the standard type of transaction that occurs in all money exchanges, and in all traded goods—which leads us to our first general principle:

A single transaction is a zero-sum event;
therefore, all transactions are zero-sum events;

therefore, in terms of trade, the entire economy must operate as a zero-sum system.

Previous economic theories have assumed that since it is possible for everyone in an economy to create new products, it is possible for everyone in an economy to 'make money'. Zero-sum Economics demonstrates that this is not so.

So, if the economy is limited as a zero-sum system, how is it that the value of an economy can increase?

Let's say we have a group of people. The first person has $100 and everyone else has $0.

Value	$0	$0	$0	$0	$0	$0		$0
	○	○	○	○	○	○	...	○
Money	$100	$0	$0	$0	$0	$0	...	$0

The first person hires the second person to help them build a house, and the second person ends up with the $100.

Value	$100	$0	$0	$0	$0	$0		
	🏠	○	○	○	○	○	...	○
Money	$0	$100	$0	$0	$0	$0	...	$0

The next day, the second person hires the third person to build another house.

86

Value	$100	$100	$0	$0	$0	$0		$0
	🏠	🏠	🧍	🧍	🧍	🧍	...	🧍
Money	$0	$0	$100	$0	$0	$0	...	$0

And so on.

Value	$100	$100	$100	$0	$0	$0		
	🏠	🏠	🏠	🧍	🧍	🧍	...	🧍
Money	$0	$0	$0	$100	$0	$0	...	$0

…

Value	$100	$100	$100	$100	$100	$100	
	🏠	🏠	🏠	🏠	🏠	🏠	🧍
Money	$0	$0	$0	$0	$0	$0	$100

What this means is that the 'Value' in an economy can increase at a rate close to to the amount of money that exists in the economy. In the previous example, there is a total of $100 of money in the economy, and the value of the houses in the economy increases every time there is a transaction. The problem with this situation is that the amount of money in the economy quickly becomes much smaller than the amount of 'Value' in the economy.

From this we can create a distinction: 'richness' is how much money you have, whereas 'wealth' is how much your assets are worth. The more money someone has, the more options they have to purchase products. The more wealth someone has, the more money they have already spent. This suggests that wealth follows richness.

This distinction becomes important in later chapters, but at this point you just need to remember that in Zero-sum Economics, value is almost entirely ignored. What is found is that the economy can be largely understood without considering value. Also, the limiter of the growth rate in an economy is the amount of money. This is what is called a 'boundary condition' in mathematics.

4.2   Systems analysis

Systems analysis is a tool originally created by software engineers to investigate how system components interact in a software program. The practice involves determining the independent processes that can be linked together to form a system that has inputs and outputs.

Each process (its inputs, outputs, requirements and relationships with other processes) is examined to determine the overall system operation and output. This type of analysis can be used for both the design of new systems requiring particular outputs, and to examine existing systems to determine why particular outputs occur.

As seen in Figure 12, the 'Circular Flow of Money' (from macroeconomic theory) is a basic system. (Figure 13 shows a slightly more complex system involving a Government.) The Circular Flow of Money can be analysed by examining its elements and the ways in which they interact.

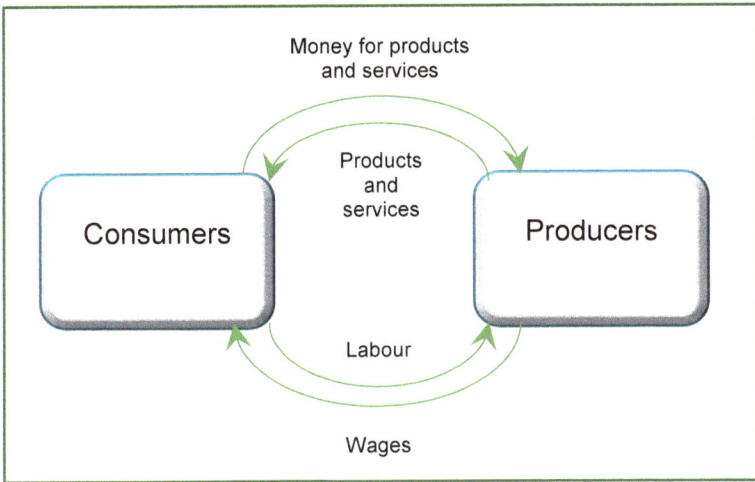

Figure 12: Circular Flow of Money

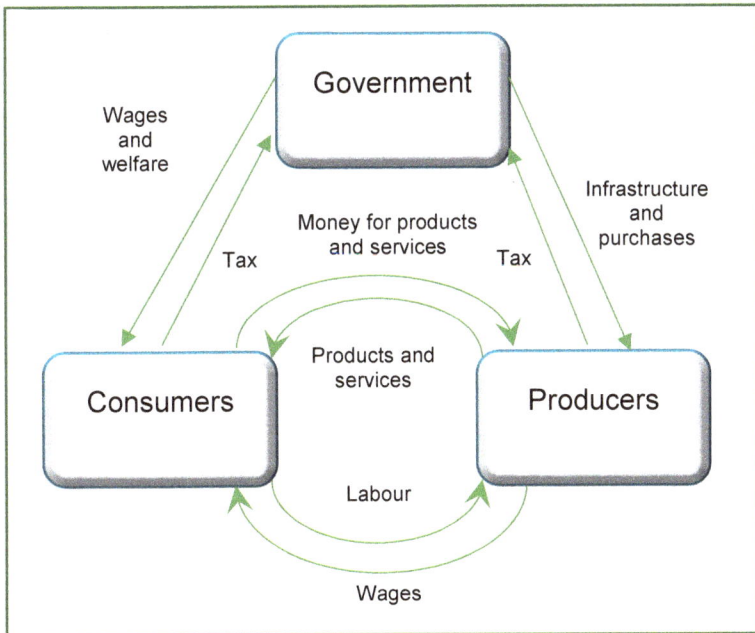

Figure 13: Circular Flow of Money with Government

Zero-sum Theory uses three main types of entities: Consumers, Producers and Governments. Each type of entity has specific characteristic interactions that are common to all entities of its type. For example, Consumers work for Producers for wages and consume products.

The types of entities can be classified further, depending on the nature of the phenomena being investigated. For the simulations developed thus far, only the three most basic types of entities have been needed. In future research if a study of exchange rates is performed, this may require a new type of entity representing a currency exchange business that allows the exchange of currencies to make a profit. Also, Banks can be modelled as a separate entity that create 'debt' via 'loans'. In the current system, they have simply been represented as Producers.

There can be more than one instance of an entity in a single model. In other words, there can be multiple Consumers, multiple Producers and even multiple Governments in a single model. The informative aspect is how these entities interact: the main way that interactions occur is via monetary (i.e. zero-sum) transactions.

An example of systems analysis for a farm is shown in Figure 14 and

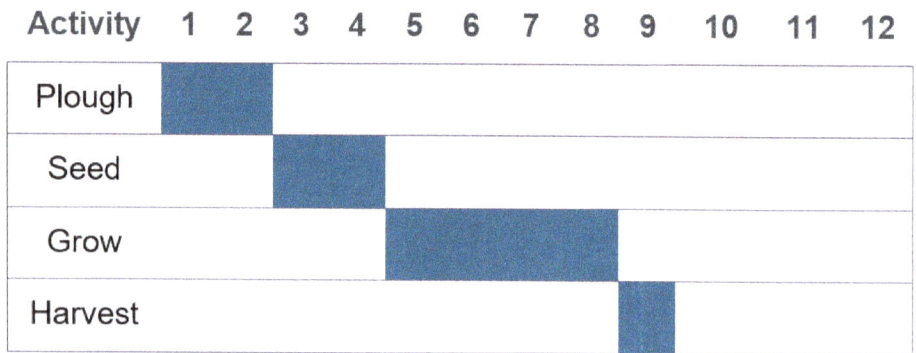

Activity	1	2	3	4	5	6	7	8	9	10	11	12
Plough	■	■										
Seed			■	■								
Grow					■	■	■					
Harvest								■				

Figure 15.

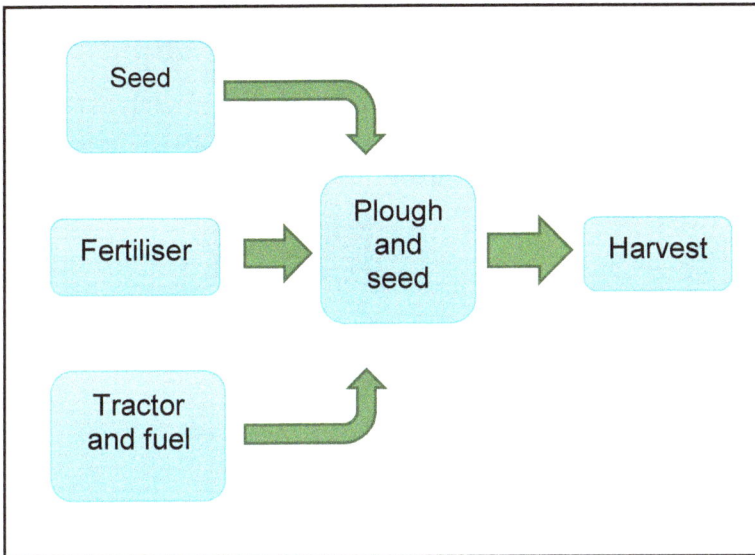

Figure 14: Farm Model

I have identified a few relationships between the various components and processes illustrated in Figure 14:

Harvest size will be proportional to the amount spent on seed, but there may be a volume discount; hence, the more purchased, the cheaper the seed will be. Harvest size will be proportional to the amount spent on fertilizer, but there may be a volume discount; hence, the more purchased, the cheaper the fertiliser will be. A tractor is a one-off cost, but fuel will be proportional to the harvest size. Harvest size will be proportional to the amount of land. The actual ploughing and harvesting will be proportional to the harvest size. These will typically be one-off costs to start the farm.

Activity	1	2	3	4	5	6	7	8	9	10	11	12
Plough	■	■										
Seed			■	■								
Grow					■	■	■	■				
Harvest									■			

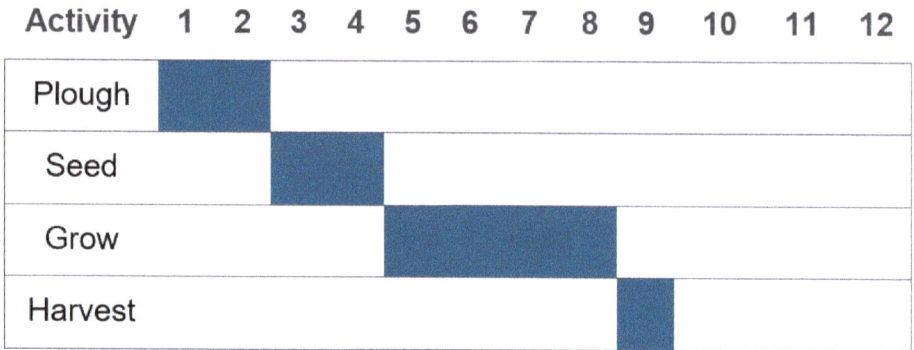

Figure 15: Farm Gantt chart

A Gantt chart shows the sequence of activities that must be performed in a particular process, as shown for the Farm Model. This chart indicates that most of the activities need to be performed in order. Payment is received only after the harvest occurs, so income is likely received only once every 12 months. Expenses, however, are ongoing over the rest of the year.

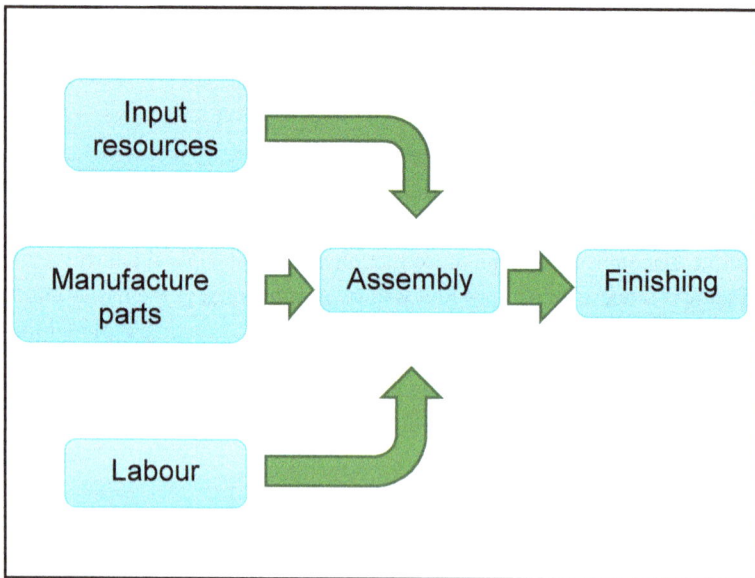

Figure 16: Manufacturing Model

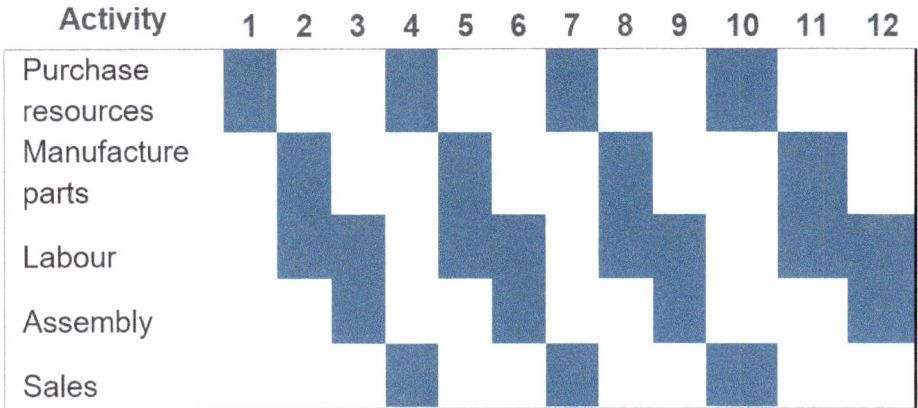

Figure 17: Manufacturing Gantt chart

Figure 16 and

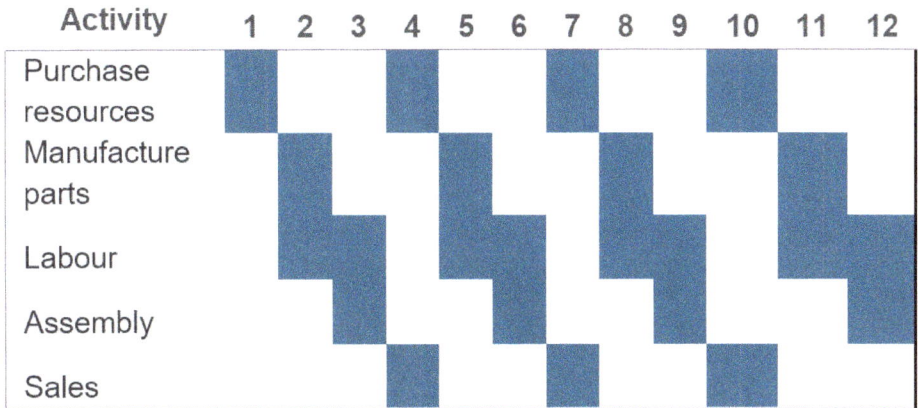

Figure 17 show a manufacturing system, which is in this case is performing batch processing. There are several processes that occur sequentially, and once batches are completed they can be sold. Thus, this type of business receives income progressively, but not necessarily continuously.

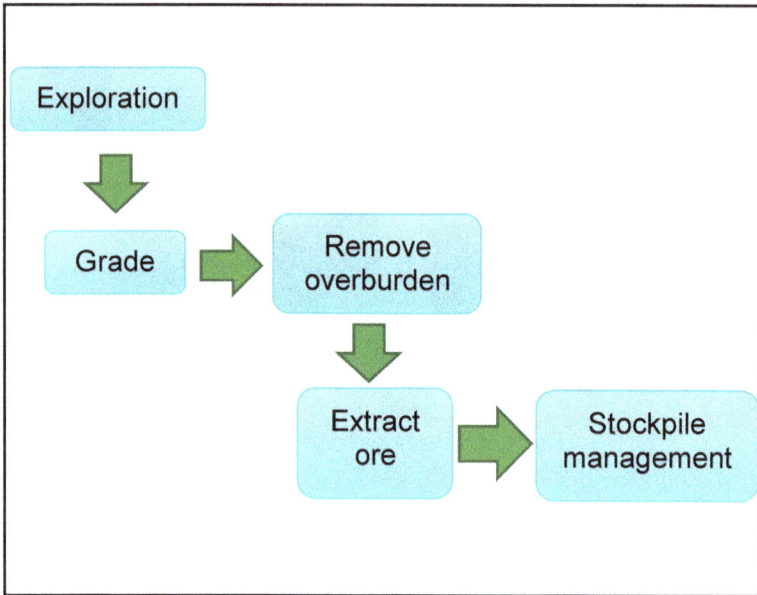

Figure 18: Mining Model

Activity	1	2	3	4	5	6	7	8	9	10	11	12

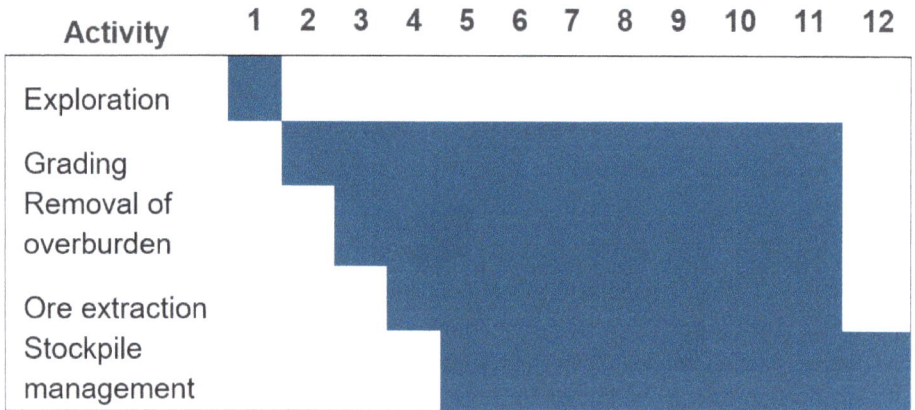

Figure 19: Mining Gantt chart

Figure 18 and Figure 19 show a mining operation that uses a combination of sequential and parallel processes. Sales also occur continuously throughout the operation of the mine, providing a continuous income.

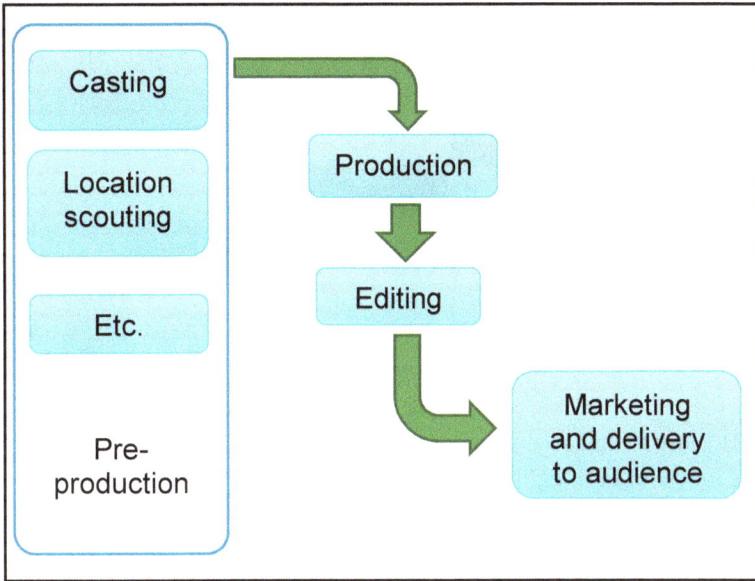

Figure 20: Movie Model

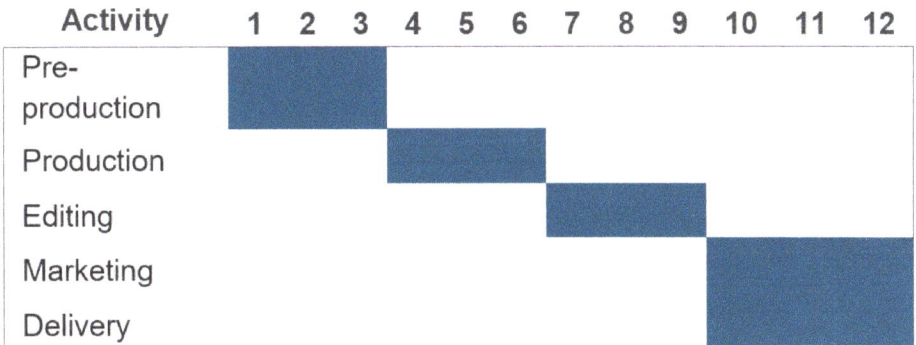

Activity	1	2	3	4	5	6	7	8	9	10	11	12
Pre-production												
Production												
Editing												
Marketing												
Delivery												

Figure 21: Movie Gantt chart

Figure 20 and

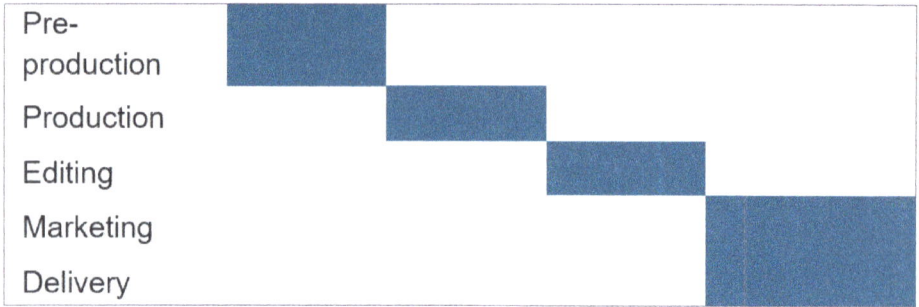

Activity	1	2	3	4	5	6	7	8	9	10	11	12
Pre-production												
Production												
Editing												
Marketing												
Delivery												

Figure 21 illustrate the production of a movie. This process has a similar structure to that of farming in that most activities are performed in sequence. Once complete, however, the movie can receive income continuously from legacy sales.

These diagrams represent the production stage of different types of businesses. They illustrate the relationships between the various activities, and help with the scheduling and costing of the process. Figure 22 is a generalised model applicable to any business. Despite the advantages, there does not seem to be a significant emphasis on this type of analysis in business or economics schools.

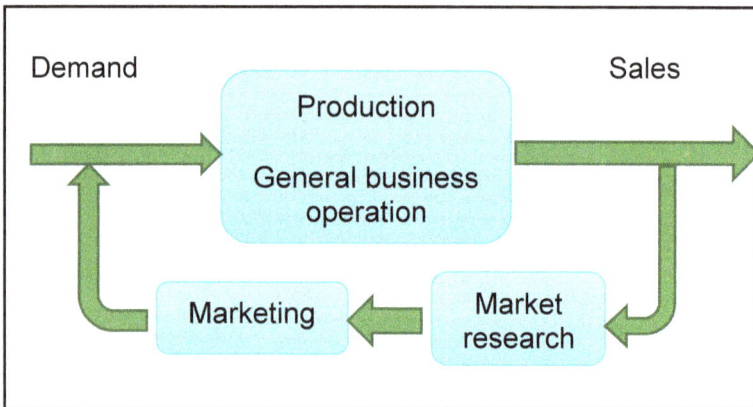

Figure 22: Generalised Business System Analysis

The three main processes depicted in the generalised system are Production, Market Research and Marketing. The objective of any business is to maximise its sales. By studying the market (Market Research), areas of demand are identified. The marketing process aims to maximise awareness in potential customers of the products available. Operation of the generalised business system can be optimised by understanding Control Theory and treating the business as a control system.

4.3 Control Theory

Control Theory is a theory that allows engineers to determine the performance of a 'system' in response to various external stimuli. It also allows engineers to modify that system in order to generate particular system responses. Analysis of the changes that occur in systems requires the use of calculus, and it can become extremely complex, requiring the use of differential equations and other complex mathematical analysis.

The mathematics for Control Theory was initially developed in the 1800s (during the 'Steam Age') by people such as Fourier, La Place and Bernoulli. It enabled engineers to develop strategies for allowing the reliable operation of machines (such as trains and cars) using mechanical devices such as governors for speed control. In modern times, Control Theory is used in everything from simple electronic devices to aircraft, spacecraft and nuclear reactors. It is widely considered to be one of the most successful and useful tools in engineering.

Zero-sum Economic Theory uses the basic macroeconomic model of the 'Circular Flow of Money' (as discussed in Section 3.2.1) and Control Theory–based mathematics to determine how money moves around an economy. There are no new relationships to be derived from the initial economic rules; Zero-sum Theory simply takes what we know about how the various entities in an economy interact, and applies engineering tools and mathematics to determine the economic system's operation.

4.4 Boundary conditions

In general terms, boundary conditions are minima or maxima that define the limits of what an entity can perform. These can be internal conditions (such as the entity's cash balance) or external conditions (such as the amount of money in the entire system). The boundary conditions can significantly change the behaviour of individual entities.

4.4.1   Mathematical boundary conditions

Mathematical boundary conditions are limits on equations. One example is that an entity (Consumer, Producer or Government) can never spend more than it has. From a mathematical perspective, the maximum money an entity can spend is its own current balance. This is observed in the CP analysis in Section 5.1.1. This maximum condition on expenses changes the nature of the equation from a simple linear equation to a much more complicated exponential decay. This is an internal boundary condition.

Boundary conditions have a habit of introducing differential components to otherwise simple equations, making them differential equations. Differential equations are equations in which the result of the equation is related to the differential of the equation itself. To solve the new equations, we need to use differential calculus.

It is possible to have an external boundary condition, such as the maximum amount of money in the economy, or an internal maximum, such as the maximum amount an entity can spend (the amount that they have).

4.4.2   Real boundary conditions in economics

Boundary conditions in the real world, specifically for economic systems, are those conditions that limit what products can be made, sold or consumed.

These conditions include:

- population
- time
- money
- products.

They all have maximum values.

4.4.2.1   4.4.2.1   *Population*

In an economy, there are a limited number of people, for example:

- Australia 24 million people
- USA 350 million people
- world 7.3 billion people.

You can't sell things to more people than there are. Hence, production and demand will always have an upper limit based on the population. At any one time, there are only going to be a fixed number of people who will want or need a product. So in terms of economics, demand will never be larger than the size of the population.

4.4.2.2   4.4.2.2   *Money supply*

The maximum amount of money in any zero-sum system is called the money supply. The maximum amount of money any single entity can have is this value. If this occurs, it also means that (due to the zero-sum nature of the system) every other entity in the system has zero money. Thus, if all of the entities add up their balances, this number will be equal to the money supply.

However, the money supply can be increased. In the real world, this can be achieved in two ways:

- A reserve bank can release more currency.
- Any bank can give a loan.

This changes the nature of the differential equations.

C is the balance of all Consumers.

P is the balance of all Producers.

CP is the amount transferred from Consumers to Producers, and PC is the amount transferred from Producers to Consumers.

Typically,

$$\frac{dC}{dt} + \frac{dP}{dt} = -CP(t) + PC(t) = 0.$$

This equation means that the rate of change of the total system balance is equivalent to the sum of changes in the system. If the money supply is constant, the total system rate of change must be zero. The boundary condition in this case is the zero.

But, the boundary condition can be a function:

$$\frac{dC}{dt} + \frac{dP}{dt} = -CP(t) + PC(t) = R(t),$$

where $R(t)$ represents the amount of money released in a given cycle.

In real terms, the maximum amount of cash is also the maximum amount of profit a single entity can make. This value is not normally reached, because that would mean everyone else would have zero cash and the entire economic system would stop.

Productivity in a real economy is measured in terms of GDP. This is the total amount of products created in a country over a period of time, typically a year.

The total amount of money in the economy is actually measured in the real world. Banks have several classifications of what is actually considered money in the economy. The various levels of money are referred to in M classifications: M1, M2, M3 and M4. M1 is physical currency; M2 includes bank deposits and is essentially represented digitally; M3 and M4 typically represent Bank reserves that are somewhat more confusing and are not often traded by individuals in the economy. The complete set of M designations are often referred to as 'broad' money; the main types of money used in the economy are often referred to as 'narrow' money and are often called the M1 + M2 money supply. Comparing data from the US Treasury concerning the M1 + M2 money supply with data on the US GDP, it is possible to see how similar the production and cash supply are over time.

GDP, personal expenses, company profits vs M1 + M2

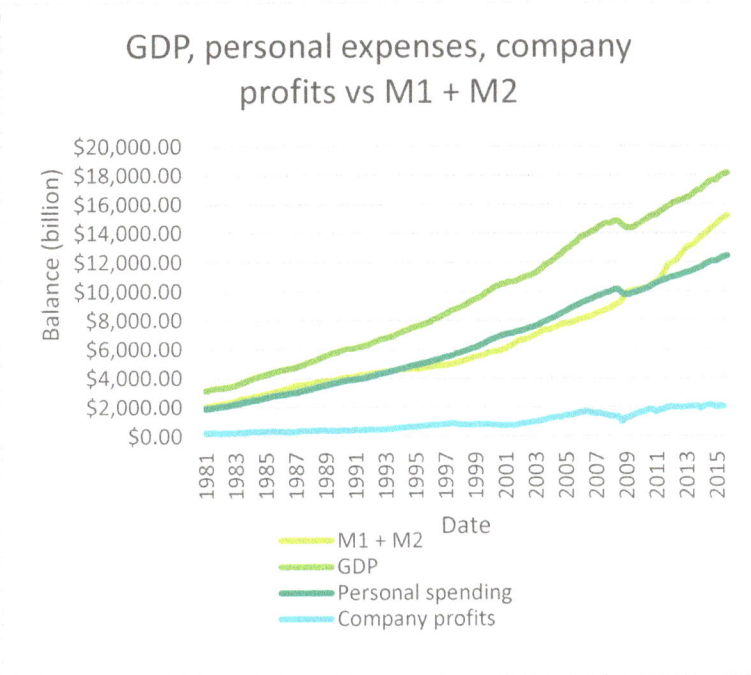

Figure 23: Raw US GDP versus M1 + M2 money supply

Figure 23 shows raw data for the M1 + M2 versus various aspects of the GDP, including personal expenses and company profits. In general, this shows that all of the personal expenses are the component of GDP that people have spent on their own needs and wants. It does not include company expenses.

According to the theory, the amount of money in the system should be an upper limit on profits. This is somewhat difficult to establish. One of the biggest points is that Company profits are significantly lower than the M1 + M2 money supply. This suggests that, while companies may be spending s significant proportion of the money supply, they are not removing the majority money from circulation in one cycle. However, we know that recessions reoccur over a period of 10 years at present. With Company profits of around $2 trillion, over 10 years would reallocate the entire money supply to be businesses.

The raw data is still somewhat confusing as everything increases. However, by dividing the different values by the M1 + M2 supply, we get the graph in Figure 24. Figure 24 shows total GDP, personal income and company profits as a percentage of the money supply. Over the period 1982–2015, US Personal

Expenses were typically within 20% of the money supply. The total GDP was as much as 180% of the money supply. This means that to produce everything recorded by the GDP, the amount of money in the economy had to cycle through 1.8 times before everything could be produced. The CP model shows that any production say from Consumer to Producer must be balanced by the opposite direction Producer to Consumer. This suggests that GDP is as much as double the amount of money that is actually circulating in the CP cycle. Alternatively, this figure might have been due to double counting of components and final products.

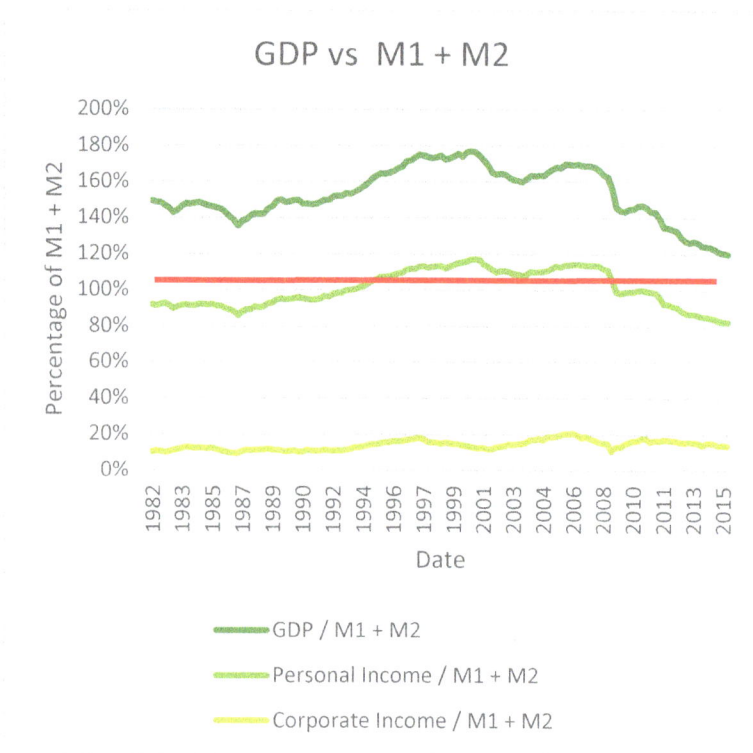

GDP vs M1 + M2

Figure 24: US GDP versus M1 + M2 money supply

Company profits are significantly lower than the money supply, peaking at around 20%. Unfortunately, it is not clear whether this is the only profit being made in the system, as most people end up spending most of any money they get.

One notable element in the graphs is that in 2008–2009 a major recession occurred. This produced a significant dip in GDP, but one of the strategies for improving the economy was to release more money, which reduced the overall effectiveness of the economy. Apparently, the US economy has not recovered since, despite the fact that in the raw figures both GDP and personal income has increased. This should mean that, despite the fact that more product is being made, less of the money in the economy is being used in the production.

The interesting thing here is that there are many reports that US companies are holding cash overseas [96–101]. The reason given in these reports is typically that companies want to avoid repatriation taxes. The problem is, again according to this theory, that the money held overseas is not circulating; hence, it is not contributing to profits or wages. The numbers reported are up to $2.5 trillion, which represents 10% of the money supply. The economy can be seen to be running as much as 20% below capacity, and this suggests that the amount of money out of circulation is as much as $5 trillion. Many of the researchers cited here have come to the same conclusion [96–98, 100, 101]. My research into these findings simply validates the theory that money operates as a zero-sum entity and needs to circulate for an economy to be effective.

Then we can consider how GDP per capita is affected over time by inflation. GDP per capita is effectively a measurement of how productive each individual is in the economy. This is shown in Figure 25 for Australia. The GDPPC graph shows that since 1960 we have increased our productivity from $25,000 per year to around $75,000 per year. Encouragingly an increase with a factor of three. Ideally, we would expect that with GDP growth would counter the effects of inflation leaving people roughly at the same level of productivity or even with the technological advancements we would be far more productive. Figure 25 shows the equivalent GDP per capita from 1960, essentially GDP divided by the total inflation since 1960. This is a much more depressing view, as it shows we are currently about 15 times less productive than in the 1960's when taking into account inflation.

GDP per capita Vs Inflation

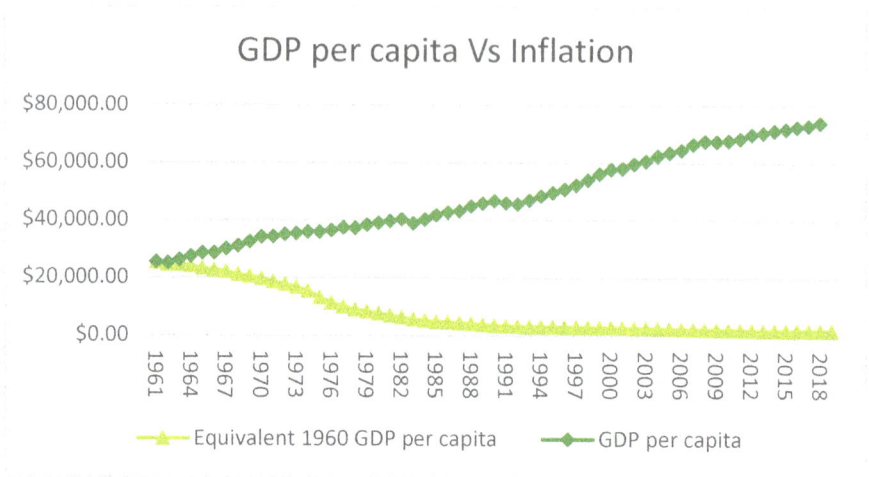

Figure 25: GDP per capita versus Inflation Australia

Clearly, we are producing far more "stuff" than in the 60's, but taking into account that personal income has stayed flat over similar periods shows individuals will not be receiving an equivalent lifestyle to that of the 1960's. Hence, for once it was definitely better in the old days.

4.4.2.3   4.4.2.3   Time

There are only 24 hours in what is defined as a day. This is a universal fact. Thus, if a particular task is required in either production or consumption, there is an upper limit to how many times that task can be performed in a given time period.

4.4.2.4   4.4.2.4   Income budgeting

Usually people have a limited income and thus cannot afford everything they want. Zero-sum Economics means that these limits are extremely important. You can't spend what you don't have.

Sensible priority queue:

1. water
2. food
3. housing

4. transport
5. luxuries
6. investments.

The queue works by fulling demand for each product in order. In the sensible queue water is the first product needed followed by food then shelter and so on. The list of priorities can be skewed and changed, for example if someone becomes addicted to drugs. Junkie priority queue:

1. drugs
2. water
3. food.

Queues can be generated for larger organisations such as businesses or governments, but they are far more varied as to the items on the list and each political faction may order the queue differently.

Budgeting for a country:

1. health care
2. defence
3. education
4. environment.

One of the most challenging things about planning a budget is that the limit (income) often changes, which means that new decisions need to be made about what the income will be spent on. Things that can be afforded at one time cannot be afforded later.

A priority list can be used to order the items on the list, and this can be used to generate a budget. The less money available, the fewer the priority items that can be purchased.

The main thing to note here is that the generation of a priority list involves choices (based on individual values), which means that it is difficult to predict what people will do.

Business choices are somewhat easier to predict because businesses have the common goal of making a profit. Nevertheless, people who run businesses also make choices.

The choices made by individuals or businesses have consequences for other people and other businesses. These are mechanical economic effects.

4.5 Zero-sum supply

To determine supply costs, Zero-sum Theory requires that a systems analysis be developed for the business processes. Use of a line or curve to represent the costs of a business can be an oversimplification that does not reflect what actually occurs.

For example, as shown in Figure 26, a factory uses a main production system when supply volume is below a certain point (described by one supply curve), but once a critical supply volume is reached, a secondary production system is used, which has a higher cost per unit.

Figure 26: Double Supply Model

4.6   Zero-sum demand

Microeconomic theory is aimed at optimising individual businesses with respect to maximising their profits. It does not seek to create enough product for everyone. When Producers cannot make enough of a product, prices increase, until only the Consumers who can afford the product buy it. Economics is not about maximising production—it is about figuring out who gets to have the products when there is a limited supply; these will be the people who have the most money. This relates back to Subjective Value Theory. Each person can value different products differently, and if they have a limited amount of money there is a limited amount that they can spend.

One of the tools commonly used in microeconomics is the supply-versus-demand graph. Despite the frequency with which this tool is used, rarely is an explanation given for how the demand curve is generated. The following methods have been developed to demonstrate how a demand curve can be calculated.

One way to generate a demand is to consider constant income requirements. For a person or business to maintain a constant income with a variable quantity of items, the price becomes inversely proportional to the Quantity as Shown in Table 11 and Figure 27.

Table 11: Constant income Demand

c	$5	$10	$20	$50	$100	$500	$1000
Quantity	200	100	50	20	10	2	1
Total Income	$1000	$1000	$1000	$1000	$1000	$1000	$1000

Demand Curve

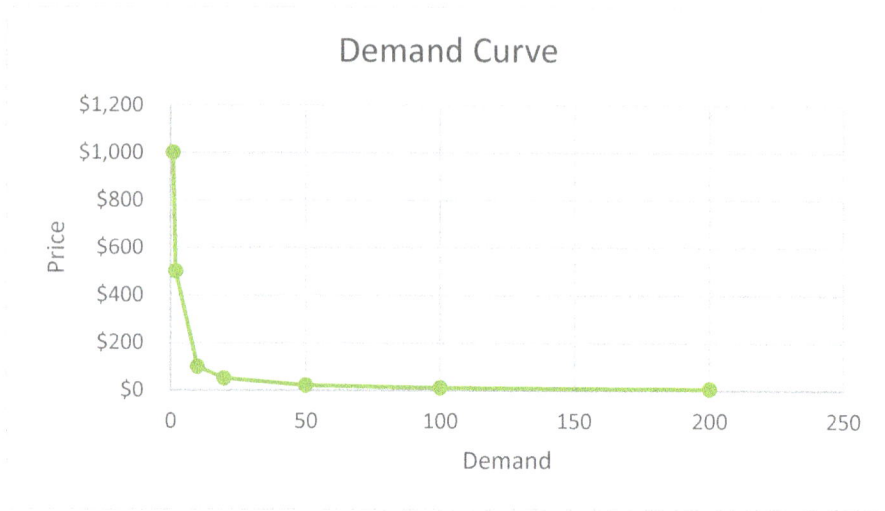

Figure 27: Demand curve from Constant income

And Analytically:

$$Income = Price \times Quantity$$

$$P = I / Q$$

This produces in inverse relationship between Quantity and Price, which is consistent with Marshallian demand.

Another method to determine a demand curve is to consider a typical product survey. Product surveys attempt to find out how many people are willing to pay a particular price for a product. An example of the type of data obtained is shown in Table 12.

Table 12: Customer price survey

Price	$5	$10	$15	$20	$25	$30	$35
Consumers	0	6	14	21	9	2	0
Total Consumers	52	52	46	32	11	2	0

A supply-versus-demand graph can be mapped from this data by graphing the total number of Consumers who would be willing to pay a particular price. For example, 14 people have stated they would be willing to pay $15 to buy the product. Adding the number who would pay more than $15 (21 who would pay $20, 9 who would pay $25, and 2 would pay $30) gives a total of 46 people who would agree to purchase the product at $15. These numbers can be projected across an entire population to give an estimate of the demand curve for an entire population. Plotting the price against the number of people willing to purchase the product at a particular price, gives a graph as shown in the demand curve (Figure 28).

Demand curve

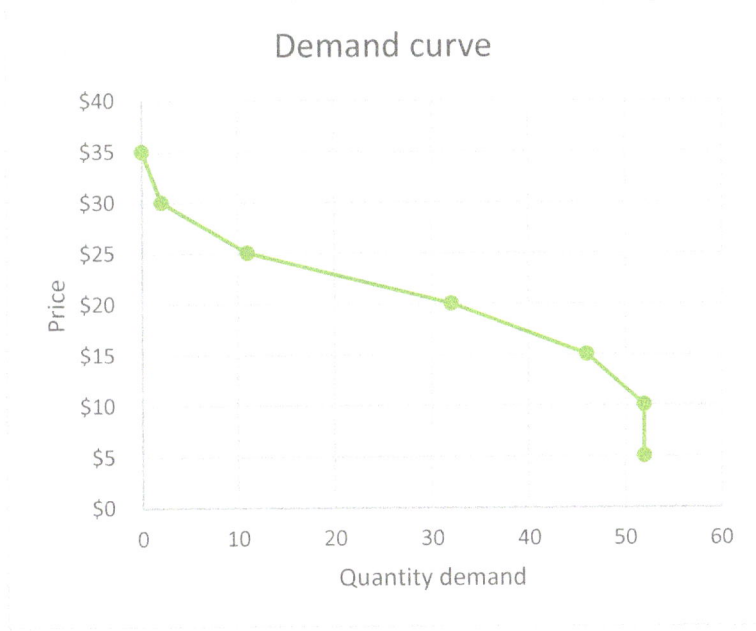

Figure 28: Demand curve from Survey

This curve looks similar to the typical demand curve presented in economics textbooks and in research papers. There are a few notable differences, these being at the limits of the data collected. The differences are that there is an absolute maximum price that a population will be willing to pay for a product, and that the maximum number of sales would be the size of the population itself, assuming one unit will satisfy each customer. If customers wish to purchase more than one unit, this can be taken into the calculations.

The demand curve can also be generated from income, as shown in Figure 29, which shows a world income distribution. Using this data, a world 'continuous' demand curve can be developed, as shown in Figure 30.

World annual income distribution for 2000

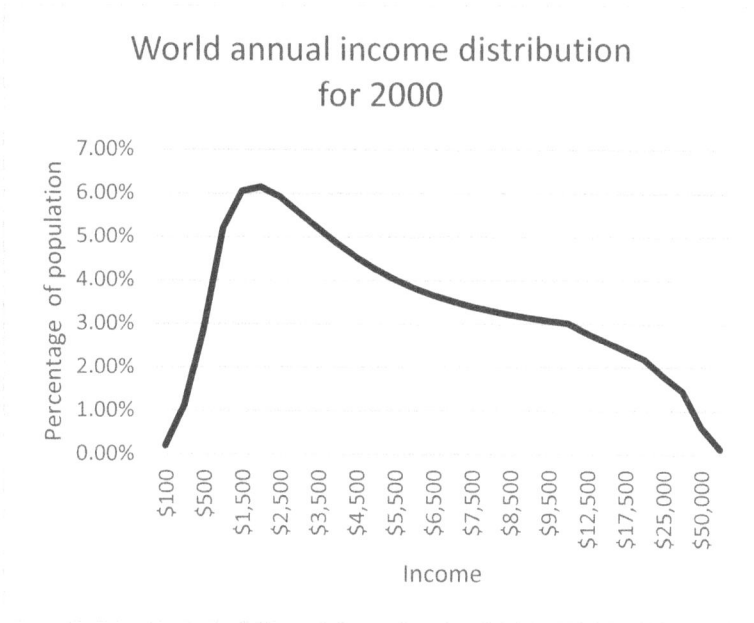

Figure 29: World annual income distribution 2000

World continuous annual demand curve for 2000

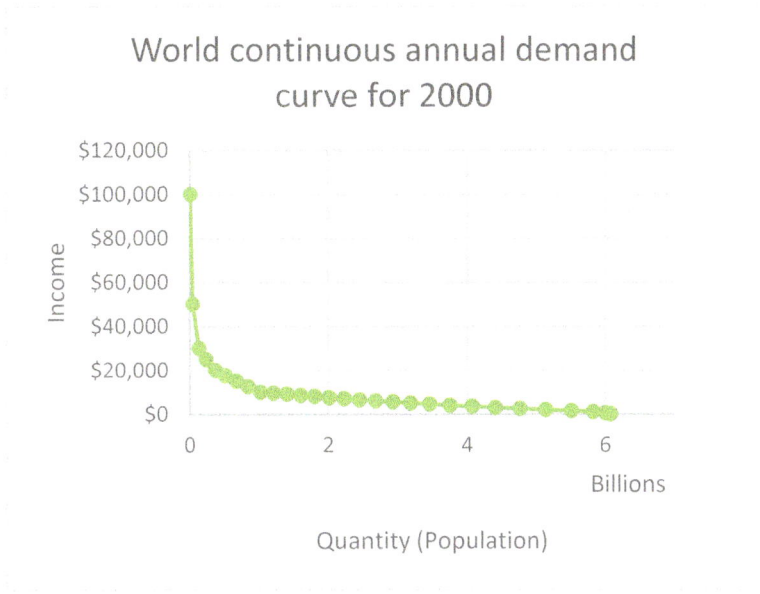

Figure 30: World continuous demand curve for 2000

The boundary conditions of demand curves are defined by the population and the maximum price. One of the problems caused by trade is that as the money held by Producers accumulates due to profits, the demand curve changes. Every transaction shifts the demand curve, which is developed from the cash distribution. When some people have collected more money than others, they have more opportunities to purchase production assets, which in turn allows them to collect more money. This is a reinforcing effect that accelerates the movement of money to those people who already have more money, i.e. "The rich get richer."

The demand generation procedure developed can also be considered with respect to the Theory of Subjective Value. Each point of the demand curve can represent the amount of money or amount of income that the individual has. This can translate to the amount each person is willing to pay for their lifestyle or its 'value'. Each person has a different amount of money; hence, the amount they are willing to pay for a product is different.

The result of this is the same as the theory of marginal value. Hence, the Marginal Value Theory, which compares supply cost with demand, is still valid but has a slightly different interpretation.

4.7 Spending priorities

The value of water is that you can drink it and survive; without it people die. This is an inherent value, not a monetary value. Thus, the value of water can be determined independently of the price. The argument that "prices are required by the Consumer in order to make evaluations" is based on the circular reasoning of the concept of 'non-subjective value'.

When considering the more rational concept of 'subjective value', the prices people are willing to pay for products are ultimately set by the availability of money to buyers, not by any inherent value. This effect can be seen in modern times in the housing market. When banks increase the amount of money available for loans, more people attempt to buy houses; hence, the average price of houses increases.

One of the major oversights of the current economic theories is that all products can be considered equally. People *need* some products for survival; other products are useful but not necessary for survival; and many products are simply desirable. According to the survival guides [102–104], there are three things a human being needs in order to survive. These are, in approximate order of priority (depending on the weather conditions):

- water
- food
- shelter.

These 'products' are essential to a human being's long-term survival. Most survival guides claim that a human will die if they don't have water for 3–7 days. In hot weather, this figure can be reduced to hours.

If water is available, a human being will still die of malnutrition after approximately 30 days without food.

Shelter is required in extreme weather conditions, such as in snow or extreme heat. It also provides safety and security from external threats. From an economic perspective, shelter also allows people to keep belongings that they value safe, and hence to collect assets and develop a more personalised space in which to live.

These 'products' are necessary for people's survival and will be given high priority in Consumer spending. It is somewhat nonsensical to consider these products in the same category as say ice-cream or luxury cars. You probably won't die if you don't have enough ice-cream. (Instead, too much of it can cause health problems!)

Once the basics (water, food and housing) are covered by a person's income, most other things can be considered a luxury. If the person's income does not cover the cost of housing, they will need to share with someone else or they will become homeless. If they don't have enough income for food, they will die within 30 days, according to the survival guides. Without water, they will die within 3 days (according to the survival guides) (although in most modern cities water can usually be obtained from free drinking taps, and the people there don't often die from lack of water).

The next 'level' of priorities, referred to here as maintenance products, includes power, transport and communications. These products are required for people to 'maintain' the operation of a modern civilisation, but individual people will not die if they don't have them.

In more general terms, all products can be categorised as needs or wants, then subsequently prioritised in relation to income. I have considered products in certain categories (water, food, housing, transport and luxuries/investments), prioritised them and plotted them against income, as shown in Figure 31.

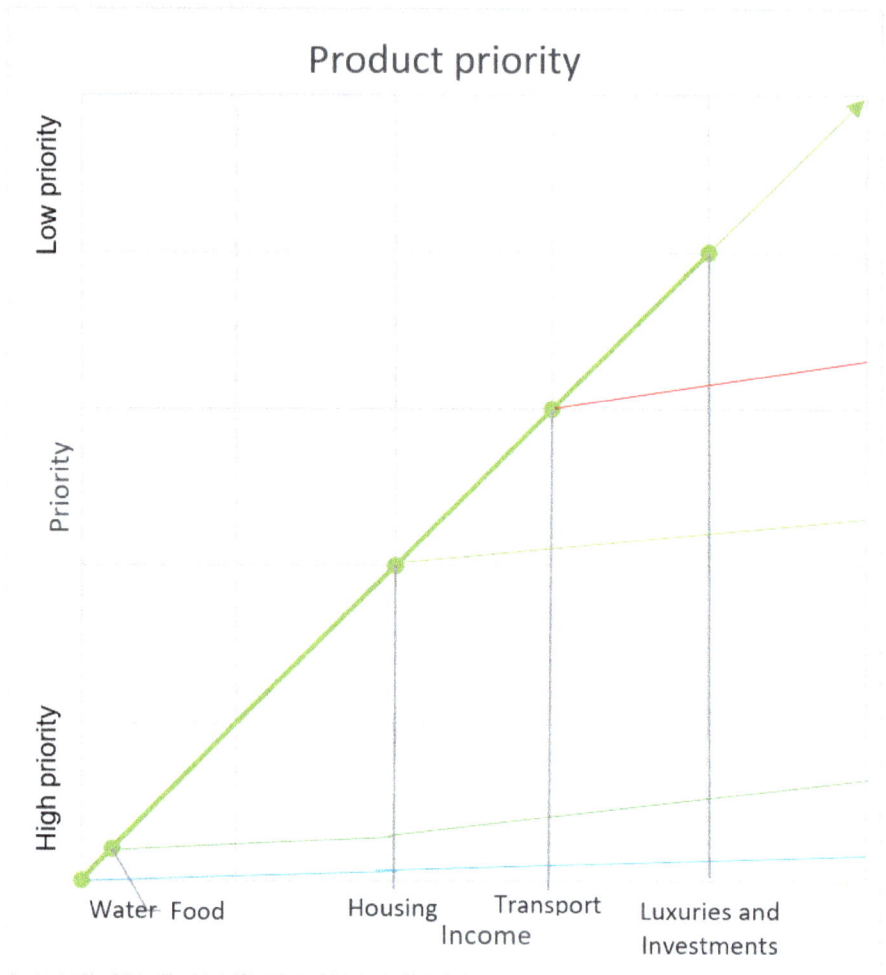

Figure 31: Product priority

This figure shows that as income increases, people can afford more of the products they need, and eventually also the transport and other luxuries or investments that they want. The cost of products can be totalled to yield the cost of living.

Finally, we have luxuries and investments. Luxuries can be described as things we don't need but want, or as more expensive versions of things we need.

Investments become another option when people have surplus money available. These investments are intended to increase income and reduce reliance on a wage. Investments can be used to develop new technologies or new businesses, or simply to invest in an existing business in return for some of the income of that business (i.e. dividends). However, there is usually no guarantee that an investment will be successful.

In general terms, a person or business will attempt to purchase items from their highest priority to their lowest priority, limited by income, but spending priorities can change. For example, the further someone works from where they live, the more reliance they will have on transport.

The constants are the needs: food, water and shelter. The variables are income and the available resources. The objective for any individual is to maximise the 'value' obtained in spending their income by prioritising their spending.

Different entities have different product priorities. Consumers require food, water and shelter; Producers can require energy, labour, mineral resources and a wide variety of other secondary products. To model multiple products, each entity (Consumer or Producer) requires the implementation of a 'shopping list'. They must have connections to multiple supply entities, and employees must be able to produce more than one unit of product. To accomplish this requires much more in-depth simulation detail; at present, the models use a single product because this simplifies the modelling process. In chapters 5 and 6 Zero-sum modelling is used to simulate some behaviours of macro-scale economics that only require a single product to describe.

4.8   Loans and debt

Despite the detail the banking industry descries its money and debt creation processes, as discussed in Section 3.2.11.5, the operation of debt and money in the economy does not seem to match the description. There are several problems that the banks don't seem to describe. One is interest and the other is the actual debt and money rations we can see from Figure 32.

When people put money into bank accounts, it can earn interest. The interest is available because the bank can then loan out the money, which creates a debt. A debt is a contract requiring that the loan amount is repaid over time, with interest. Banks are businesses that are out to 'make money', and the way they make money is by making sure that the money received from the interest on their loans is larger than the interest they pay out on savings accounts. The difference becomes the bank's profit.

The interesting thing is that when banks loan out money, they do not decrease the savings in accounts. Technically, this is a zero-sum violation, as it effectively increases the amount of money in the world by the amount loaned out. Traditional economic theories also argue that loans increase the amount of money. While this is technically true, especially if a reserve bank creates the money to finance the loan, it is problematic in several ways.

The first problem is that the loans need to be paid back with interest, which means that more money needs to be paid back than has been created. The interest charges mean that debt can increase to the point that more debt needs to be paid than the amount of money that exists in the economy. At that point, if all of the money in the world is given back to pay off the loan, the loaner will have all the money and the debtor will still have debt—and the entire economy will stop! However, the economy generally has problems before it stops completely, and typically, people have difficulty repaying the loans.

As of 2016, there was an estimated US$237 trillion in debt worldwide [122]. The current worldwide estimate of the broad money supply is approximately US$85 trillion, and of the narrow money is approximately $35 trillion [123]. As of 2020 Australia's total Debt is approximately $9.8 Trillion and the money supply is $2.43 Trillion.

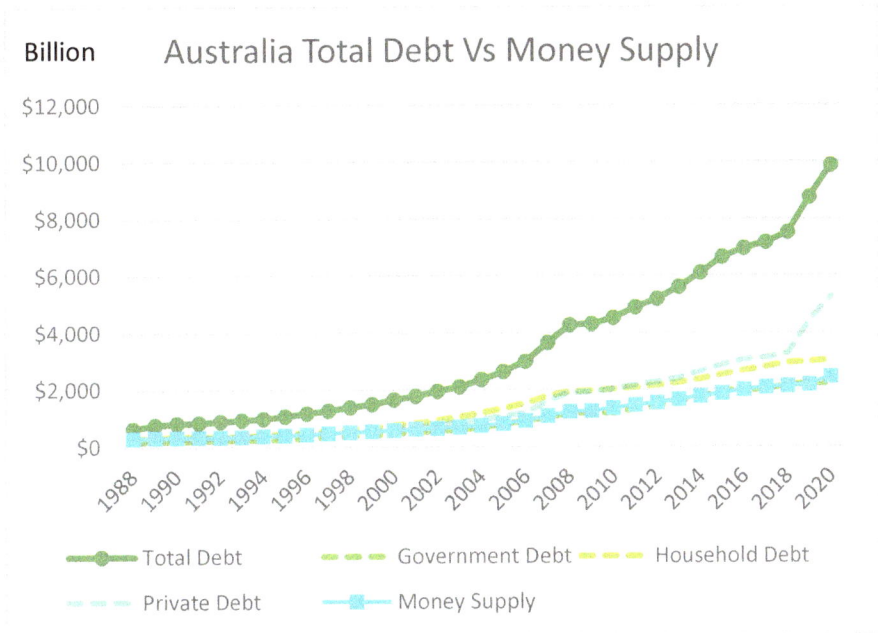

Figure 32: Australia Total Debt Vs Money Supply

This shows that, despite the banks assurance that debt should create money, the amount of debt is almost a factor of 4 times higher than money.

The final problem is that once the bank has loaned out the money, whoever gets the loan puts the money in a bank. That bank can use this as an opportunity to loan the money out again, because it views the amount of cash it has as related to the maximum rate of loans it can create, even if there is more debt than money.

Mathematically for banks:

$$Current\ cash = \Delta\ Debt$$

This means banks can continuously create debt without bound, and since banks charge interest on the debt, they are guaranteed that the debt growth will accelerate. These problems can cause what can be described as a 'Debt shock'. If one debt fails to be repaid, it is written off, which in turn reduces income for other banks and makes it impossible for them to finance their debts; the problem continues back to the original source of the debt. This can cause financial crises and bankrupt banks, as banks are typically the source of the debt.

It is possible to estimate when a debt shock will occur using the total debt (D), the interest charges (I) and the amount of money in the economy (R). Essentially, if the interest payments on the debt are larger than the amount of money in the economy, there is going to be a debt crash. It gets even worse. We know that the total amount of money in the economy is not distributed equally. This means that if the 'debtors' do not have enough money to pay the interest payments, we get a debt crash. If we factor in business cycles, which reduce the amount of money debtors have available, the formula becomes the following:

if $(D \times I > R_C \times (1 - M))$ ➜ Debt crash,

where Rc is the cash held by the debtors and M is the profit margin in the economy.

The upper limit of debt is reduced further when considering wages. According to the US social security, the average wage in 2015 for the USA was $48,098.63 [124]. In 2015, according to the US Bureau of Labor statistics, there were 157,130,000 jobs. This means there was $7.55 trillion being cycled through US employees. This can be compared with the interest on the debt. If this value represents the maximum interest on the debt, then the maximum debt would be the reciprocal of the interest rate. For example, if the average US debt was charged at 10%, the maximum debt the workers in the USA would be able to support would be $75.5 trillion. It is likely that any amount of debt close to this value would cause a debt crash, as the workers would not be able to afford to buy basic necessities and also to pay off any debt. However, workers are not the only people who have to pay debts, so there can be more debt than just that of the workers.

This means that to pay off the debt, everyone who owes money would have to receive all of the money in the world and pay it back, and the owners of the debt would then need to spend the money in such a way that all of the debtors received all of the money and would still have to spend it again. For Australia, this cycle would have to be repeated 4 times for broad money. It's not gonna happen!

According to many textbooks [4, 35–38] and other sources [14, 108–111], excessive debt was the cause of both the Great Depression of 1927 and the 2008

'Global Financial Crisis'. These events show that debt might look like a temporary solution, but it will always come back to cause problems. Hence, a general rule for running an economy should be to avoid using debt, wherever possible.

4.9   Zero-sum entities

For the moment, let us consider just the three basic types of entities active in zero-sum systems: Consumers, Producers and Governments. The entities differ in their capabilities and requirements, but have features in common—the main one being that any entity can own an amount of money (their 'bank balance', or just 'balance').

For now, we will include the banks that supply loans (and the financial institutions that allow money to be exchanged) in the Producers group. They are like Producers who are making a profit by providing banking services.

The following sections describe the capabilities of the three basic entities.

4.9.1   Consumers

The primary goal of Consumers is survival. They need to collect all of the products they need in order to do this. These products are supplied by Producers. Consumers can also invest their money in Producers in an attempt to receive extra income. Consumers can receive a wage from Producers and can receive welfare from Governments.

4.9.2   Producers

Producers create products for Consumers and pay Consumers a wage for creating products.

Consumers can invest in Producers, and Producers can invest in Consumers.

4.9.3   Governments

There can be multiple Governments in a system. Each Consumer and Producer works with a particular Government. All non-Government entities pay income tax to a Government. Governments pay Producers to create infrastructure. Governments are responsible for cash releases. (This simplifies the modelling somewhat, so that banks are not required as a separate type of entity.)

4.10 Zero-sum supply versus demand

The problem with supply versus demand calculations is that they are calculated entirely in favour of businesses. In general, supply versus demand calculations are sensible as long as the data used is correct. Demand should be calculated from real measurements of what people are willing to pay for a product, and most businesses should be able to use their own systems analysis to ensure that their costs are accurate. The main thing to remember is that the 'equilibrium' point as described by previous economic theories is the optimum point *with respect to businesses*, because this point maximises the number of sales for the maximum price, as shown in Figure 33.

The ideal point for Consumers in the supply-versus-demand curve is maximum supply (the point at which all of the Consumers' needs are fulfilled) at zero cost. In contrast, the ideal point for Producers is the point at which they sell the product to the entire population of Consumers for the maximum amount of money possible.

Ideal supply vs demand

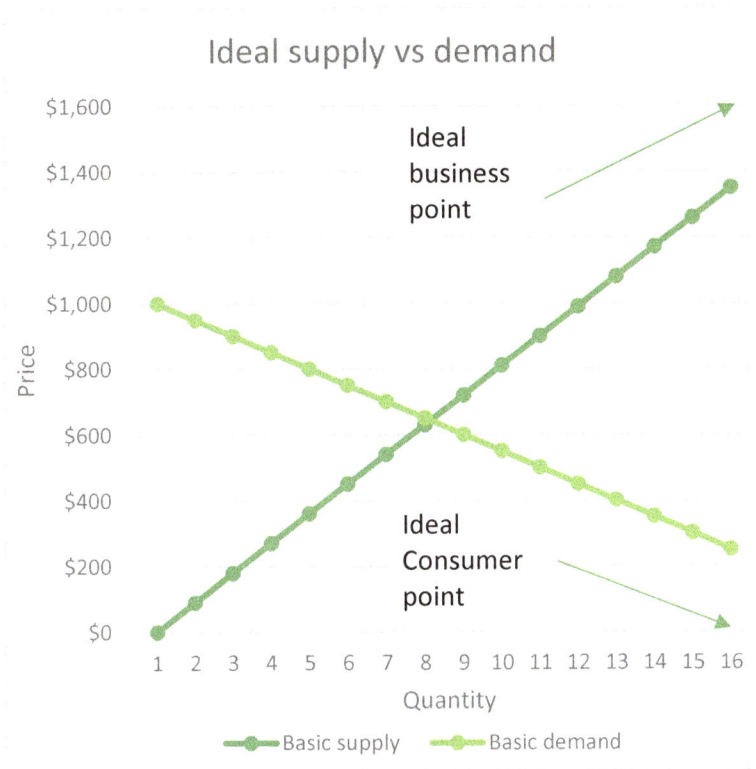

Figure 33: Zero-sum Ideal supply versus demand

4.11 Zero-sum equilibrium

The equilibrium point of a supply-versus-demand system is the point of maximum income and hence maximum profit. In a zero-sum system, at this point Consumers have the maximum loss. The main criticism I have for equilibrium models is that the equilibrium points are chosen for the benefit of Producers—definitely not for the benefit of Consumers! The ideal situation for Consumers would be zero price combined with a supply for the entire population. Clearly, this is not the ideal situation for Producers!

Supply-vs-demand equilibrium

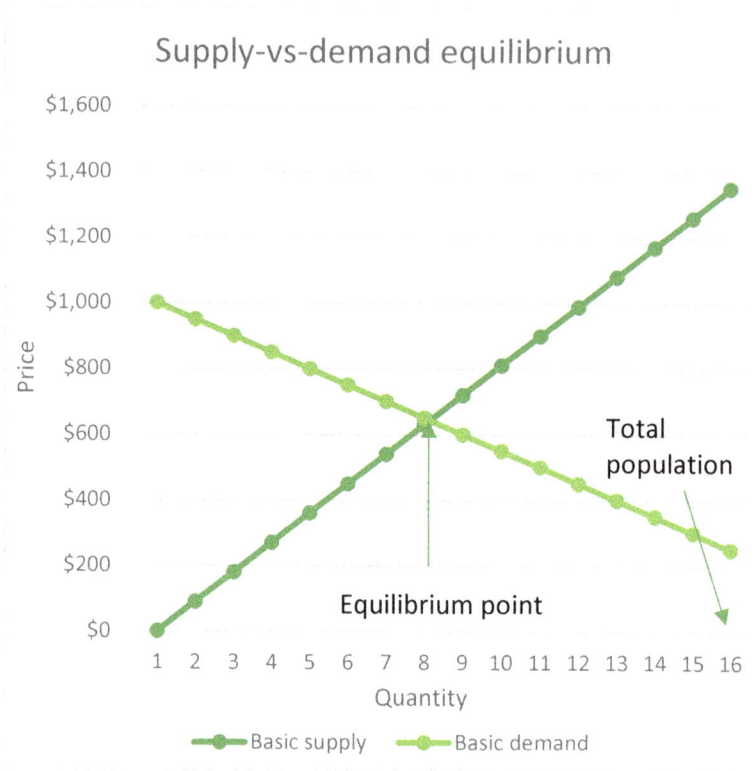

Figure 34: Supply vs demand equilibrium

Figure 34 shows us that if Producers optimise sales to the equilibrium point, many of the Consumers will miss out, as shown in Figure 35. They could miss out on essential products from the list of priorities discussed in Section 4.7 (water, food or shelter). The most likely product people will miss out on is shelter, as this is the most expensive. This provides an explanation as to why poverty occurs. Businesses do not need to sell products to an entire population in order to make a profit or to maximise their profit, which makes it likely that some people will miss out on essential services, especially if supply is limited.

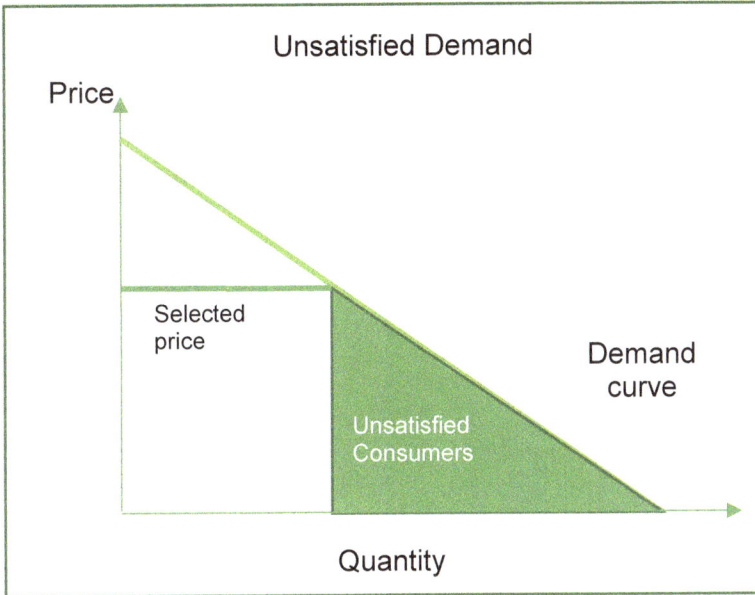

Figure 35: Unsatisfied demand

In zero-sum systems, there is no 'equilibrium', only an optimum point for businesses. However, one part of the solution presented in Chapter 6 is to adjust the optimum point for Producers so that it moves towards the ideal point for Consumers, i.e. enough for everyone and as cheap as possible.

4.12 Employment and unemployment

Employment is a major component of any economy, and it plays a significant part in determining how Consumers and Producers interact. In zero-sum terms, Consumers work for Producers for a wage. In the modelling, a single Consumer's work only creates the resources for a single Consumer to live on. This is for several reasons that are specific to the modelling. The goal of the models is to determine how many Consumers can be employed and to find out who does not have enough money. Hence a 1:1 ratio is used. More productive ratios were examined, but ultimately they made the employment rate decrease and the outputs unrealistically low.

Examining the real world (as opposed to simulated) industries of several countries shows the distribution of employment within their populations (Tables

11–13). These tables show how many people are actually required to supply the entire population with the products made by particular industries. Table 13 shows that, in 2014, only 11.57 million people out of a population of 23 million were employed. This means that only 48% of the population of Australia was employed. Supposedly, during this time the unemployment rate was 5–6%. When you look at figures like this, it is hard not to question the unemployment statistics. As it turns out, those surveyed to determine the unemployment statistics generally only include people aged 18 to 54 who are fit for work and either employed or actively looking for work. This means that these statistics tell us little about what is actually happening in the economy. When the broader employment situation is considered, the participation rate (percentage of the population either employed or actively seeking employment) of most countries is approximately 65% [129]. The difference can be accounted for by considering people outside the age range of 18-54 The percentage of the population employed is close to 50%, as shown in Table 13 (for Australia), Table 14 (for the UK) and Table 15 (for the USA). This means that the unemployment figure should be in the range of 15%, or 3.75 million people in Australia, 9 million in the UK and 52.5 million people in the USA.

Table 13: Australian employment by industry

Population 2014			23,460,000
Industry	% jobs	% pop.	Total employed
Agriculture, forestry and fishing	2.79%	1.38%	323,100
Mining	2.45%	1.21%	283,900
Manufacturing	8.20%	4.05%	949,500
Electricity, gas and water and waste services	1.37%	0.68%	158,800
Construction	8.88%	4.38%	1,027,200
Wholesale trade	3.48%	1.71%	402,200
Retail trade	10.85%	5.35%	1,255,300
Accommodation and food services	6.59%	3.25%	762,700
Transport, postal and warehousing	5.16%	2.55%	597,600
Information media and telecomm	1.64%	0.81%	190,200
Financial and insurance services	3.43%	1.69%	397,000
Rental, hiring & real estate services	1.64%	0.81%	189,800
Professional, scientific and technical services	7.61%	3.75%	880,300
Administrative and support services	3.43%	1.69%	397,400
Public administration and safety	6.60%	3.26%	763,700
Education and training	7.84%	3.87%	907,900
Health care and social assistance	12.25%	6.05%	1,418,300
Arts and recreation services	1.72%	0.85%	199,500
Other services	4.07%	2.00%	469,400
Total	100.00%	49.34%	11,573,800

Table 14: UK employment by industry

Population 2017			65,511,098
Industry	% jobs	% pop.	Total employed
Agriculture, forestry & fishing	1.20%	0.58%	379,831
Mining, energy and water supply	1.70%	0.82%	537,961
Manufacturing	9.17%	4.43%	2,900,518
Construction	7.38%	3.57%	2,335,578
Wholesale, retail and repair of motor vehicles	13.07%	6.31%	4,133,867
Transport and storage	4.93%	2.38%	1,558,177
Accommodation and food services	5.52%	2.67%	1,747,271
Information and communication	4.19%	2.02%	1,325,759
Financial and insurance activities	3.78%	1.83%	1,197,320
Real estate activities	1.17%	0.56%	369,573
Professional, scientific and technical activities	7.42%	3.58%	2,347,312
Administrative and support services	4.90%	2.37%	1,550,462
Public admin and defence; social security	6.17%	2.98%	1,950,507
Education	10.44%	5.04%	3,303,788
Human health and social work activities	13.36%	6.45%	4,227,657
Other services	5.6%	2.70%	1,768,096
Total	100.00%	48.29%	31,633,677

Table 15: USA employment by industry

Population 2014			318,900,000
Industry	% jobs	% pop.	Total employed
Goods-producing, excluding agriculture			
Mining	0.56%	0.26%	843,800
Construction	4.08%	1.92%	6,138,400
Manufacturing	8.10%	3.82%	12,188,300
Services-providing			
Utilities	0.37%	0.17%	553,000
Wholesale trade	3.87%	1.83%	5,826,000
Retail trade	10.20%	4.82%	15,364,500
Transportation and warehousing	3.08%	1.46%	4,640,300
Information	1.82%	0.86%	2,739,700
Financial activities	5.30%	2.50%	7,979,500
Professional and business services	12.69%	5.99%	19,096,200
Educational services; private	2.27%	1.07%	3,417,400
Health care and social assistance	12.00%	5.66%	18,057,400
Leisure and hospitality	9.77%	4.61%	14,710,000
Other services	4.25%	2.01%	6,394,000
Federal government	1.81%	0.86%	2,729,000
State and local government	12.71%	6.00%	19,134,000
Agricultural wage and salary	0.92%	0.43%	1,384,000
Agricultural self-employed workers	0.50%	0.24%	754,300
Non-agricultural self-employed workers	5.70%	2.69%	8,590,200
Total	100.00%	47.20%	150,540,000

One of the main benefits of modern economics is known as specialisation. Specialisation allows people to focus on one type of work and trade their output for money so that they can purchase any other products or services they need or want.

One of the major benefits of specialisation is in agriculture. In pre-industrial eras, most people worked in agriculture to produce enough food for themselves to survive, so the rate of employment in agriculture would have been close to 100% for most countries. Now if you examine the tables for agriculture and related fields, you find we only need 1.38% of the population employed in this sector in Australia, 0.58% in the UK and 0.67% in the USA. If we extrapolate these figures worldwide, this means that, on average, around 1 in 100 people in the world today are needed to produce all of the food we need to survive.

However, there is a downside to this … What do we do with the other 99% of people? If people were willing to live in hovels, we could all survive with only 1% of the population working in agriculture. Admittedly, we still need a few other industries to support the highly mechanized agriculture, but in a modern society we only need a fraction of the products we actually produce. It might feel like you are going to die without a cell phone, but in reality you won't. Businesses and industries in general are efficient enough to produce everything people need while employing less than 50% of a population. With better automation we could do better—possibly much better.

Despite the efficiency of businesses, there is a general world view that "Everyone needs to work." We don't actually need everyone to work in order to produce everything, but everyone needs an income to buy the products they need or want.

This brings us to the participation rate. There are only a limited number of jobs, and businesses are effectively attempting to minimise these through automation. These jobs are shared among the entire population. The problem is: what are the rest of the population doing for income?

4.13 The Problem with GDP

GDP is the total value of goods produced in a country over a period of time, typically a year. This measurement is useful for determining how well the economy of an entire country is performing over time.

The Problem with GDP is that it counts multiple levels of the supply chain. For example as shown in Figure 36, if we have a set of suppliers each will supply a product to the next stage at increasing cost. GDP adds up the cost of the entire set of products. In effect, this adds the cost of each stage multiple times, as for example the cost of products already includes the cost of resources.

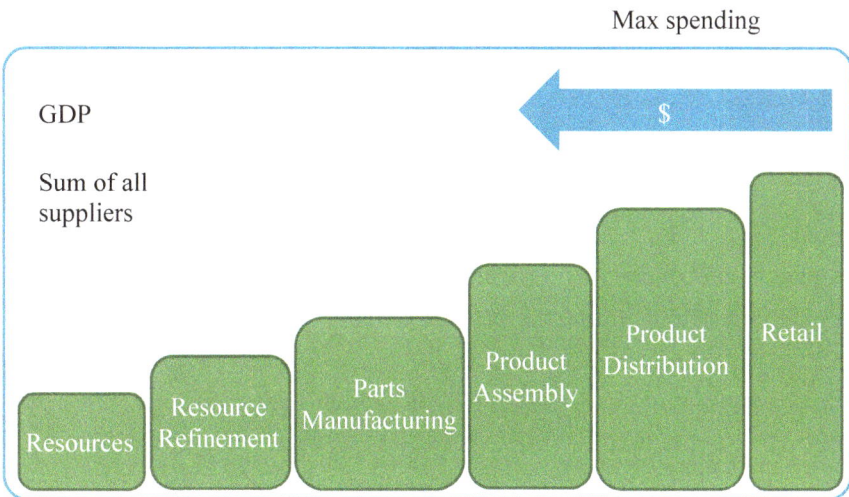

Figure 36: Supply Chain Vs GDP

What we should be considering is the maximum spending input into the system. This measurement should be the total amount that consumers can spend.

As mentioned previously the money in the economy cycles through both consumers and Producers, so GDP should be expected to be double money circulating in the CP cycle. If we halve the 1.8 Factor to 0.9 and multiply this with the Money supply of $20 Trillion US (2016) we find the value of around $9 Trillion which is close to the total wages paid in 2016. While this is not definitive, it is a reasonable indication that Max spending GDP/2 is a sensible measurement of the operation of the economy.

The important implication here is that the max spending is a better measure of the money circulating in the economy. This value have further implications for the operation of the economy as a whole. The main problem being it is impossible to change max spending (increase or decrease) without causing cascading changes in the rest of the economy. If any part of the economy has a decreased income, consumers end up with reduced income. If wages increase there is the potential for increased inflation. As far as I can tell this value is a central control value or perhaps even the central control value of the economy. My guess is that whatever value this is changed to the rest of the economy will scale to.

4.14 Growth vs Bloat

Economists and politicians have a tendency to look at "growth" as a major metric of the economy. But, is it Growth?

Inflation simply makes the same products more expensive. Arguably, products like shares purely rely on inflation to increase their value. The "share" does not change the nature of the company it represents, it simply changes in price.

So if growth represents an increase in price effectively the same products are being sold and purchased for more money. It does not mean the economy is being more productive.

4.15 Everyone can be productive

It is possible for everyone in existence to be productive. They can:

- grow their own food
- read books
- write books
- create a YouTube video
- make music
- and so on.

Many of these products could be distributed widely and used as a basis for a business. The problem is that in a zero-sum environment with limited money, it is not possible for everyone to make a profit from their productivity.

4.16 Can everyone be rich?

Assume for a moment that everyone who exists has an equal share of the wealth. Let's say everyone has the equivalent of $100,000. Supposing there are 7.5 billion people in the world; this would mean that there would be $75 trillion in the world.

If everyone made a 10% profit over say a year, they would each have $110,000. This would mean that there would now be a total of $82.5 trillion in the world. To accomplish this, the Government(s) of the world would have to release $7.5 trillion. In the real world … they don't! And the money is certainly not distributed in such a way.

Is it possible for everyone to make a profit? The answer is definitely 'No!'

4.17 Summary

The evidence and arguments presented in the previous sections show that many aspects of economies operate as zero-sum systems. While there are arguments that an entire economy is not a zero-sum system, when we focus on the use of money there are significant and well-structured experiments that show that the economy *is* limited by zero-sum conditions. It is possible to model an economy, using the boundary conditions of a zero-sum system, and to interpret and predict the properties of that economy. Such predictions turn out to be accurate as shown is chapter 5.

PART II

This section takes the theory of Zero-sum Economics and develops several numerical models for economies, examining the performance of these models under various conditions.

5   Zero-sum Economic Simulation

The purpose of producing the models discussed here was to determine the response over time of the entities involved in an economy; the simulation measured the amount of money each entity had and revealed how the figures changed over time.

5.1   Zero-sum Modelling

To model an economy as a zero-sum system requires that the entire economy be modelled, not just a subset of its components. A Zero-sum Model needs to include every single entity involved in the economy. If any component is left out of the model, the system will not operate correctly.

Through the Zero-sum Economic Models, I aimed to demonstrate what occurs in an economy, assuming there are zero-sum limitations. These models are based on several key assumptions:

- The only interactions that occur are zero-sum monetary transactions.
- There is a finite amount of money in the economy.
- Money can be released at any point by a Government. (Technically, this should be a bank, but using the Government simplifies the modelling.)
- Entities cannot spend more than they have.

When the simulation results were analysed, several behaviours emerged that had not been displayed using other models.

The following sections describe the various system models (including the CP and CPG Models) and samples of the system responses (both with and without business cycles).

5.1.1   Zero-sum CP Economic Model

I have assumed that the most basic operation in an economy is the 'transaction'. One person gives money to another.

This can be modelled mathematically as follows:

$$[A_{i+1} = A_i + T \,|\, B_{i+1} = B_i - T],$$

where entity A receives money from entity B, presumably for the transfer of a product or service. A_i and B_i represent the initial balance of the 'savings accounts' of A and B, respectively. A_{i+1} and B_{i+1} represent the respective balances of A and B after the first transaction T.

Notably, this is a zero-sum system, as shown below:

$$(+T) + (-T) = 0.$$

Thus, for all transactions that occur in the economy:

$$\sum T = \sum T_A + \sum T_B = 0.$$

$$\text{If } \sum T_A > 0,$$

then:

$$\sum T_B < 0.$$

Using the simplified model of the Circular Flow of Money from Figure 37, the transactions can be expressed as:

$$\sum T = \sum T_{\text{Consumers}} + \sum T_{\text{Producers}} = 0.$$

One of the major features of Producers, or of people in any type of business, is that they want to make profits. If a business is not profiting from its activities, eventually that business will fail and stop producing the product.

So again:

$$\text{if } \sum T_{\text{Producers}} > 0,$$

then:

$$\sum T_{\text{Consumers}} < 0.$$

We also know that Consumers need to eat and drink for basic survival, which means, typically:

$$\sum T_{\text{Consumers}} < 0.$$

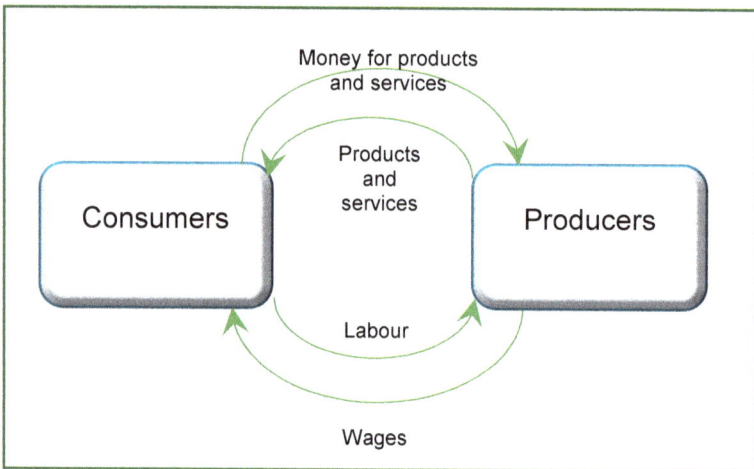

Figure 37: Basic Zero-sum CP Economic Model

It is possible to model the basic Circular Flow of Money concept presented in economic theory as a closed system. I make the assumption that the amount of money in the system is constant, i.e. $P + C = R$,

where R is the cash reserve,

P is the Producers' cash account total and

C is the Consumers' cash account total.

The interactions between these entities are well established:

134

change in *P* is proportional to increase in Consumer spending and also to decrease in the cost of labour (wages);

change in *C* is proportional to decrease in Consumer spending or increase in the cost of labour (wages);

	P	**C**
P	PP	CP (purchases)
C	PC (wages)	CC

PP represents internal transfers between Producers; these transfers do not change the amount of money collectively located among the Producers,

and

CC represents internal transfers between Consumers; these transfers do not change the amount of money collectively located among the Consumers.

CP represents transfers from Consumers to Producers.

PC represents transfers from Producers to Consumers.

$CP = -$ units sold $\times$ cost per unit, and

$PC =$ population $\times$ wages.

When *C* is reduced to a certain amount, Consumers can no longer afford to buy any more products, and Producers both increase prices and reduce wages to compensate.

Businesses need to make a profit. Thus:

$$CP - PC > 0,$$

and the profit margin can be expressed by:

$$M = \frac{CP - PC}{CP}.$$

135

Assuming that Consumers start with all of the reserve cash (R), over time t:

$$C(t) = R - (CP \times t) + (PC \times t), \text{ and}$$

$$P(t) = (CP \times t) + (PC \times t).$$

Thus, the change in C can be expressed as:

$$\frac{dC}{dt} = -CPt + PCt.$$

However, if Consumers can't afford to pay for the products, they stop buying them and the businesses lose profits.

So CP can never be greater than the current Consumer cash balance (C),

i.e.

$$CP = C$$

and

$$PC = (1 - M) \times CP,$$

where M is the desired profit margin.

The result is simplified to:

$$\frac{dC}{dt} = -CPt + (1 - M). -CPt$$

$$\frac{dC}{dt} = -CPt + CP - M.CP.t$$

which limits $\frac{dC}{dt}$ to:

$$\frac{dC}{dt} = (-M)C(t)$$

Solving for this differential equation using $C(0) = R$:

$$C(t) = R_0 \, e^{-Mt}$$

and

$$P(t) = R_0 \, (1 - e^{-Mt}).$$

The CP model is the most basic systems model of an economy, as shown in Figure 37. This model is commonly found in economics textbooks to demonstrate 'the cycle of money' in an economy. The experiments with this model show the basic system response for varying Producer profit margins.

A numerical model of the basic CP system produces the system response shown in Figure 38.

Basic economic system response

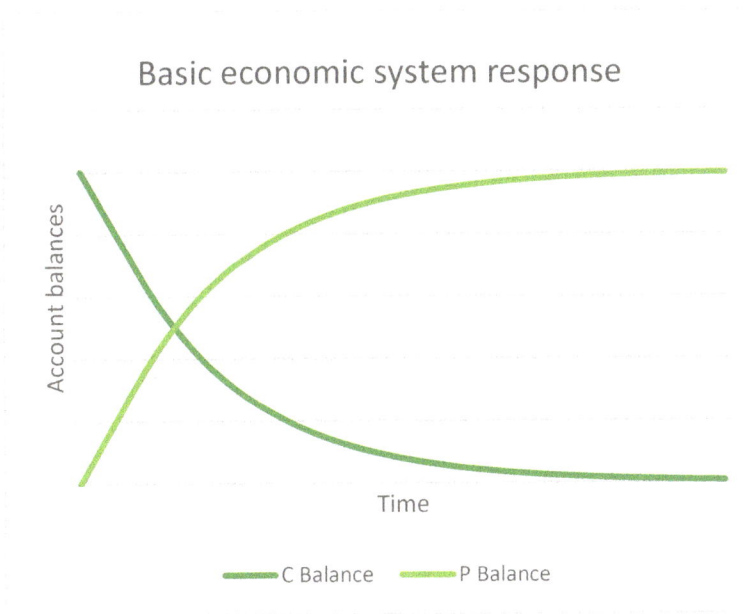

Figure 38: Zero-sum CP system response

This basic CP Zero-sum Economic Model reveals the relationship between Consumers and Producers in a closed system with a finite amount of money.

Such a system operates in two distinct modes:

1. Stable

When Consumers have enough money for purchasing all of their required goods from Producers, the system is stable. Producers have a constant income, and while Producers make a profit, the Consumers' balance is continually reducing.

2. Decaying

When Consumers do not have enough money, a decay in Consumer spending occurs, which results in a decay in Producer income; however, the Producers' balance represents the vast majority of the wealth in the system.

5.1.1.1   5.1.1.1   Summary

The purpose of this research was to demonstrate that an economic theory can be developed based on the zero-sum interaction between simple entities. The CP Model is derived from the most basic economic model presented in standard macroeconomic theory, the 'Circular Flow of Money'. This model, which shows the simplest types of entities that exist and how they operate in isolation, was analysed both mathematically and numerically, revealing that, in the CP system, if Producers make a profit they accumulate money at the expense of Consumers. The model was run with a fixed amount of money to demonstrate the interaction of the entities without influence from money creation sources.

5.1.2   CPG Model

Figure 39 illustrates the introduction of the Government entity into the system. The relationship between Consumers and Producers is the same as in the CP Model, but now the Government entity is receiving taxes from both Consumers and Producers, and also spending money on both Consumers and Producers. Consumers can be Government employees receiving wages, or Consumers receiving unemployment benefits (or other forms of welfare) when they are in need. Producers are frequently used to build or to manage infrastructure.

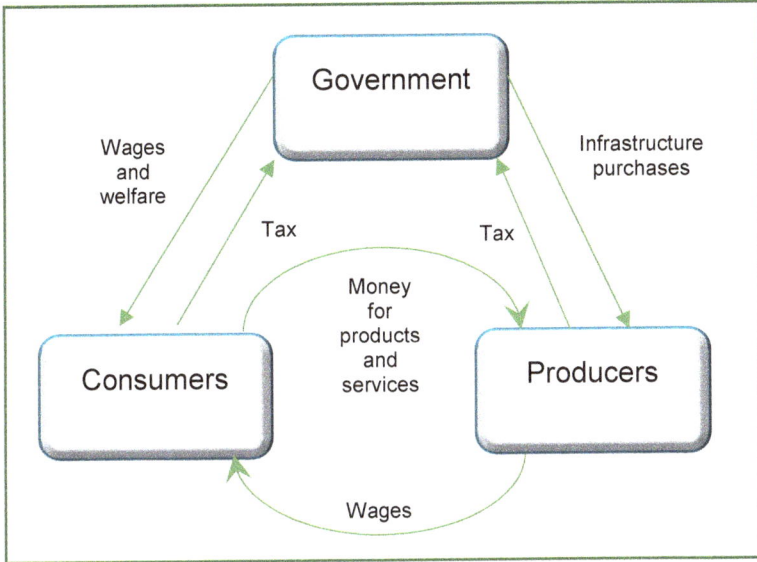

Figure 39: Zero-sum CPG Economic Model

Adding the Government into the system adds four new transaction types.

Transactions	C	P	G
C	0	CP	CG
P	PC	0	PG
G	GC	GP	0

CP represents the sum of the Consumer purchases from Producers.

CG represents the sum of the transactions from Consumers to Government ('taxes'), which are typically determined as a percentage of income, and can be averaged to a single tax value.

PC represents the sum of payments of Producers to Consumers for labour.

PG represents the tax paid to Governments, but this time from Producers.

GC represents the Government payments to those Consumers who are Government employees, and also welfare payments to Consumers who are unemployed.

GP represents payments from the Government to Producers, in return for infrastructure.

These transactions can be represented by three equations:

$$C(t) = R - CP.t - CG.t + PC.t + GC.t$$

$$P(t) = +CP.t - PC.t - PG.t + GP.t$$

$$G(t) = +CG.t + PG.t - GC.t - GP.t$$

R is the total cash reserve, and we allow Consumers to start with all the cash.

Businesses need to make a profit. Thus:

$$CP - PC - PG > 0,$$

and the profit margin can be expressed by:

$$M = \frac{CP - PC - PG}{CP}.$$

We know that Governments use income tax from both Consumers (T_c) and Producers (T_p), so

$$CG = T_c\, PC, \text{ and}$$

$$PG = T_p\,(CP - PC).$$

T_c and T_p vary depending on the country, but for a numerical example we have used 0.3 (30%) for both.

For a profit margin, *M*,

$$PC + T_p\,(CP\!-\!PC) = 1 - M.CP$$

140

$$C(t) = R - CP.t - CG.t + PC.t + GC.t$$

$$P(t) = +CP.t - PC.t - PG.t + GP.t$$

$$G(t) = +CG.t + PG.t - GC.t - GP.t$$

GC is modelled as a constant plus any amount of cash for welfare payment to Consumers, if it is required.

Thus, if $C < CP + CG - PC$,

$$GC = C - CP + CG - PC.$$

GP is modelled as a constant payment to Producers, but is limited to ensure Government cash is greater than zero.

$$\frac{dC}{dt} = -CPt + PCt.$$

However, if Consumers can't afford to pay for the products, the Producers lose profits.

CP can never be greater than the current Consumer Cash balance (C).Hence, the boundary condition:

$$CP = C$$

and

$$PC = (1 - M) \times CP,$$

where M is the desired profit margin.

The result is simplified to

$$\frac{dC}{dt} = -CPt + (1 - M) \times CPt$$

$$\frac{dC}{dt} = -CPt + CP - M.CP.t,$$

which limits $\frac{dC}{dt}$ to

$$\frac{dC}{dt} = (-M)C(t).$$

Solving this differential equation using $C(0) = R$ gives:

$$C(t) = R\, e^{-(M-Tax)t}$$

$$P(t) = R\, (1-e^{-Mt})$$

$$G(t) = R\, e^{-(Tax)t}.$$

The CPG Model adds in the Government entity and uses income tax as the basis for Government income, as shown in Figure 39. Governments also give Consumers a constant amount of wages and welfare when they do not have enough money to purchase the goods they require.

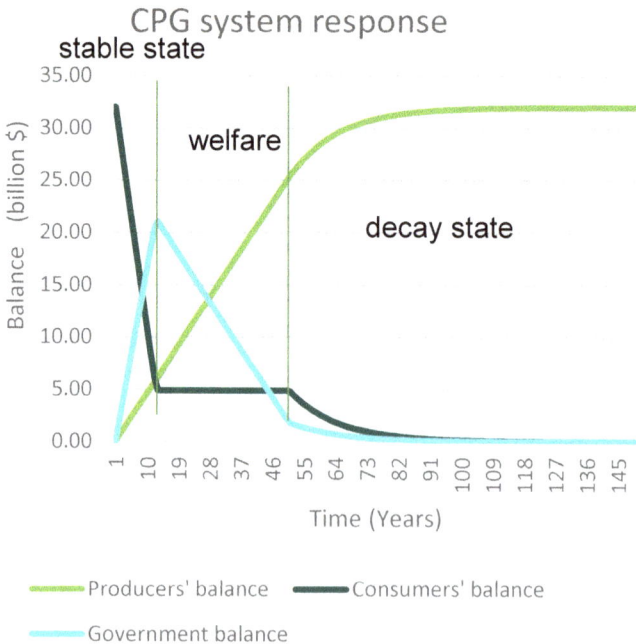

CPG system response

stable state

welfare

decay state

Producers' balance   Consumers' balance

Government balance

Figure 40 CPG system response

Including Governments in the CP system shows the effect of taxation and welfare on the economic responses. The CPG Model response shown in

Figure 40 portrays the three states: stable, welfare and (finally) decay. During the stable constant-income state, Governments receive income from both Consumers and Producers, thus allowing those Governments to accrue a considerable balance. This phase, however, is short-lived. As soon as Consumers cannot afford the products they need, the system enters the welfare state. During the welfare state phase, the Consumers can maintain a constant balance, but this is at the expense of the cash balance that the Governments have accrued. Once the combined Consumer and Government balance is not enough to pay for the required Consumer products, the economy enters the decay state. During this state, both Government and Consumer balances decay to nothing, and Producers accumulate all the cash in the economy.

5.1.2.1   5.1.2.1   Summary

The purpose of this research was to demonstrate that an economic theory can be developed from the basic zero-sum interaction between simple entities. The CPG Model is derived from the 'Circular Flow of Money Model' of standard macroeconomic theory. The mathematical and numerical analysis of the CPG Model shows how Producers and Consumers operate in a system incorporating a Government entity that controls taxation and welfare.

The CPG Zero-sum Economic Model shows the relationship between Consumers, Producers and Governments in a closed system with a finite amount of money. This type of system operates in three distinct states:

1. Stable state
    Producers have a constant income, Governments have a constant income and Consumer balances are constantly reducing.
2. Welfare state
    As Consumers do not have enough money, the Government pays them welfare to keep the system running. The Consumer balance is constant, the Government balance is decaying, and the Producers' income is decaying.
3. Decaying state
    All three collections of entities have decaying incomes, but the

Producers' balance represents the vast majority of the money in the system.

Obviously, the economy has not completely decayed away, but the Basic CP/CPG Models require something extra to keep going. We need to add something that allows the money to keep circulating and moves it from the Producers back to the Consumers. That something is simply put: investment. When investment is combined with a decaying system, business cycles can occur.

5.1.3 Business cycles

Using the basic Zero-sum CP Economic Model, business cycles can be considered. In the previous section, it has been established that the incomes in an economy decay during the decay state. This does not occur in the real economy as Producers faced with falling incomes, but high cash can invest. In business cycle research [18, 22, 25, 30, 68, 69]. it has been shown that the economy recovers during an investment phase of the cycle. Considering the system model the investment phase must somehow provide consumers with more money as Producers spend money on something they believe will improve their income and ultimately profits.

As such an 'Investment' term can be added to the equation for the Producers' income becomes

$$P(t) = CP(t) - W(t) + I(t),$$

(Equation 1: Business cycle derivation)

where wages $W = MC(t)$

$CP(t)$ max $= C(t)$.

A system model of this could be as shown in Figure 41.

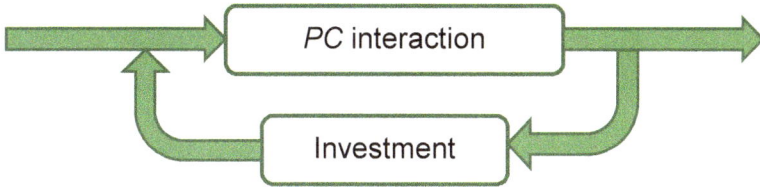

Figure 41: Control system diagram

The response of the system is illustrated in Figure 42 and Figure 43. The thing to note in this graph is that Consumers have a critical point in the balance where oscillations begin. This point is equal to the cost of living. In this simulation, the value becomes the number of Consumers (N) multiplied by the price of the products they need (C_{pu}).

$$C_0 = N \ C_{pu}$$

(Equation 2: Critical point).

This is referred to as the critical point or C_0, which is the minimum amount of cash Consumers need to purchase their required products. These values can be shown graphically from the system response of a CP or CPG system, as shown in Figure 42.

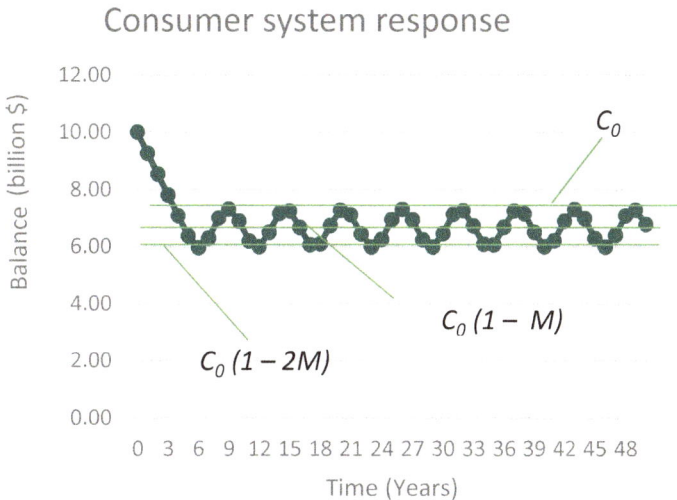

Figure 42: CP Consumer system with business cycles

The basic differential equation comes from the CP system:

$$P(t) = R_0 - C(t) + I(t).$$

If we have an investment strategy that dictates an increase in investment with a decrease in the change in income, where K is the investment factor, we create a second order change:

$$I(t) = -K\frac{d^2P(t)}{dt^2}$$

(Equation 3: Business cycle investment strategy)

$$P(t) = R_0 - C_0(1 - M)e^{-Mt} + (1 - M)P(t) - K\frac{d^2P(t)}{dt^2}$$

$$P(t) - (1 - M)P(t) = R_0 - C_0(1 - M)e^{-Mt} - K\frac{d^2P(t)}{dt^2}$$

$$MP(t) = R_0 - C_0(1 - M)e^{-Mt} - K\frac{d^2P(t)}{dt^2}$$

Using the CP result as a forcing function, gives:

$$\frac{K}{M}\frac{d^2P(t)}{dt^2} + i(t) = R_0 - C_0(1 - M)e^{-Mt}$$

(Equation 4: Business cycle differential equation with CP forcing function)

$$a\frac{d^2P(t)}{dt^2} + b\frac{dP(t)}{dt} + cP(t) = 0$$

The roots of the equation are:

$$r_{1,2} = \frac{-b \pm \sqrt{b^2 + 4ac}}{2a}$$

$$r_{1,2} = \frac{0 \pm \sqrt{0 - 4\frac{K}{M}}}{2\frac{K}{M}}$$

$$r_{1,2} = \frac{2 \pm \sqrt{4\frac{K}{M}}}{2\frac{K}{M}}$$

$$r_{1,2} = \pm\sqrt{\frac{M}{K}}$$

This differential equation is solved to determine the Producer balance (P), as shown below:

$$P(t) = R_0(1 - M)e^{-Mt} + A\,\text{Sin}\left(\sqrt{\frac{M}{K}}t + \phi\right) + B\,\text{Cos}\left(\sqrt{\frac{M}{K}}t + \phi\right)$$

Given $P(0) = 0$ gives B = 0 and $\phi = 0$.

$$P(t) = R_0 - C_0(1 - M)e^{-Mt} + C_0(1 - M)\text{Sin}\left(\sqrt{\frac{M}{K}}t\right)$$

(Equation 5: Final business cycle time domain)

This function is described by the curve shown in Figure 43 as the Producers' balance. The graphs presented for the whole system response were generated numerically. There could be multiple mathematical solutions, with slightly differing responses. These variations could be due to the use of different expressions for investment, or to slight variability in the interactions between Consumers and Producers.

CP system response

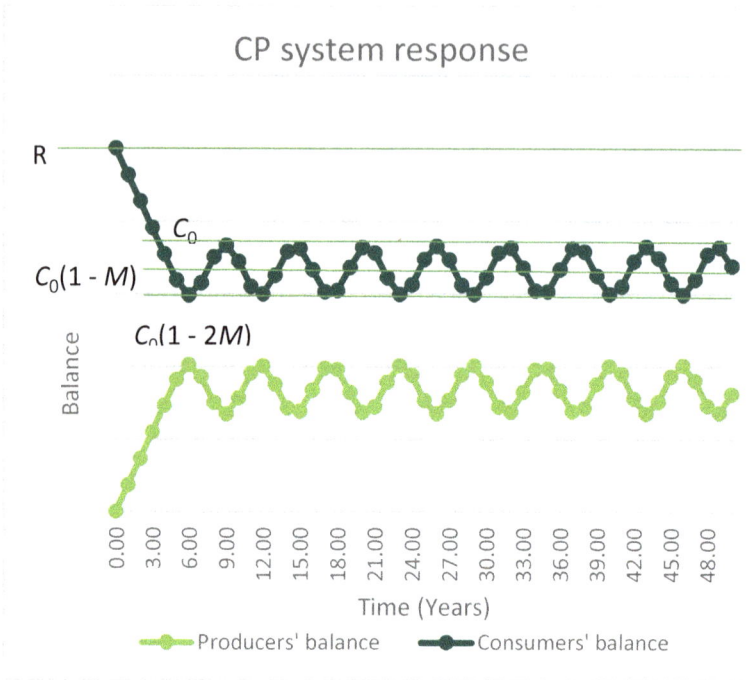

Figure 43: CP System with business cycles

During the decay state, the Producers need to 'invest' money, and this money must ultimately end up in the hands of Consumers. Such action results in the system response being sinusoidal, with a calculable resonant frequency (f) or period (T), as shown in (Equation 6 and (Equation 7.

$$f = \frac{1}{2\pi \sqrt{\frac{K}{M}}}$$

(Equation 6: Business cycle frequency)

$$T = 2\pi \sqrt{\frac{K}{M}}$$

(Equation 7: Business cycle period)

The model and analysis thus indicate that an economy will continuously oscillate at a particular frequency defined by the investment factor K and the profit margin M.

Mathematically the main controlling factor of the frequency is something called Lag. This is the lag between the decay from profit making and the investment. A lag of say 1 year results in a period of 2π years. A lag of 6 month results in a period of π years. This is a difficult concept to understand the theory and measure in the real world.

One way to think of this is to follow the curve on the decay cycle. The longer investors wait to begin the recovery, the longer the decay remains and the worse the recession is. It also means investors need to spend more to recover the economy.

Taking lag (L) into account the Period becomes:

$$T = 2\pi \, L \sqrt{\frac{K}{M}}$$

(Equation 8: Business cycle period)

This shows that an increase in lag will result in an increase in the period between recessions. As shown in

Table 16 there have been several changes in the average period between recessions in the real world. This may also be due to increased difficulties in creating investments over the years, Increases in bureaucracy for both government and corporations over the years may have also added to the lag in investment.

Also, there is no guarantee that Producers will invest with the constant strategy shown in (Equation 3. However, it is guaranteed that if investors do not invest enough in Consumers, the economy will not recover.

There have been many researchers who have investigated Business cycles [18, 22, 25, 30, 68, 69]. The economy continuously cycles through periods of decline and investment. These cycles have been observed in the US economy, as shown in

Table 16.

These data come from a long-standing research project of the National Bureau of Economic Research (NBER). While an NBER committee officially declares the dates when recessions begin and end, the following rule will almost always predict what they are going to do: "If real (inflation-adjusted) GDP declines for two consecutive quarters, a recession has begun; when real GDP begins to rise, the recession is declared over." [130]

Table 16: Dates of peaks and troughs of business cycles in the USA, 1854–1997 [130]

Peak	Trough
???	December 1854
June 1857	December 1858
October 1860	June 1861
April 1865	December 1867
June 1869	December 1870
October 1873	March 1879
March 1882	May 1885
March 1887	April 1888
July 1890	May 1891
January 1893	June 1894
December 1895	June 1897
June 1899	December 1900
September 1902	August 1904
May 1907	June 1908
January 1910	January 1912
January 1913	December 1914
August 1918	March 1919
January 1920	July 1921
May 1923	July 1924
October 1926	November 1927
August 1929	March 1933
May 1937	June 1938
February 1945	October 1945
November 1948	October 1949
July 1953	May 1954
August 1957	April 1958
April 1960	February 1961
December 1969	November 1970
November 1973	March 1975
January 1980	July 1980
July 1981	November 1982
July 1990	March 1991

March 2001	November 2001
December 2007	July 2009

From this data, the average time between troughs is 4.52 years (with a standard deviation of 1.96 years). If we split this table at 1927, when social security was introduced, the pre-Depression average becomes 3.84 years (with a standard deviation of 1.52 years).

In the post-Depression era, this average increased to 5.88 years (with a standard deviation of 2.44 years). This analysis suggests that the introduction of social security reduced the frequency of the business cycles. The post-Depression era can be split into two further groups: 1927–1990 and 1990–present. This gives averages of 5.00 years and 8.3 years for the periods, and standard deviations of 0.63 and 1.74 years, respectively, as shown in Table 17.

From these measurements of the real economy, it is possible to calculate the profit–investment ratio (K/M) for each period; the values obtained are listed in Table 17:

Table 17: Profit-investment ratio

Period	Measured period (T)	K/M
Pre 1927	3.84	0.3732
1927–1990	5.00	0.6341
1990–present	8.3	1.7439

The important thing to remember is that 'investments', as defined in this model, are the amount of money that returns to Consumers.

These data suggest that the profit-investment ratio was extremely low before 1927. (Only about one-third of the money collected from profits was reinvested.)

In 1927, the USA introduced social security, which effectively paid Consumers. As could be expected, the amount of money available to Consumers increased, and the frequency of the business cycles decreased.

In 1990–2001, significant investments were made into both computer systems and software development. As a result, the profit-investment ratio significantly changed—almost twice the amount of money was being invested as was being made in profits.

While the total of the investments is difficult to determine precisely, the link between business cycles and investment is demonstrated with real-world data. Thus, Zero-sum Theory can be used to predict and verify the existence of business cycles in an economy. The accuracy of such prediction would be based on how accurately the data for investment and company profits can be measured.

In both CP and CPG Models, Producers end up accumulating the money in the economy, irrespective of taxation methods. When a critical point is reached, the Producers' income is reduced because Consumers no longer have enough money to purchase the goods they require.

In the previous models, this behaviour was allowed to continue until both Consumers and Governments completely ran out of money.

In the Business Cycle Model, at the point where Producer income starts decaying, the Producers start investing. The result of this investment is that Consumers end up receiving some of the investment money.

The main variables tested here are again the profit margin of Producers, and a new one—the investment rate. The investment rate is a factor of the accumulated losses from the decay in income.

Adding an investment factor proportional to the amount of lost income during decay states produces the system response shown previously in Figure 43.

The distress of Consumers, illustrated in

Figure 44, is represented by the percentage of people who cannot afford to buy all of the products they need. During decay states, the percentage of distress is determined by how much money is in the system, and by how much profit Producers attempt to make. In

Figure 44, the profit margin is 10% and the distress peaks at approximately 20%.

Consumer distress

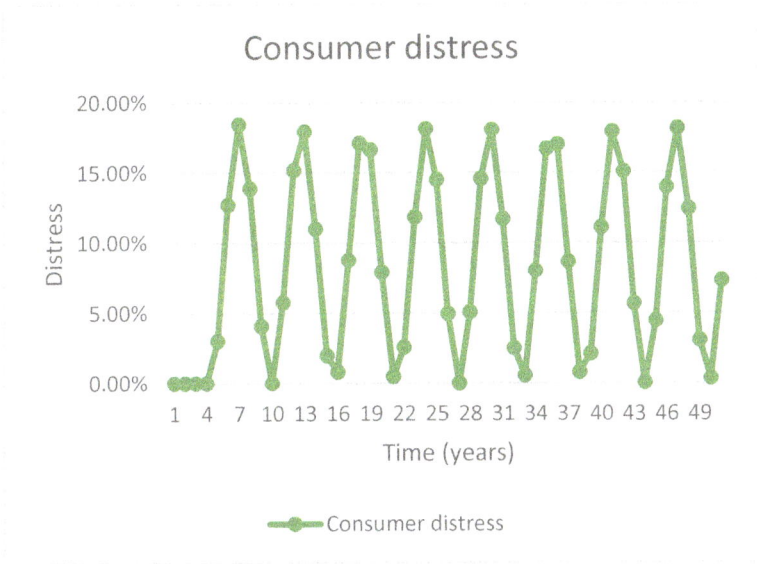

Figure 44: Consumer distress with business cycles

Figure 45 shows the CPG Model with business cycles. Again, the investment factor added to the Producers' balance is proportional to the amount of money lost during decay cycles. As with the CP Model, during the decay state the business cycles again become evident.

CPG system response

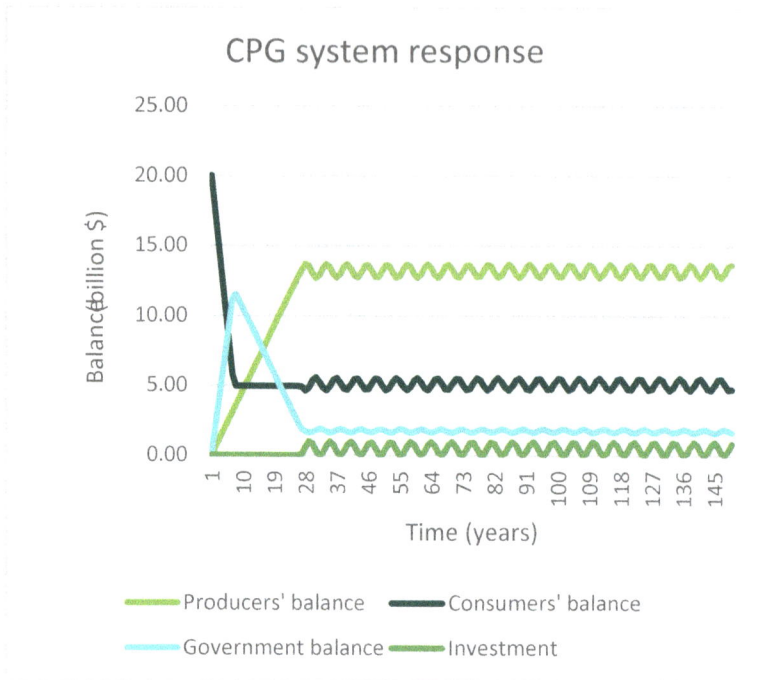

Figure 45: Zero-sum CPG system response with business cycles

5.1.3.1   5.1.3.1   *Maximum income*

The maximum income of the system is the total amount of money in the system. Business cycles show that the maximum income can be reached if all of the money in the system is spent. If the maximum money is not spent, this may cause a recession.

5.1.3.2   5.1.3.2   *Stagflation*

(Previously Lock in State)

While researching the CP models, it was discovered that the model could obtain a state in which investment and Consumer losses balanced out, resulting in a state of the economy in which there was high unemployment and Consumer distress, but no business cycles, as shown in Figure 46. This state is caused by the investments exactly matching the Consumer expenses. Notably, this state could also occur when high unemployment and low productivity exist. The problem with this state is that the distress remains constant, as shown in Figure 47.

This behaviour occurs mathematically when the investment rate (K) is less than the reciprocal of the profit margin (M). $K < 1/M$. Under these conditions, investment is not enough to recover the economy. The good news is that as far as we can tell from a historical perspective, investors have always eventually put in enough money to keep the economy running. Hence, this may just be a mathematical curiosity of the simulation. It's probably not something we want to experience.

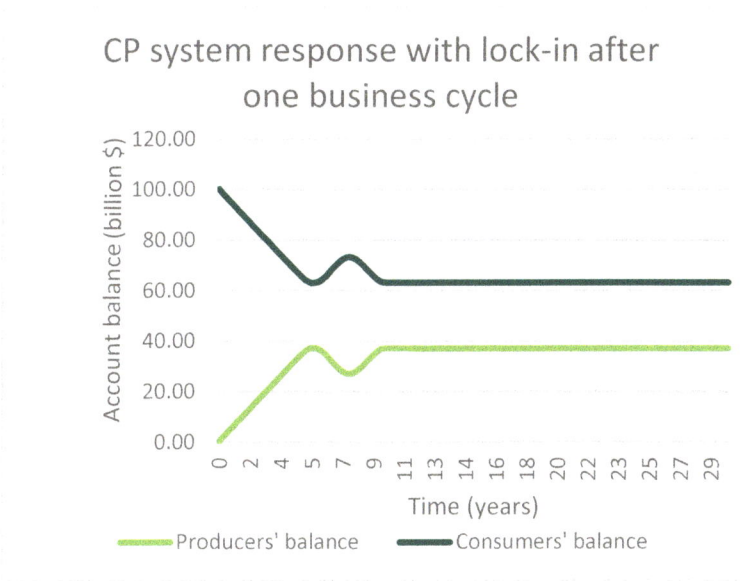

Figure 46: CP system response with lock-in after one business cycle

Figure 47: CP system distress with lock-in after one business cycle

However, if they do not invest enough, we can enter a period of a "lock in". This results in the economy running permanently at a reduced capacity equal to 100% minus the Business Profit margin, as shown in the graph below. If the Average Profit margin is 15%, the economy will run at 85%, leaving 15% of the Consumers in a permanent state of poverty.

The CP system response shown below uses an initial balance of $100 Billion for Consumers. They require a minimum of $73 Billion to buy all their required products. This used a profit margin of 18% and results in the consumers having around $62 Billion.

CP system response

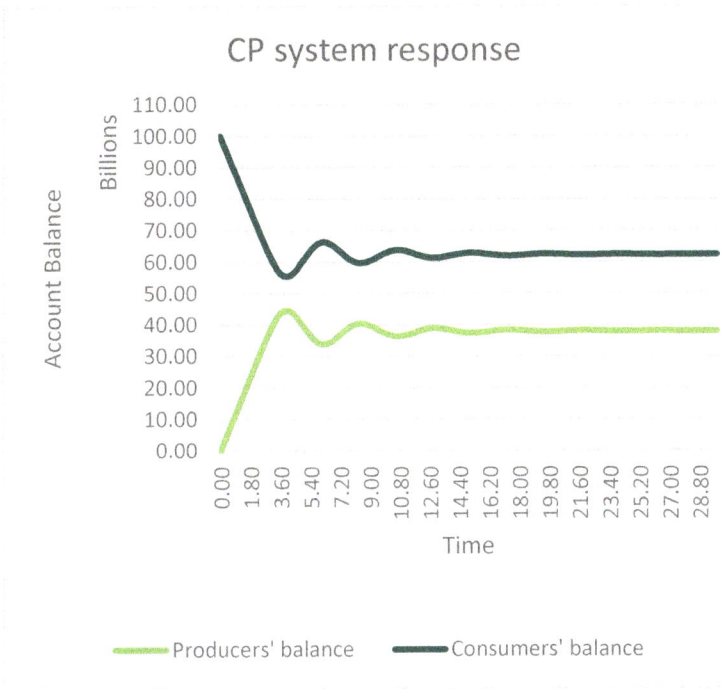

Figure 48: CP system response

A profit margin of 18% results in a distress (or unemployment) of close to 15% in simulation as shown below.

Distress %

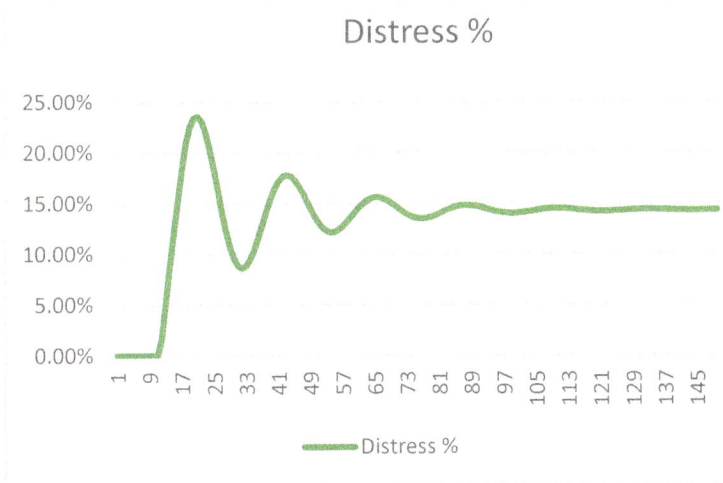

Figure 49: CP system distress

This shows that irrespective of the amount of effort people put into education, networking, or any other activity that gets jobs, and irrespective of their work ethic, we are guaranteed that around 15% of the population will continue to be unemployed, and will as such be stuck being poor.

Stagflation is a term for when the economy experiences both high unemployment and high inflation. The "Lock-in" state may be related, as during this period the economy experiences high unemployment. As the models do not make an estimate of inflation, it is possible that during a lock in state inflation could increase, as purchases would be reduced.

5.1.3.3   5.1.3.3   *Asymmetric Business cycles*

Sometimes in research, you can be surprised by what is discovered when you do research. Part of the problem is having expectations. The following images show the typical model I was expecting. Once consumers run out of cash, and the investment cycle kicks with a nice continuous sinusoid.

CP System Response

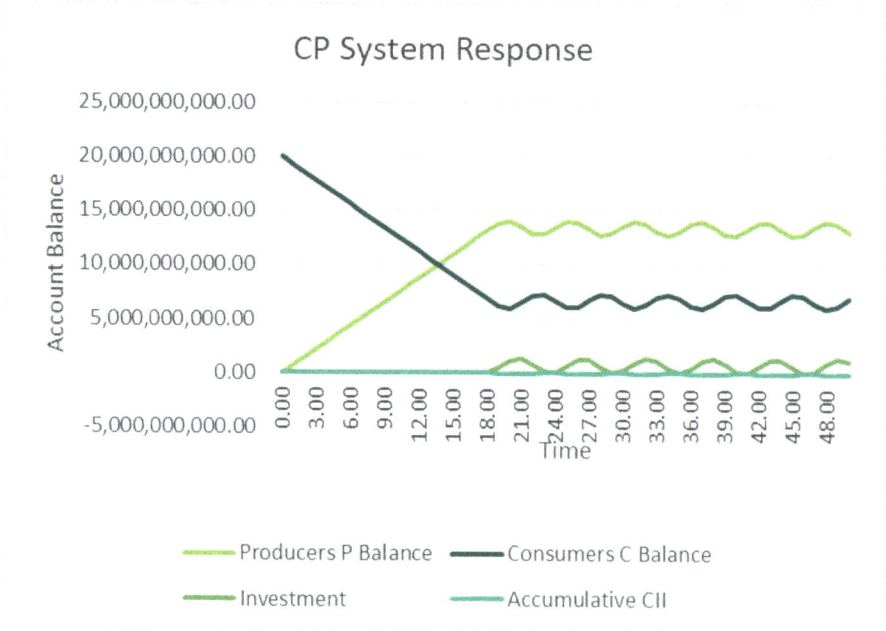

Legend: Producers P Balance — Consumers C Balance — Investment — Accumulative CII

Figure 50: CP System with Business Cycles

The distress shows the same thing, zero until the investment cycle kicks in and creates a nice looking sinusoid.

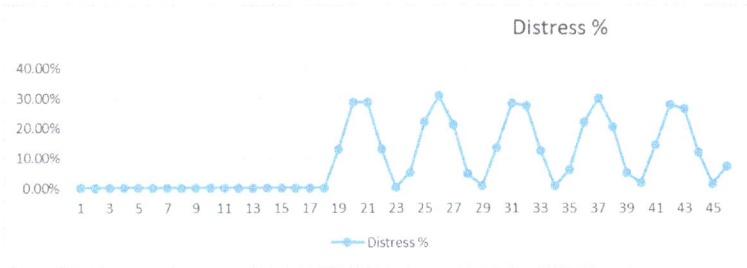

Figure 51: CP System Distress

In the models, the nice sinusoids only occur when the investment rate is exactly the reciprocal of the profit margin. (1/profit). When the investment rate is increased, the sinusoids turned into triangular or saw tooth waves.

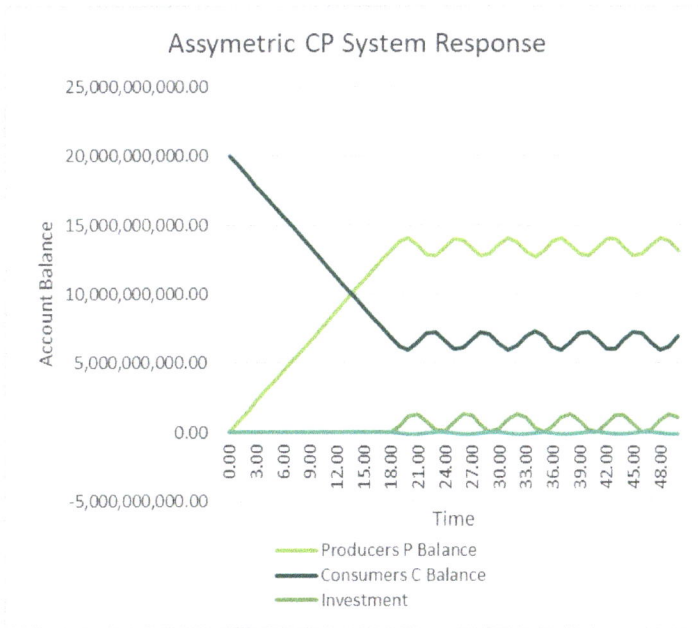

Figure 52: CP System with Asymmetric Business Cycles

159

When this is completed the distress only occurs as spikes towards the end of the business cycle.

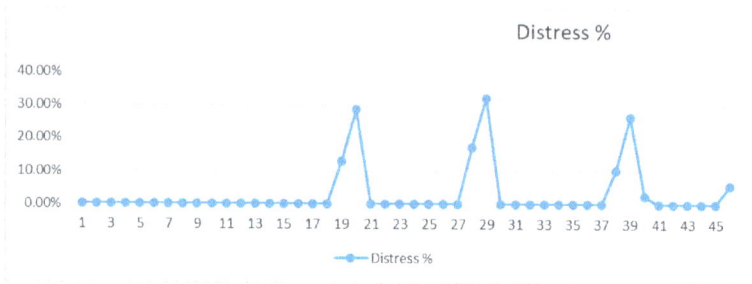

Figure 53: CP System with Asymmetric Business Cycles Distress

Frankly I thought that this kind of data was wrong and simply a function of how I was implementing my simulation. Then I looked at the US unemployment.

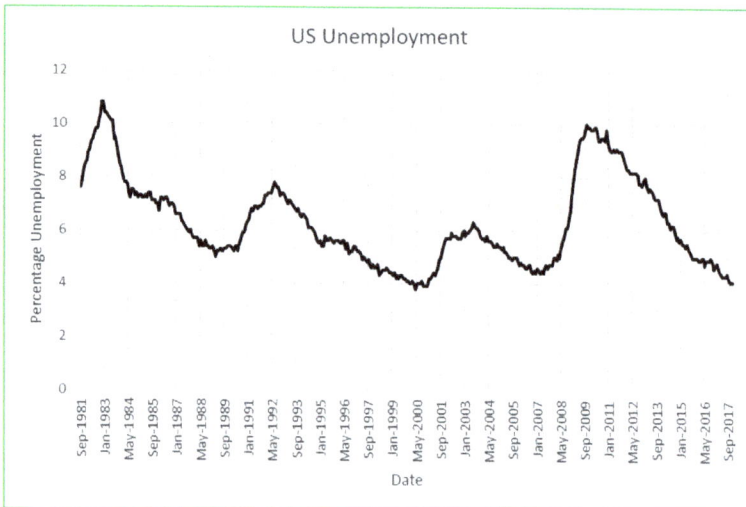

Figure 54: US Unemployment

Can you see the similarity? We have at least 4 cycles there with what you would call a triangular or "saw tooth" wave. When you adjust for the frequency and overlay the Consumer balance, the signals are extremely close. When consumers are suddenly receiving more cash producers are investing and attempting to cut back on their expenses by reducing employment, which is where shape of the curve comes from.

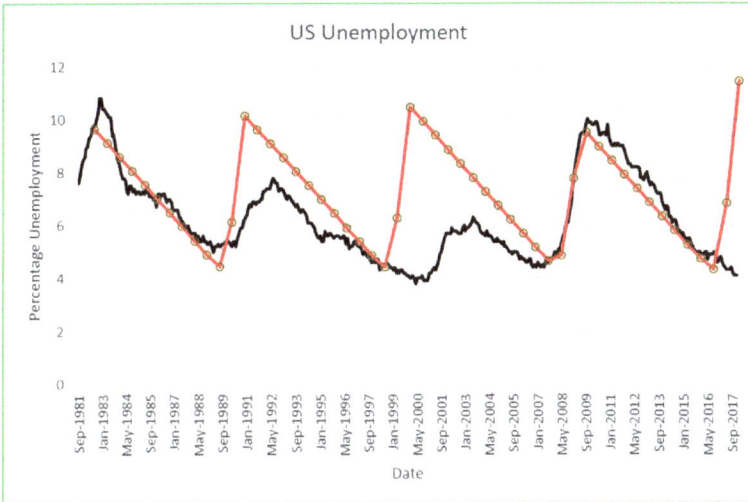

Figure 55: US Unemployment with CP System Response Overlay

This is another example of me being surprised by how much sense these simulations seems to make and gives me a lot more confidence in the simulations. The difficulty with this is that real data is far more complicated than simulated data. I was not expecting to find this kind of data. The reason this works is that the US economy is far more independent of external pressures and hence seems to give a much more "natural" looking data.

Which is exactly why this is a serendipitous discovery and shows why objective assessment of your measurements and data is so important.

5.1.3.4   Producer condensation

A striking phenomenon in economics is that in any market there is a tendency for markets to be dominated by a few large businesses, with many other smaller businesses. This 'Producer condensation' phenomenon can be caused by the biggest and most profitable businesses in a market buying out other Producers in the same market to increase their market share (rather than other types of investments, such as building new shops or developing new products).

A production company may be purchased by another company; the owners of the first company would then become Consumers permanently, transferring the money received back to the Consumers. After this, the Producers' balance would increase constantly, as consumers can once again afford everything they need. However, in the decay state of a CP or CPG Model, the Producers' income still decays. This would result in the value of the production company decaying as well. At some point, the value of the production company will be less than the amount of money accrued by another Producer, in which case the high-wealth Producer may 'buy out' the other Producer, resulting in fewer Producers and what is known as 'Producer condensation'.

5.1.3.5   5.1.3.4   *Comparison with previous theories*

Business cycles have been the subject of much discussion since economic theory was first established. Some of the greatest contributors to economics have dissected and discussed the possible causes [18, 22, 25, 30, 68, 69], but none have successfully developed a model that explains them satisfactorily.

It is useful to compare the models developed for Zero-sum Economics with models developed from previous theories to determine whether the previous theories still have merit. It is helpful to see where the theories agree with one another, and even to determine whether any improvements can be made to any theory by taking into account the different factors and conditions present in an economy.

Marx noted that financial crises had occurred regularly, and that they had a tendency to leave people unemployed and impoverished. Schumpeter [40, 50, 51] and Keynes [30] also investigated the phenomenon. Despite the amount of research, there is not a lot of consensus in modern economic theories as to why business cycles occur.

One major early theory was that business cycles develop from external effects, such as an increase in workload due to changes in working conditions. For example, in mining it may become more difficult to gain access to a mineral deposit because it becomes necessary to mine deeper underground, or because of a reduction in available resources. Zero-sum Economics, on the other hand, shows that business cycles are usually due to the internal processes present in any economic system that is profit driven. However, it should be noted that external factors such as those mentioned can lead to higher rates of inflation and higher costs, and thus can exacerbate business cycles.

Technological change (in the form of new products and improved efficiency) has been suggested as another potential cause. The creation and development of new technologies requires the investment of a lot of money and time. A significant proportion of this money is paid to people who have technical skills but who are not Producers. In the Zero-sum Model, these people would be considered Consumers, and the money would be considered an investment in technology. The downside is that technological change can and does cause unemployment. As processes become more efficient, fewer people are required to perform the same work. Once a market is saturated, fewer people are employed.

Investment in the more general sense was identified by Keynes as a factor playing a role in the business cycle. Investment is said to have occurred when someone who has cash available buys another business, or pays people to do something or to build something they want but which doesn't exist at the time of the transaction. In terms of Zero-sum Economics, the investment only affects the system output if money is transferred between entities. For example, a useful investment in terms of recovering the economy occurs when a Producer creates a new product and pays Consumers to perform research and development. An ineffective investment in terms of recovering the economy would be when a Producer buys a factory or other asset from another Producer.

The Zero-sum models show three major features of business cycles:

(i)   While Producers are making a profit, Consumers are always losing money.
(ii) Economic activity decays as the Consumers run out of money.
(iii) Recovering from the recession requires money to be invested in Consumers.

A number of the earlier theories identified investment as integral to the recovery stage of the business cycle, and this continues to be confirmed in modern economic theory.

This explanation does not preclude other causes of business cycles. As found by previous researchers [22, 69, 73–75], external factors will still cause recessions. Also, as previous researchers have noted, excessive debt can also cause recessions. These factors would still occur in a Zero-sum–based economy and could trigger a recession or make one worse if they coincided with a natural downturn in economic activity. What seems to have been missed in previous theories is the idea that *profits cause the decay in economic activity*.

5.1.3.6   5.1.3.5   *Summary*

The purpose of this research was to demonstrate that an economic theory can be developed from the consequences of zero-sum interaction between simple entities.

The Business Cycle Model is derived from the Circular Flow of Money Model as presented in standard macroeconomic theory. The addition at this point is that Producers are allowed to make investments, whereby money they have accumulated can be transferred back to Consumers. The Zero-Sum business cycle models, developed in this section, compare a Producer's current income with the maximum income previously received.

This model has been investigated both mathematically and numerically, and it has been determined that if their current income decreases, Producers will increase their investment based on their perceived accumulated loss. This pattern results in business cycles with distinct states of natural decay and investment recovery.

The CPG Zero-sum Economic Model with investment included shows the relationship between Consumers, Producers and Governments in a closed system with a finite amount of money. This type of system operates in three distinct states, in a similar fashion to that of the basic CPG Model.

1. Stable state
   Producers have a constant income, Governments have a constant income and Consumer balances are constantly reducing.
2. Welfare state
   As Consumers do not have enough money, the Government pays them welfare to keep the system running. The Consumers' balance is constant, the Government's balance is decaying, and the Producers' income is decaying.
3. Decaying state
   All three collections of entities have an oscillating balance and income.

This model has been applied to existing data on the dates of recessions in the USA. The period under consideration can be divided up into three phases: pre-1927 (average period between recessions 3.84 years), 1927–1990 (average period between recessions 5.0 years) and 1990–present (average period between recessions 8.3 years).

The Zero-sum Business Cycle Model shows that the ratio of investment:profit determines the period of the recessions, as given by the following formula:

$$T = 2\pi \sqrt{\frac{K}{M}}$$

The more investment there is compared with profits made, the longer the period between recessions.

This is consistent with actual records from the real world. In 1927, during the Great Depression, the US government created a form of social welfare that paid Consumers.

During the 1990s, the computer revolution started, which encouraged much more investment in technology development. While these technologies eventually produced significant changes in overall efficiency, from a business cycle perspective, the investment slowed the rate of the cycles. After the first recession, in around 1990, the next major financial event occurred in 2000 with the 'dot com bubble'. This was followed by the Global Financial Crisis in 2008. Business cycles can be considered as a systemic behaviour. The individuals involved in the system (Consumers and Producers) do not 'decide' to start a recession. It simply occurs due to the nature of the system. While Consumers and Producers have a choice about where they invest any profits they have made, the recession only stops when some of the money they have accumulated is returned to Consumers.

5.1.4   Inflation

We need to understand one basic fact about inflation: it does not happen 'by magic'. A person in a business must make a decision to increase the business prices. If we are talking about inflation, we are talking about people making business decisions. Thus, inflation needs to be considered as having a psychological cause as well as a mechanical effect. The mechanical effect of inflation changes prices and people must pay more. How and why do business people make such business decisions? The main motivation for businesses changing prices is to maintain profits.

Previous researchers investigating inflation have typically considered the relationships between inflation, unemployment, GDP and other measurable statistics, without presenting an underlying model that might explain why the inflation occurs. The research presented here uses the Zero-sum System Model and makes the basic assumption that businesses always attempt to maintain their profit levels.

One of the main points to remember in economics is that the only receiver of money is another person. If you think about buying a car, it is nonsensical to think you give the money to the car. You give the money to the previous owner of the car. All monetary transactions involve two or more human parties.

Consider a supply chain, with products being transferred between suppliers. This creates a 'legacy of transactions' in which the final purchaser of a product is in effect purchasing all of the previous transactions plus the profit made by the retailer. Figure 56 illustrates how the price paid by each 'person' equals the price paid by the previous person plus the profit made.

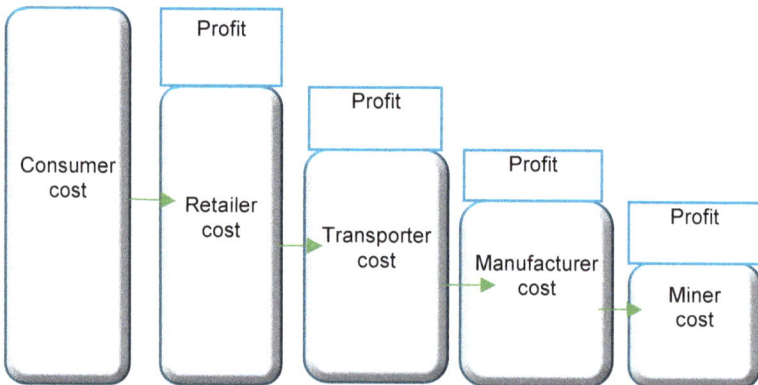

Figure 56: Legacy of transactions

A miner is also a Consumer: if they need to buy a mining product from a retailer, they need to pay for the transportation, the manufacturing and the mining that they themselves performed previously. This makes it obvious why inflation occurs: every generation throughout the legacy of transactions needs to make a profit.

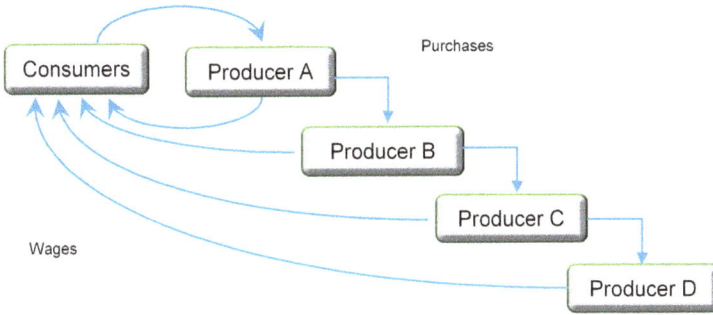

Figure 57: Supply Chain Zero-sum CP Economic Model

Furthermore, the legacy of transactions becomes cyclic, as shown in Figure 57, when the Consumers' wages are added to the model. When this behaviour becomes cyclic, it becomes a somewhat ridiculous situation, where everyone is paying for their own work from previous years.

The CP model can be used as a basis for examining inflation. This model incorporates the relationships required to examine Producer profits, wages and product prices.

P_t = total profit; C_t = total cost; W_t = total wages; P_{pu} = profit per unit; C_{pu} = cost per unit; W_{pu} = wages per unit; N = population; S = sales; S_e = sales to employed Consumers; S_u = sales to unemployed Consumers; E = employed; U = unemployed.

$$S = S_e + S_u$$

$$P_t = C_t - W_t$$

$$W_t = W_r E$$

$$P_{pu} * N = C_{pu} * N - W_r E$$

$$C_{pu} = P_{pu} + \frac{W_r E}{N}$$

$$C_{\text{pu}} = P_{\text{pu}} + W_r \frac{E}{(N)}$$

The cost per unit is proportional to the ratio between unemployment and employment.

$$C_{\text{pu}} \propto \frac{E}{N}$$

(Equation 9: Inflation versus unemployment)

This expression results in the inflation rate being calculated with respect to unemployment, and it will be unit-less.

Inflation vs employment

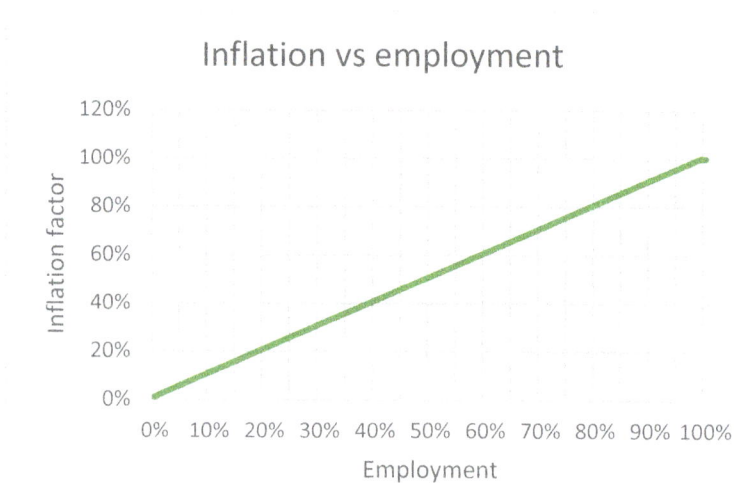

Figure 58: Inflation versus unemployment graph from the CP Model

The graph in Figure 58 shows that inflation is at a maximum when employment is maximised. Conversely, when employment is maximised, unemployment is minimised.

From this observation, we can construct an alternative model for inflation, which shows two groups of Consumers, one group of which are employed and the other unemployed, as shown in Figure 59.

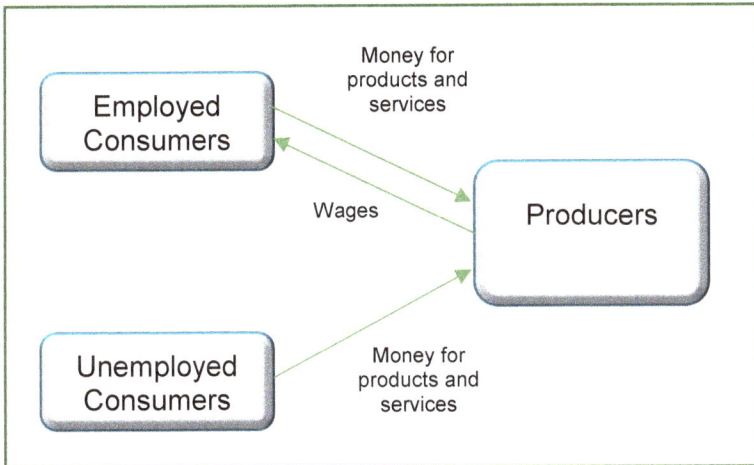

Figure 59: CP Economic Model with unemployment

This shows that wages are only paid to employed Consumers, even though unemployed Consumers still have to pay for their products. This means that the unemployed Consumers' savings will be continually drained, and eventually these people will not be able to buy any products. Since the Producers do not have to pay the unemployed Consumers a wage, they make far more profit from them—almost 100%! It would be possible to conclude that Producers *prefer* unemployed Consumers, but this would probably be a systemic, rather than intentional, outcome.

Current research identifies at least three causes of inflation:

- demand pull
- cost push
- exchange rates.

In addition to these factors, the Phillips curve relates unemployment to inflation.

From the formula developed previously, the entire cost of a product is given by:

Zero-sum Economic Simulation

$$C_{total} = (P_{total} + W_{total} \frac{E}{N}) X$$

(Equation 10: Phillips curve inflation breakdown)

Demand pull becomes the P_{total} term.

Cost push is the W_{total} term.

The Phillips curve is related to the ratio of employed to unemployed, i.e. $\frac{E}{N}$.

The entire cost function can be multiplied by the exchange rate, X, if the transaction occurs across currencies.

Also, the cost of products must be paid for by employees; hence, C_{total} must be equal to W_{total}:

$$C_{total}(T+1) = W_{total}(T).$$

With this limitation, if profits (P_{total}) are greater than zero, wages (W_{total}) must be reduced to compensate over time.

Hence, if $P_{total} > 0$, $\Delta C_{total} > 0$. This means that prices must increase while profits are greater than zero.

Using inflation rate data from the USA from 1969 to 2014 (source: World Bank data [131]), together with the dates of recessions during this period (as shown in Section 5.1.3), possible correlations can be identified. In the period 1969–2014, there were a total of seven recessions: in November 1970, March 1975, July 1980, November 1982, March 1991, November 2001 and July 2009.

As shown in Figure 60, most of the recessions correlate closely to peaks in inflation. These results suggest that inflation is related to the Consumer–Producer money cycle. While Producers are making a profit, Consumers are losing money and reducing spending. Producers attempt to recover their income using two possible mechanisms: reducing costs (i.e. reducing employment) and increasing the price of their products (i.e. inflation). The previous CP and CPG Models use cost reduction alone to increase profits.

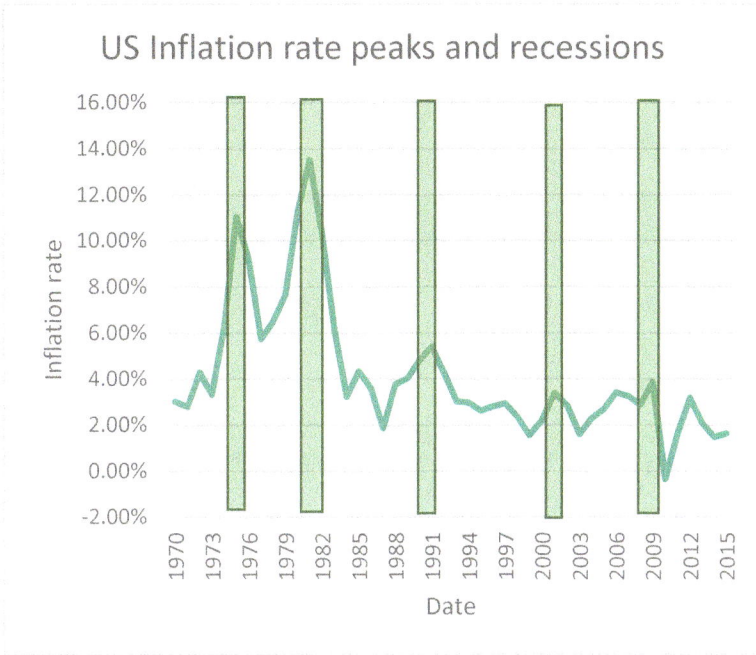

Figure 60: US Inflation rate (yellow line) peaks coincide with recessions (indicated by blue lines)

The relationship described by the Phillips curve is a fundamental observation of macroeconomics that can be derived from mathematical analysis of a Zero-sum CP Model. This shows that zero-sum analysis is consistent with this aspect of existing macroeconomic theory.

Business people use inflation of their product prices as a means of maintaining their profit margin. As shown previously, the equations for the cost of a product show that there are several causes of inflation.

$$C_{total} = (P_{total} + W_{total}\frac{E}{N})X$$

(Equation 11: Inflation breakdown)

The profit margin (P), the wages (W) and any exchange rates (X) all contribute to the price of the product.

Wages are to some extent determined by the difficulty of the process of creating a product. The more difficult the process, the greater the cost of producing the product.

$$W_{total} = W_{Rate} \times H,$$

where W_{Rate} is the wage rate of the workers.

H is the number of hours the workers must work to generate a product.

- Real inflation

Real inflation occurs when products become harder to acquire, i.e. the number of hours required to produce a product increases. This means that more work is required to obtain the same amount of product. This has occurred with oil and mineral resources. When minerals run out in one location, mining companies need to spend money on resource exploration As prices increase, mining companies may attempt to develop more labour-demanding resources. Thus, in the overall scheme of the business, the wage rate may stay constant, but the number of hours the workers need to operate increases.

- Cost inflation

If the number of hours worked by employees stays the same but the wage rate increases, this increases the overall cost of products. The wage rate is the most common cause of industrial disputes.

- Profit inflation

If companies wish to earn more money, they can simply add the cost of their desired profit to the cost of a product. Surprisingly, this does not occur often (at least anecdotally). Managers are often sensitive to workers' needs, and show some compassion by avoiding needless decreases in wages. They also try to avoid increases in prices just to increase the company's income.

- Legacy inflation

Legacy inflation can be considered to be a type of profit inflation. The price of a product increases due to a series of people attempting to make a profit on it by repeated transferring of ownership. This occurs with most trade. A Producer distributes their product through retailers, who often use shipping companies. At each stage, the cost of the product increases, but there is no increase in the amount of the product produced. Housing prices are one of the most notable examples of legacy inflation. Over many years, the same house can be bought and sold many times. As a rule, the price people sell a house for is always higher than the price they bought it for. As a result, housing prices steadily increase. The greater the number of transactions, the higher the cost involved; from this we deduce: "To cut costs, eliminate the middle men." Legacy inflation is an unproductive process, and no new products are produced when the product is sold. The price simply goes up.

- Exchange rate inflation

Exchange rates have been established so that trade can occur between countries. There have been many cases in which the exchange rate with other countries has decreased so significantly that the purchasing power of the currency does not allow Consumers to purchase the products they need. These collapses occurred in Germany in 1924 and 1931, in Asia in 1997, in Russia in 1998 and in Zimbabwe in 2009. There can be a few different reasons for this phenomenon, including excessive debt and excessive trade deficits.

Hyperinflation is a state in which the price of goods in a country experiences rapid inflation of maybe several 1000% over a matter of days. This can occur when the majority of money from a particular country is outside the country, and the country is relying on trade for basic Consumer products (food, water, shelter). In that situation, a Government will often release more cash so that its citizens can afford their basic products. This creates a feedback cycle in which everyone needs more money to pay for basic goods; this money is then sent overseas to other countries. According to recent analyses [77, 80, 82, 83], exchange rate inflation is the primary cause of hyperinflation. This occurred in Germany after World War I (1924, 1931), and more recently in Zimbabwe (2009). In these cases, the result was that the currency was abandoned altogether.

These forms of inflation are types of cost-push inflation. Cost-push inflation always raises the price of products.

The main reason for discussing the various forms of inflation is to determine whether the causes can be considered external or internal to the economy. Real inflation is the only source of inflation that is external to the economy. All of the other sources are effectively internal to the economy. Since an economy operates with a Circular Flow of Money, internal inflation becomes self-reinforcing. Inflation in one part of the economy leads to inflation in other parts of the economy. It should be possible to minimise the effects of numerical inflation within an economy by eliminating the initial stages of inflation.

It should also be noted that increasing prices in a business cycle is completely ineffective at recovering from a recession. In Section 5.1.3, it is shown that the cause of business cycles is that the Consumers are running out of money. This is a problem that is external to businesses; hence, any modification of the business itself is going to be completely ineffective as a solution. This is an example of systemic behaviour and local information. Business owners only have local information about how their businesses are operating. They do not have any information about the state of Consumer funding. Due to their limited information, business owners do not realise that the problem with their business is due to external conditions, and this causes a systemic behaviour whereby businesses increase prices. By increasing prices, businesses are chasing their own tails. Higher prices mean a higher cost of living, which means paying higher wages.

5.1.4.1   5.1.4.1   Future work

This book introduces the development of a new theory; much work is yet to be done to extend the theory to take account of additional complicating factors. However, the basic CP system can take into account pricing and inflation. The design could be further modified to allow for external inputs to the economic system, including the effects of technology and the full complexity of work.

Such a design is illustrated in Figure 61: the Producers have control of their pricing through a supply-versus-demand mechanism. This requires two inputs: the number of Consumers, and the distribution of money among the Consumers. The Producers decide to set pricing by examining a supply-versus-demand curve. As noted in Section 4.6, when people purchase products, the demand curve shifts; over time it could be expected that due to the supply-versus-demand curve, the 'equilibrium' point would move in the direction of increasing prices. This suggests a reason why there is constant inflation, but the idea requires confirmation via further research.

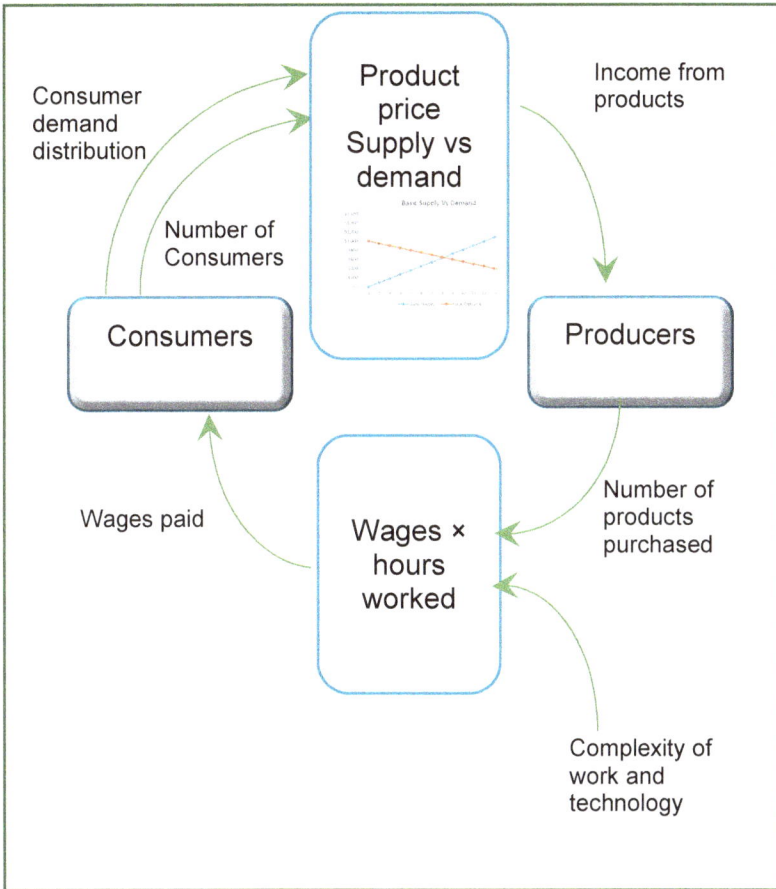

Figure 61: Zero-sum CP Economic Model with inputs

5.1.4.2   5.1.4.2   *Summary*

The purpose of this research was to demonstrate that economic phenomena can be explained from the interaction of basic zero-sum entities. By considering the mathematics of the Zero-sum CP Model, it has been demonstrated that this theory can be used to develop an equation that is consistent both with the current forms of inflation recognised in macroeconomics (demand-pull and cost-push) and with the Phillips curve. The Phillips curve is an economic phenomenon that relates inflation to unemployment. CP Model analysis shows that this relationship can be driven by the money flow in an economy going to a Producer. This money flow can be divided into money coming from those Consumers who are employed by a Producer, and money coming from those

Consumers who are unemployed. The mathematical formula developed shows that the more people who are unemployed, the greater the amount of money coming from sources external to Producers (in general terms, the government), and hence the more profit Producers can make. This means the CP system will favour people becoming unemployed, because that provides external income for Producers.

The equation developed for inflation ((Equation 11) was further investigated and used to calculate a number of different types of inflation, including cost, profit, legacy and exchange-rate inflation. The results were compared and found to be consistent with existing inflation statistics and with the generally recognised causes of the major financial crashes. This demonstrates that Zero-sum Economic Theory is consistent with both current macroeconomic theory and with past observations of inflation.

5.1.5   Cash Distribution Model

One of the most striking features of the current economy is the disparity in wealth between the rich and the poor. It is often observed that the top 1% of the population own 50% of the wealth in the world [13]. This disparity causes huge problems in terms of purchasing products, poverty and social unrest.

One of the primary reasons why people created economics was to determine who would get resources when their availability was limited. The main way in which this is sorted is through wealth: only the wealthy can afford to buy the rarest resources; thus, these resources have the highest price.

Despite the fact that, with our current technology, the human race can create everything required for people to survive (primarily food, water and housing), a significant proportion of the population still cannot afford the basic necessities. Current economic theories do not explain why wealth does not become evenly distributed, even when everyone is employed.

The graph in Figure 62 shows the cash distribution in Australia in 2013–2014 [132]. Notably, cash (along with wealth) has a highly skewed distribution, with nearly 60% of the cash being owned by the richest 20% of the population.

Cash distribution in Australia 2013–2014

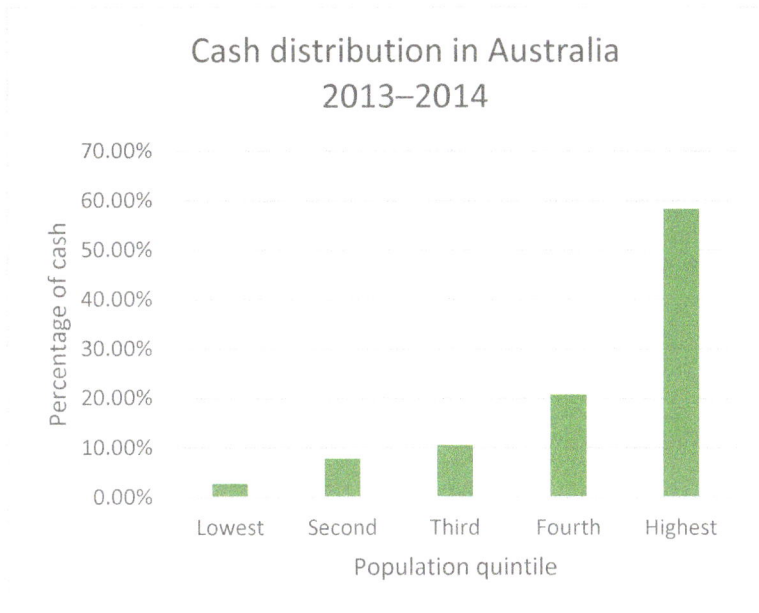

Figure 62: Cash distribution in Australia 2013–2014

Disparity in wealth is measured by the GINI Index.

An equal society is one that uniformly receives same income (G = 0) while an unequal society is one where an individual receives 100% of the income (G=1– 1/N). Income distribution of a region or a country does not follow the simple function rule. The function gives a measurable analysis of the income distribution of a region. A clear case of income distribution distinguishes levels of income as high income or low income. The Gini coefficient can, therefore, be calculated using discrete probability distribution, continuous probability distribution, or Chi-square distribution among other methods. The Gini coefficient can be represented mathematically on a Lorenz Curve which plots the proportion of … [a] … population's income earned cumulatively by a bottom percentage of the population. The Gini coefficient of income is obtained for both the market income and disposable income basis while the coefficient of market income is obtained from pre-taxed income and transfer. The Gini coefficient of the whole world ranges from 0.60 to 0.68.

World Atlas [133]

The Cash Distribution Model sought to determine whether a Zero-sum Economic Model can be created that automatically generates a similar wealth distribution to that observed in the real world.

For this purpose, a model was created, shown in Figure 63, in which the Consumers were grouped into levels, from Consumers Level 0 to Consumers Level 10; it was predicted that the higher levels would accumulate wealth from the lower levels. The Producers were also grouped into different levels. In general terms, Producers can be considered to be people who own businesses. When modelling wealth distribution, we can consider Producers to *be* the actual businesses, which can be owned by Consumers. When a Producer (business) accumulates money, it can be automatically transferred to the owner of the Producer (the Consumer).

The Cash Distribution Model shows that when Producers are ordered according to profitability, and higher-tier Consumers receive income from these Producers, the wealth naturally flows to the upper tiers. This produces a Gini Index that approaches 1.0 over time, even if wealth is evenly distributed initially (Gini Index of 0.0).

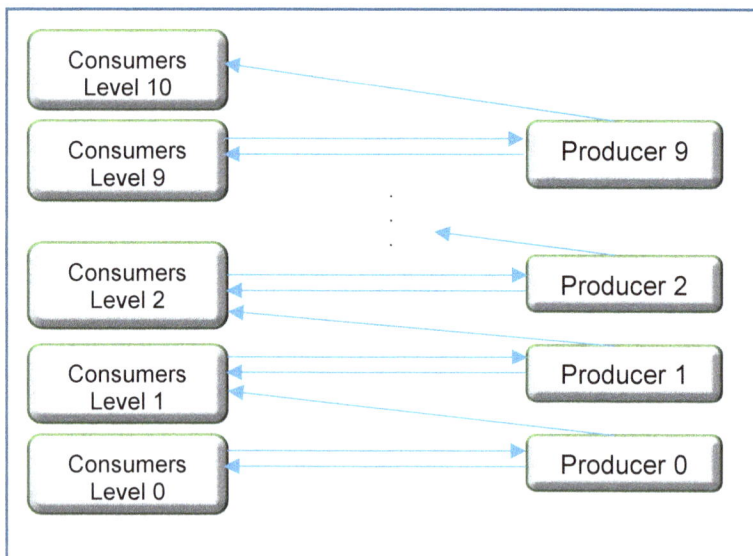

Figure 63: Wealth distribution in the Zero-sum Economic Model

Cash distribution over time

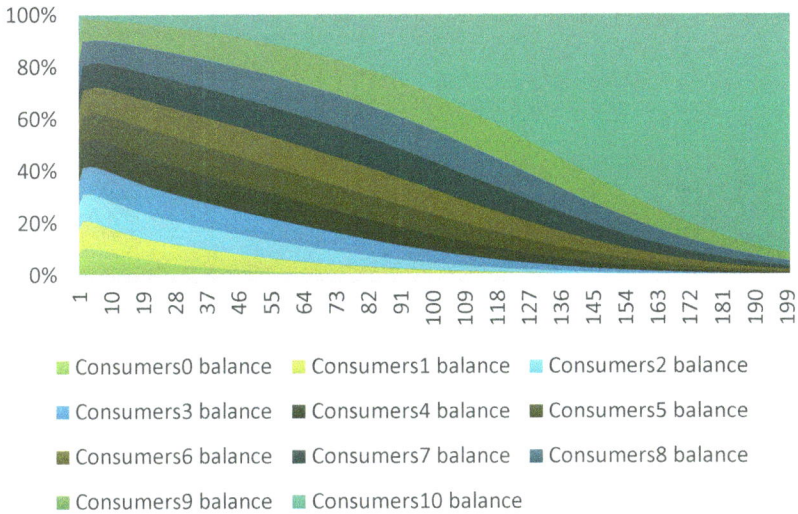

Figure 64: Cash distribution in the Zero-sum Economic Model response

Figure 64 demonstrates that the cash distribution among a group of Consumers who receive income from the ownership of Producers will favour the Consumers who have the most profitable businesses.

If the distribution shown in Figure 64 is examined in a particular year, for example in year 100 ($T = 100$), the cash distribution in Figure 65 is observed.

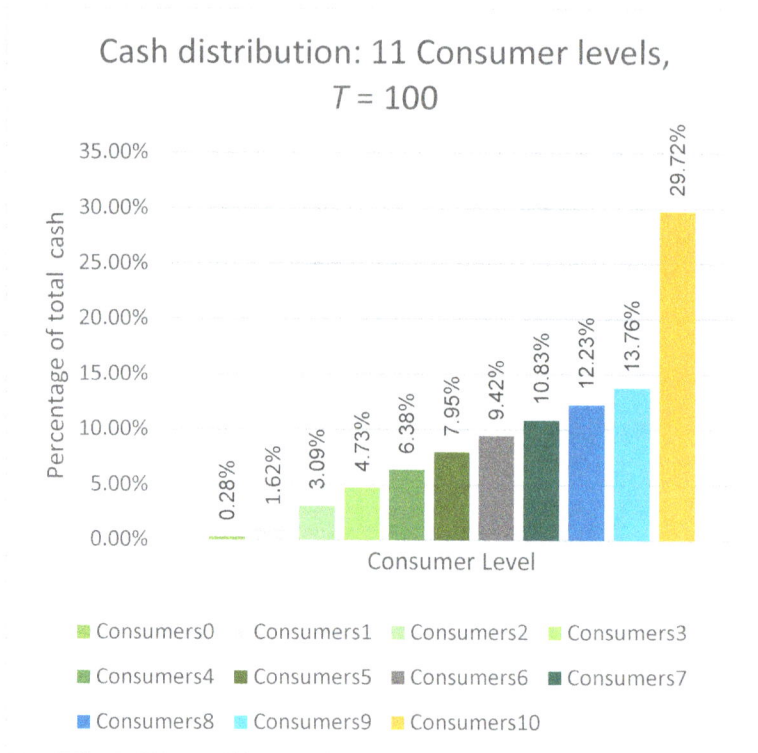

Cash distribution: 11 Consumer levels, $T = 100$

Figure 65: Cash distribution at $T = 100$

This shows that the Zero-sum Theory can produce a cash distribution similar to that found in the real world. In the Cash Distribution Models, each level of Consumers purchases a particular level of product and is paid a particular level of wages. By creating four levels of pricing and wages, Consumers can be sorted into cash distribution levels equivalent to the real distribution shown in Figure 62.

The final group of Consumers starts with their share of cash, then accumulates money from a lower-level Producer. These Consumers purchase their products from a Producer that they own; as a result, any money they pay to the Producer they receive back through ownership.

This simulation shows the cash distribution of Consumers, but not of Producers, because there is the possibility that the distribution could be varied by money that is allocated to Producers. The difficulty with testing this model is that there are very little data available that include a combination of Consumer and business data. Hence, the focus here is on Consumers and how cash is distributed among them.

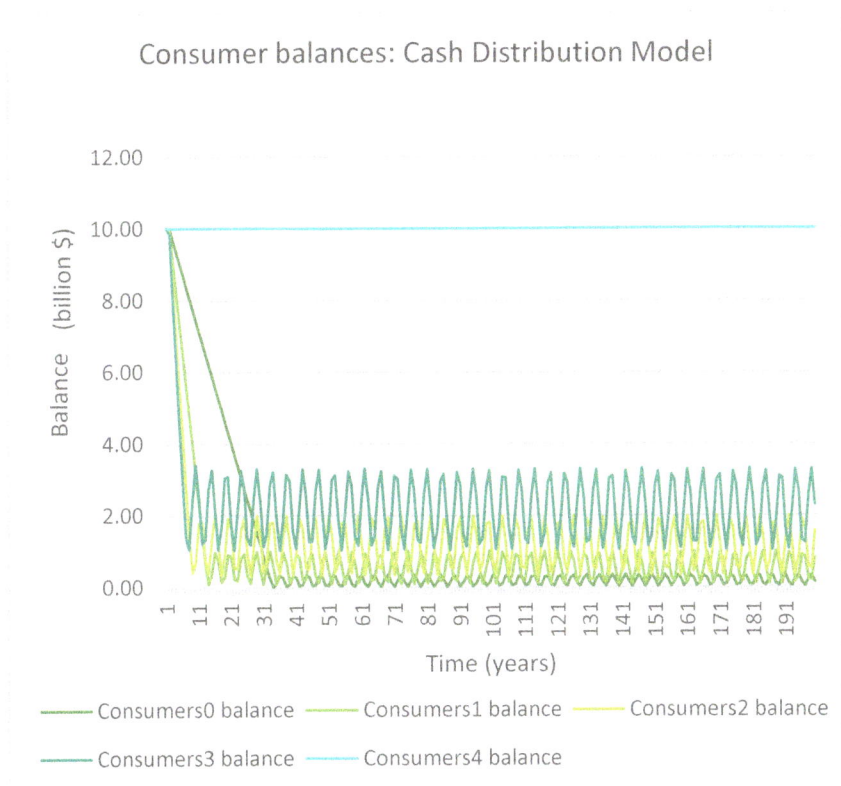

Figure 66: Cash Distribution Model: Consumer balances

Figure 66 shows the system response of five groups of Consumers, Figure 67 shows the total cash distribution over time, and Figure 68 is a histogram of the final cash distribution. All Consumers start with $10 billion in cash. From there, the distribution naturally develops. The objective of this model was to reproduce the Australian cash distribution shown in

Cash distribution in Australia 2013–2014

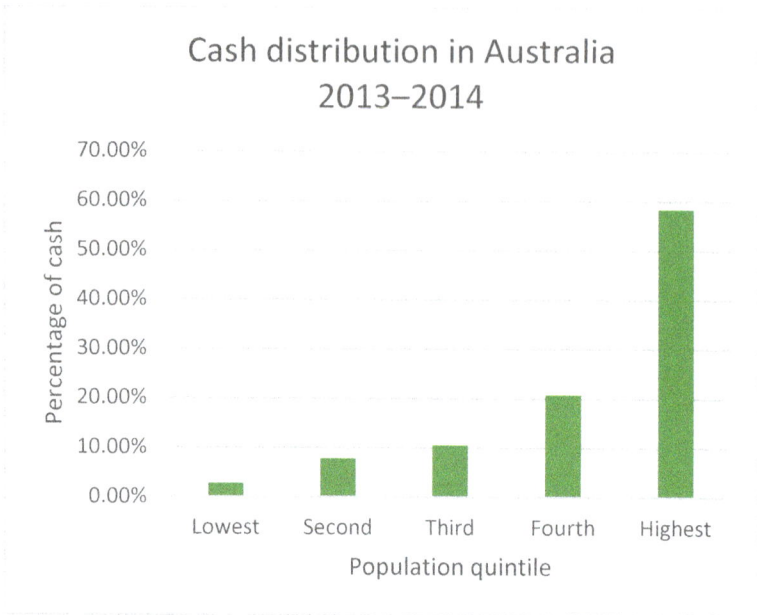

Figure 62: Cash distribution in Australia 2013–2014

Accumulative cash: Cash Distribution Model

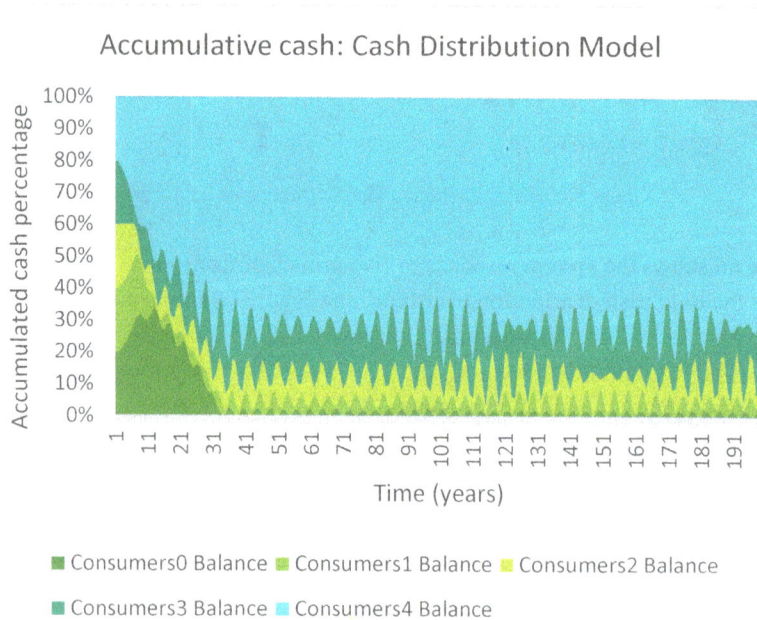

■ Consumers0 Balance ■ Consumers1 Balance ■ Consumers2 Balance
■ Consumers3 Balance ■ Consumers4 Balance

Figure 67: Cash Distribution Model: accumulative cash

Figure 68 shows the final cash distribution, which is very close to the real-life cash distribution illustrated in Figure 62. It was surprisingly easy to generate this distribution. The main determining features were found to be product price and wages. All that was required was to identify the appropriate price and wage levels consistent with the distribution.

Cash distribution outcome: Cash Distribution Model

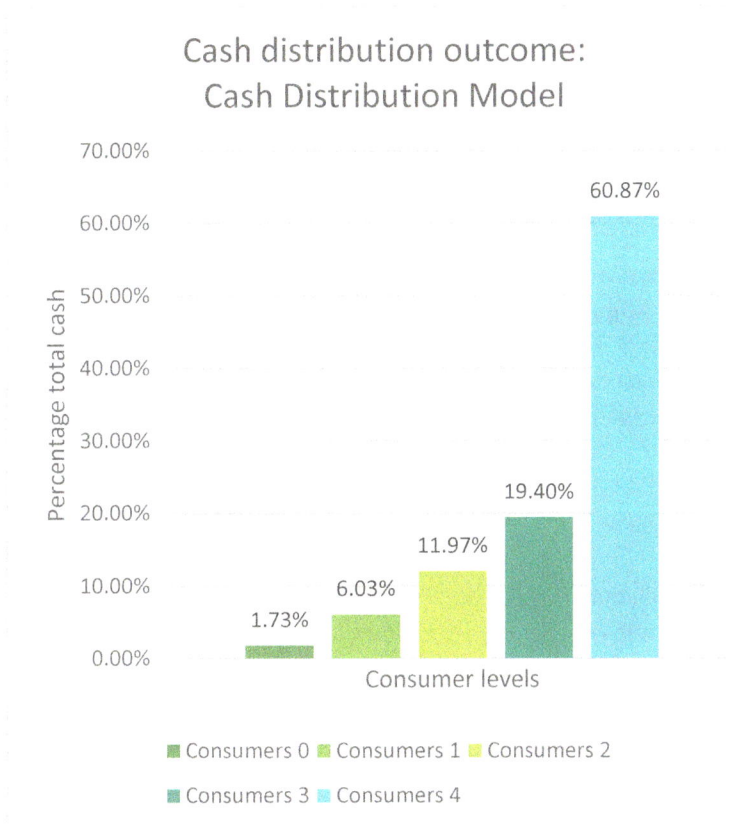

Figure 68: Cash Distribution Model: cash distribution histogram

Other researchers have suggested that initial conditions may have a significant effect on the final cash distribution. This simulation showed that the initial conditions do not appear to be a significant factor in the final distribution. People just end up with a standard of living commensurate with their income. For the most part, people in the real world live within their means, without either overspending or underspending.

5.1.5.1   *What does this mean for the real world?*

There are always going to be some differences between what happens in the real world and what happens in a simulation. Here, I found that product pricing and wages were the main factors determining the outcome of the simulation. In real life, it is most likely that wages have the biggest influence on cash distribution.

The simulation is limited in that it does not allow people to move within the distribution. In the real world, it is possible for people to 'move up'. This can happen when people get a better job. Alternatively, they can live on less than their wage and save up to invest, allowing them to acquire more income. In that scenario, what would most likely occur is that someone else higher in the cash distribution would drop down to a lower position in the distribution due to zero-sum limitations.

As mentioned previously, the top 1% of people own 50% of the cash. It is likely that these same people own as much as 50% of the Producers. The Producers themselves are much more varied in the real world, and each Producer would actually employ multiple 'levels' of Consumers. Each level of Consumers would represent people with a different type of training, expertise and/or experience level.

5.1.5.2   *Summary*

The Cash Distribution Model seeks to demonstrate how cash will be distributed among a set of zero-sum entities (Consumers and Producers). The output of the model is consistent with current cash distributions found in the real world. From this it can be concluded that the Zero-sum Model is capable of generating a cash distribution consistent with real-world data.

5.1.6   *Global Labour Model*

In recent times there has been a tendency for western companies attempting to increase their profit margins to outsource labour to less affluent countries with lower labour rates. This situation has caused a significant amount of tension in the origin countries.

It is informative to compare the real cost of living in China, India and Australia with the cost of labour in those countries.

Table 18 shows the costs of living in Melbourne (Australia), Goa (India) and Zhubhai (China). These statistics were collected from the Numbeo website, which collects economic data on countries around the world to calculate the cost of living, the CPI and other statistics.

We can see that the average monthly wage in Melbourne is $6000, four times higher than in Goa ($1500), and 2.4 times higher than in Zhuhai, China ($2400). In a global economy, when business people make a decision about where to create a new factory or to set up a new business, they need to take into account the cost of labour. Research into labour outsourcing indicates that business people prefer to create these new businesses in (or move old businesses to) areas where labour is cheap [91–94, 117, 118]. The result is that profits increase for the company, and people in less advanced countries get new jobs; however, in line with zero-sum predictions, workers in the higher-cost-of-living countries lose jobs.

Table 18: Cost of living comparison (from Numbeo.com [136]).
All values in equivalent $AU.

	Melb., Aust.	Melb/ Goa	Goa, India	Melb/ Zhuhai	Zhuhai, China
Average monthly wage	6000	4.00	1500	2.40	2500
Restaurants					
Meal, inexpensive restaurant	$15.00	4.81	$3.12	3.77	$3.98
Meal for two, mid-range restaurant, three-course	$80.00	5.70	$14.03	6.11	$13.09
McMeal at McDonalds (or equivalent combo meal)	$9.00	0.87	$10.39	1.48	$6.08
Domestic beer (0.5 litre draught)	$7.50	6.00	$1.25	4.46	$1.68
Imported beer (0.33 litre bottle)	$8.00	5.30	$1.51	3.32	$2.41
Cappuccino (regular)	$3.77	2.42	$1.56	0.71	$5.34
Coke/Pepsi (0.33 litre bottle)	$3.07	5.69	$0.54	3.99	$0.77
Water (0.33 litre bottle)	$2.46	8.20	$0.30	4.24	$0.58
Markets					
Milk (regular), (1 litre)	$1.16	1.23	$0.94	0.38	$3.04
Loaf of fresh white bread (500 g)	$2.72	5.55	$0.49	1.44	$1.89
Rice (white) (1 kg)	$2.23	2.28	$0.98	0.67	$3.35
Eggs (12)	$4.25	4.25	$1.00	2.16	$1.97
Local cheese (1 kg)	$10.63	1.46	$7.27		
Chicken breasts (boneless, skinless) (1 kg)	$10.94	3.29	$3.33	0.87	$12.57
Apples (1 kg)	$3.95	1.63	$2.42		
Oranges (1 kg)	$3.30	2.28	$1.45	1.57	$2.10

185

Zero-sum Economic Simulation

Tomatoes (1 kg)	$4.48	6.14	$0.73	2.67	$1.68
Potatoes (1 kg)	$2.62	3.32	$0.79	1.78	$1.47
Lettuce (1 head)	$2.31	1.11	$2.08	0.74	$3.14
Water (1.5 litre bottle)	$1.93	3.39	$0.57	3.06	$0.63
Bottle of wine (mid-range)	$15.00	2.06	$7.27	1.02	$14.67
Domestic beer (0.5 litre bottle)	$4.39	3.51	$1.25	4.48	$0.98
Imported beer (0.33 litre bottle)	$5.30	3.66	$1.45	3.44	$1.54
Pack of cigarettes (Marlboro)	$21.50	6.89	$3.12	5.13	$4.19
Transportation					
One-way ticket (local transport)	$3.76	8.17	$0.46	8.95	$0.42
Monthly pass (regular price)	$135.30	16.3	$8.31		
Taxi start (normal tariff)	$4.00	7.69	$0.52	1.90	$2.10
Taxi 1 km (normal tariff)	$2.00	4.26	$0.47	4.00	$0.50
Taxi 1 hour waiting (normal tariff)	$39.75	19.1	$2.08	4.99	$7.96
Gasoline (1 litre)	$1.48	1.18	$1.25	0.88	$1.68
Volkswagen Golf 1.4 90 kW Trendline/ equivalent new car	$25,995.00	1.73	$15,066.87	0.50	$52,376.77
Utilities (monthly)					
Basic (electricity, heating, water, garbage) for 85 m³ apartment	$202.77	6.58	$30.83	3.99	$50.88
Internet (6 Mbps, unlimited data, cable/ADSL)	$68.05	2.11	$32.21	4.06	$16.76
Sports and leisure					
Fitness club, monthly fee for 1 adult	$81.67	1.31	$62.35	3.90	$20.95
Tennis court rent (1 hour on weekend)	$17.38	2.23	$7.79		
Cinema, international release, one seat	$19.00	4.57	$4.16	1.58	$12.05
Clothing and shoes					
1 pair of jeans (Levis 501 or similar)	$98.46	2.02	$48.63	0.78	$125.70
1 summer dress in a chain store (Zara, H&M, ...)	$67.78	0.52	$129.89	1.62	$41.90
1 pair of Nike shoes	$148.08	2.04	$72.73	0.66	$225.22
1 pair of men's leather shoes	$152.42	4.19	$36.37	2.43	$62.85
Rent per month					
Apartment (1 bedroom) in City centre	$1,611.32	8.31	$193.96	3.27	$492.34
Apartment (1 bedroom) outside City centre	$1,176.76	7.72	$152.40	3.12	$377.11
Apartment (3 bedrooms) in City centre	$3,231.54	7.77	$415.64	3.25	$995.16
Apartment (3 bedrooms) outside City centre	$1,996.43	6.40	$311.73	2.72	$733.27
Purchase price of apartment					
Price per square metre to buy apartment in City centre	$9,033.33	8.28	$1,091.05	3.08	$2,933.10
Average		4.73		2.75	

On average, Products in Melbourne are 4.73 times more expensive than in Goa India and 2.75 times more expensive than in Zhuhai. Given these costs, it is understandable that Producers prefer to use overseas labour to help increase their profits and reduce prices.

To explore this situation, the Global Labour Model was developed, as illustrated in Figure 69: Global Labour Model. This model considers two countries with Consumers who have different costs of living. The wages required to live in each country need to reflect the cost of living. A single Producer chooses a country within which to operate his/her business, and over time decides where to hire employees.

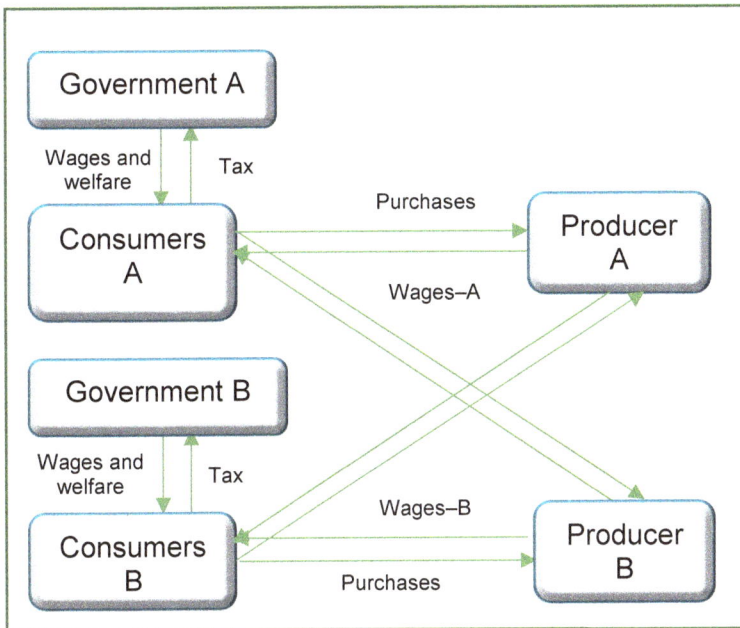

Figure 69: Global Labour Model

This simulation shows that for basic operation with no investment loop, the vast majority of money ends up with the second country's (the lower-wage country's) Producers, as shown in Figure 70.

The Global Labour Model demonstrates the Producer's preferences for hiring people from lower-cost-of-living countries. Companies prefer to hire cheaper labour. Cheaper labour is found in less industrialised nations, where the cost of living is much lower than in wealthier nations. Hence, companies prefer to hire labour from less industrialised nations.

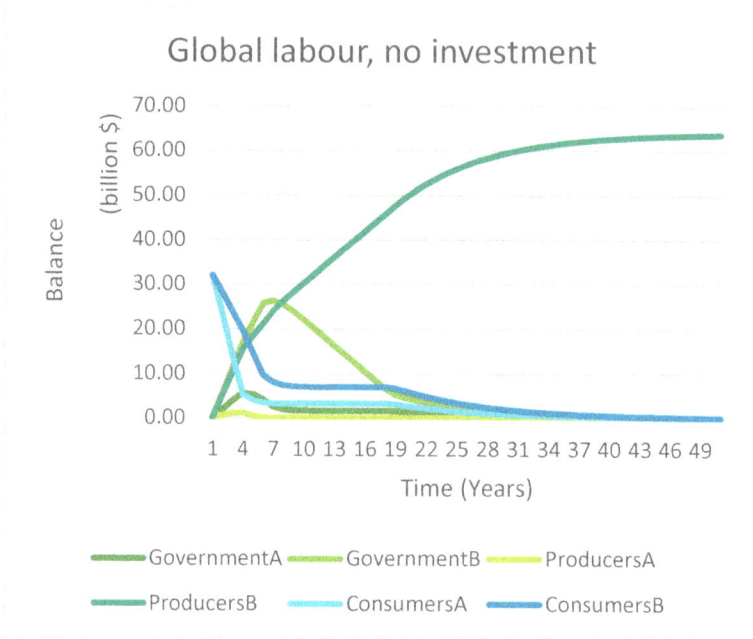

Figure 70: Global Labour Model outcomes

The problem with this approach is that this strategy literally shifts the distribution of money towards the country with the cheaper labour.

Two things then happen:

1. The Consumers in the country of origin stop buying the products, as they aren't getting paid.
2. Money builds up in the least affluent countries.

Interestingly, this model shows that there is a period of stability before the economy enters a decay state.

The Australian bureau of statistics reported that in the 2015-2016 financial year, the average commercial profit was 15.3%. There are three main industries that receive more than 18% profits [Mining (32%), IT/Telecommunications (24%) and Property (41%)]; there are two other industries (Utilities and Transportation) receiving 18% each [137]. The expenses can be paid to overseas employees. This means that, on average, as much as 84.7% of these industries' expenses can be paid to foreign countries (i.e. not Australia). More likely, this is as low as 20–50%, but it is important to realise that the money that goes overseas has no channel for returning to the source country—the people being paid overseas do not receive enough money to buy products from the source country.

The US Treasury shows that there is approximately $13.2 trillion dollars of narrow money supply (M1 + M2) in existence for the US. According to some reports, as much as $2.5 trillion of this money is in banks outside the USA.

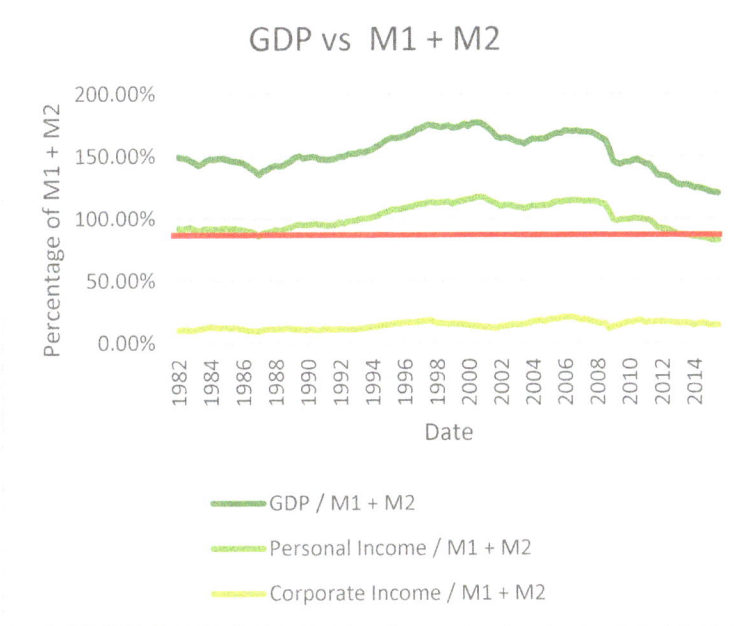

Figure 71: US GDP vs M1 + M2

This shows that nearly 10% of the money that could or should be circulating in the US economy is not; from this we can conclude that the USA is experiencing reduced monetary efficiency. This is demonstrated in several research papers [96–101] that compare US GDP with the US narrow money supply. These research papers show that from 1994 to 2009, the GDP was above the total money supply, meaning that the value of the products the USA was producing was larger than they could afford themselves. In other words, during this period, the USA was producing more products than it needed internally, and it was exporting the rest. Figure 71 shows that after the financial crisis of 2008, a significant amount of US cash was transferred to China. Zero-sum Theory suggests that the amount of money circulating in the economy creates an upper limit on production; thus, if US cash is outside the USA, this may be the cause of reduced monetary efficiency in the USA.

5.1.6.1   *5.1.6.1*   *Summary*

The purpose of this research was to demonstrate that an economic theory can be developed (from the consequences of basic zero-sum interaction between simple entities) that will predict the cash flow between countries, assuming Producers from one country can trade with Consumers from another country.

The costs of living and wages were compared between Melbourne, India and China. Significant differences between countries in both the costs of living and wages were identified.

This model demonstrated the cash flow that occurs when one country has cheaper labour than the other, when Producers are allowed to exercise a preference for cheap labour. This results in cash flowing to the country with the cheaper labour; the Producers in the cheaper-labour country finish up accumulating money. The model output was compared with current measurements of foreign reserves and productivity; this indicated that it is possible for Zero-sum Theory to reproduce the distribution of money between two countries with disparate labour costs.

5.1.7   Real-world economic model comparison

The final step in this exercise in Zero-sum Modelling was to compare the data from several economies of the world with predictions from the Zero-sum CPG Model. The model used real data for population growth, monetary growth, inflation and business cycles, and was used to investigate how money becomes distributed between the three entities. It was also used to predict Consumer distress over time.

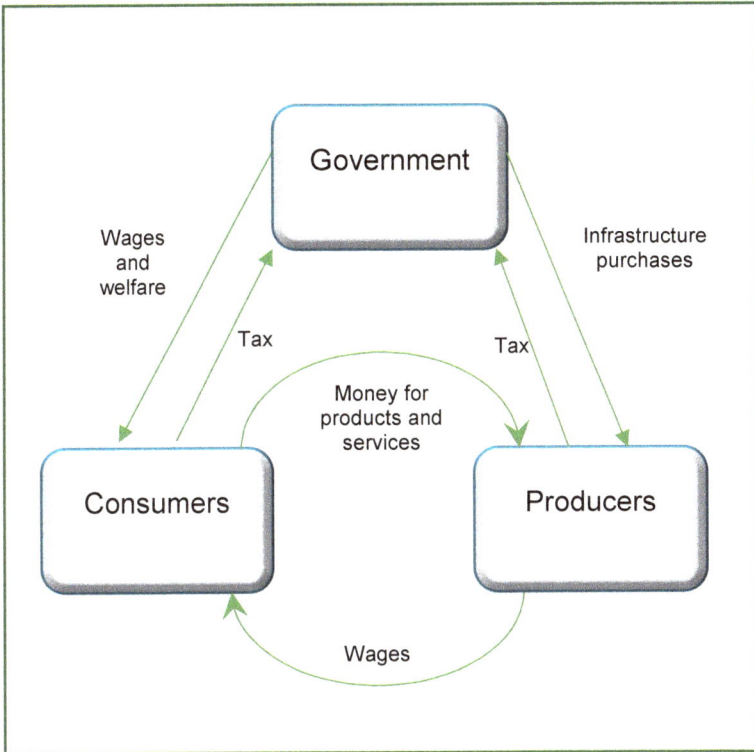

Figure 72: Zero-sum CPG Economic Model

5.1.7.1   5.1.7.1   *US simulation*

The money supply statistic used was the M1 + M2 money supply from the US Treasury [138]. The population statistics were obtained from the US Census [139], company profits were obtained from the US Bureau of Economic Analysis (BEA) [140], and inflation data was obtained from the World Bank [131].

CPG system response

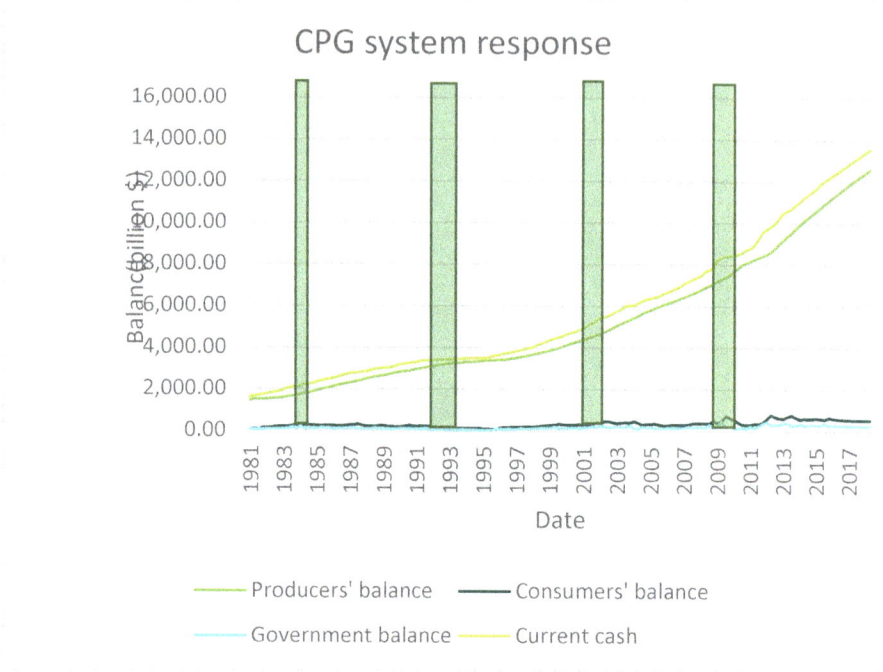

Figure 73: US Economic Model

The graph in Figure 73 shows the amount of money residing with each entity in the model. Notably, both Government and Consumers end up with a low percentage of the money in the system, while Producers retain most of the cash.

192

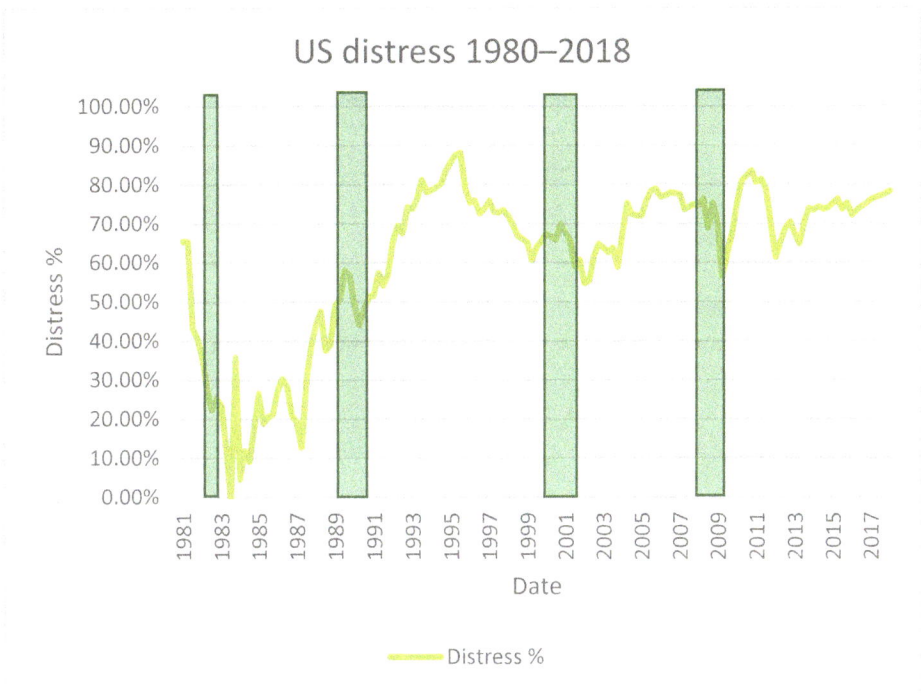

Figure 74: US simulated and real profits, with distress

The level of distress in the system is calculated from how many people in the system cannot afford to buy the products they require. Unexpectedly, the distress in the US system illustrated in Figure 58 was initially low, but it significantly increased after the 1991 recession, and has continued to remain high from 1991 to 2017.

One of the biggest changes in the economy in the early 1990s was associated with the introduction of personal computers. By the end of the 1990s, computer software had significantly progressed, and the internet had been developed to the point where online sales were occurring. During this period, according to the simulation, Consumer distress increased from a base level of 20%, peaking above 80% and stabilising at around 60–80%. This makes some sense because the new technologies allowed businesses to be significantly more efficient. In theory, this would have increased unemployment, because Producers do not need as many people to maintain existing levels of production.

The blue highlighted areas on the distress graph represent the recessions that have occurred during this period. Notably, these areas correspond to some of the periods of decrease in distress. This may indicate that during the recessions Consumers actually gain money. However, as these periods are typically temporary, it may simply indicate that Producers have lost money.

5.1.7.2   5.1.7.2   Australian simulation

The second economy simulated was the Australian economy. Population, treasury and company profits were available from the Australian Bureau of Statistics (ABS) [141], and inflation data was obtained from the World Bank [131].

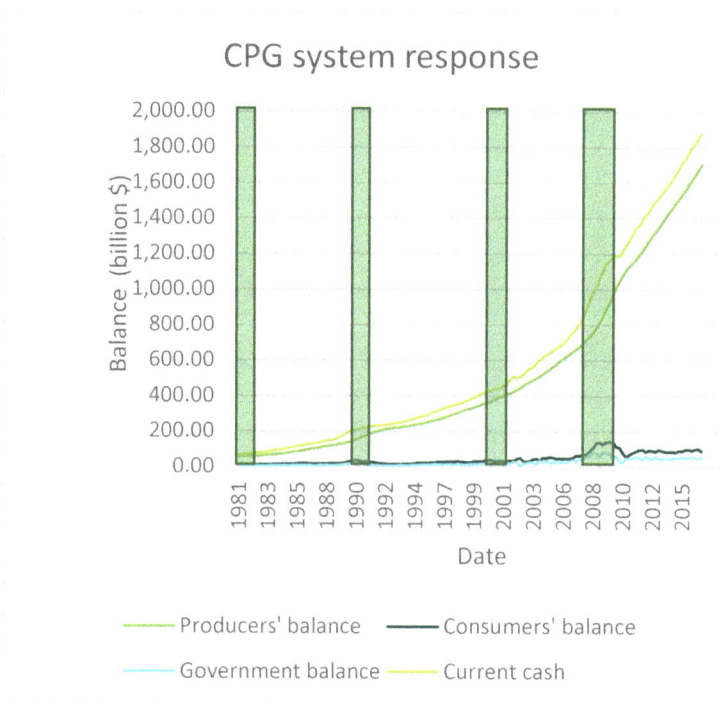

Figure 75: Australian Economic Model

The graph in Figure 75 shows the amount of money residing with each entity in the model for Australia. Again, both Government and Consumers ended up with a low percentage of the money in the system, while Producers retained most of the cash. The blue bars again represent the major recessions, the most notable of which was the 2008 financial crisis, when a large injection of cash occurred. The money appears to be have been received by both the Government and Consumers, but after the crisis it quickly drained back to the Producers.

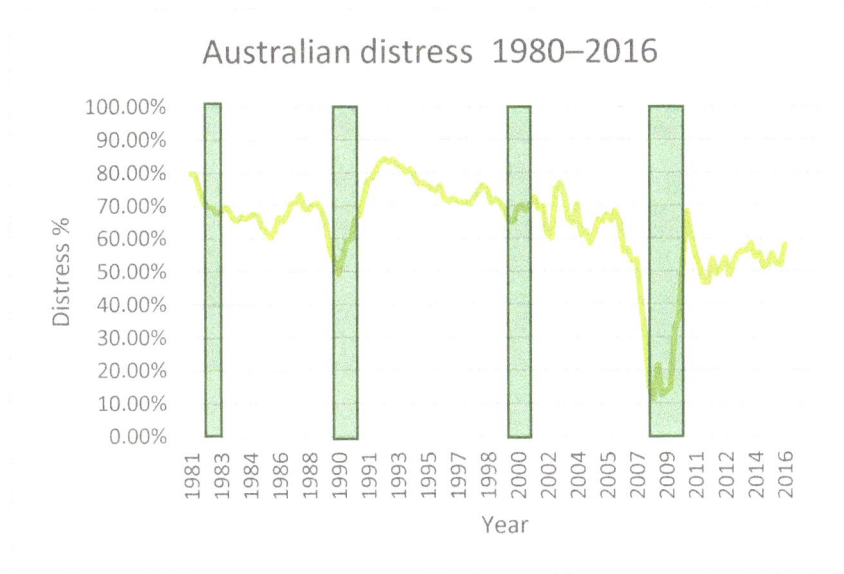

Figure 76: Australian simulated and real profits, with distress

Three of the troughs in the distress lined up with the dates of recessions (1981, 1990 and 2008), and in the other year (2000) there was a minor dip in distress. Notably, this recession did not significantly affect Consumers because it was primarily an investment collapse.

Employed population percent vs distress Australia 1980 - 2015

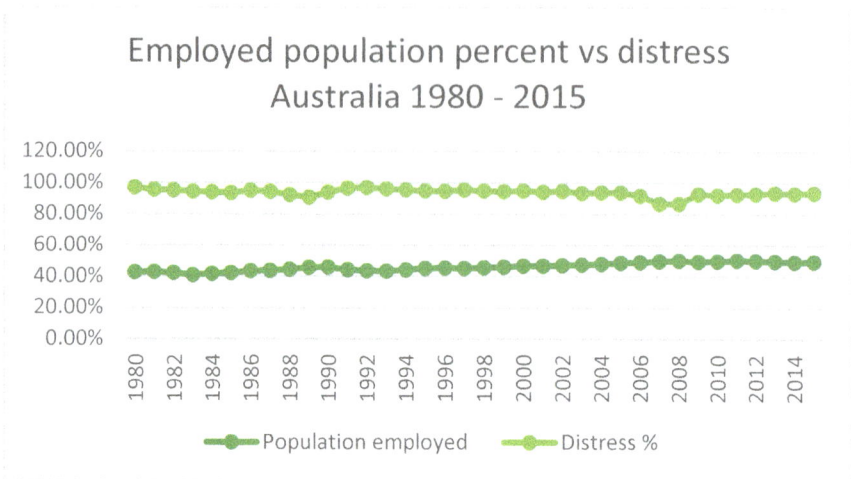

Figure 77: Australian distress versus percentage population employed

In Figure 77, distress does not directly correspond with employment. However, the employment statistics do not show how much money people have or whether this changes during recessions.

The measurement of distress does, however, correspond with some major recessions, suggesting that it may still be a useful metric for economic analysis. As distress decreases during a recession, this may represent the distress of Producers, because Producer distress = 1.0 – Consumer distress. This is also equivalent to employment. Alternatively, it may simply be a measurement of the overall 'stress' in the economy.

Figure 78 shows Real employment versus 0.52 – (Distress/10.0). This suggests that the simulation is focusing on the lowest 10% of people who are employed, (perhaps 20% of the total population). These two datasets have a correlation of 0.763. This suggests that the employment corresponds with the lowest tenth of the employed population.

Employed population percent vs Simulated Employment
Australia 1980 - 2015

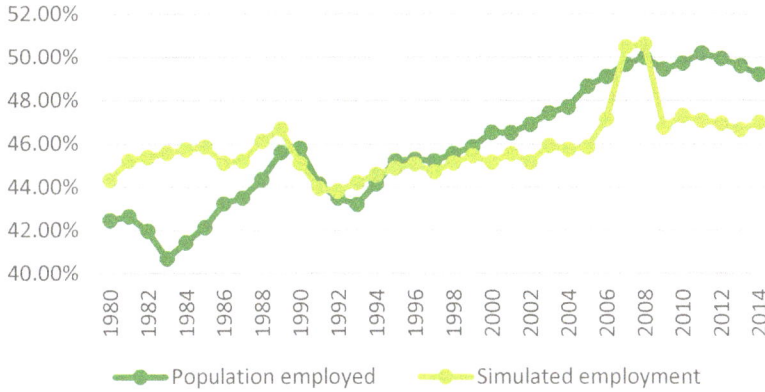

Figure 78: Employment versus simulated employment

Figure 79 shows an adjusted version of the graph shown in Figure 78. In this version, the inflation rate was reduced by a constant 1.2% per quarter. This resulted in the average gradient of the simulated population employed to be closer to the real data. This increased the correlation to **88%**. This adjustment suggests that the gradient of employment is related to the inflation rate, which is consistent with the Phillips curve. However, both the inflation rate and employment were collected from real statistics. This suggests that there are still some differences between how the simulation works and what happens in the real world.

Adjusted Employed population percent vs Simulated Employment Australia 1980 - 2015

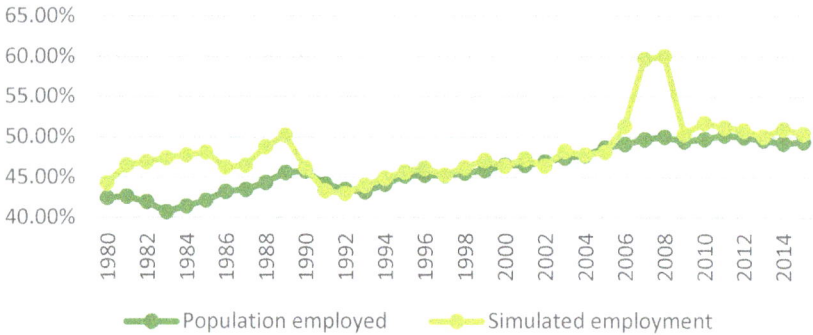

Figure 79: Adjusted employment versus simulated employment

There are clearly other factors are involved; what these factors could be is not clear. They could be due to limitations of the simulations, in terms of population. Some of the differences could be due to employment conditions in the upper levels of employment. The other possibility for why the differences occur could be that business people make decisions based on psychological reasons, or simply have to delay making decisions until appropriate information is available. Further investigation is required to examine this phenomenon.

5.1.7.3   5.1.7.3   *Summary*

The purpose of this research was to demonstrate that an economic theory can be developed from analysis of the consequences of basic zero-sum interaction between simple entities to predict the cash flow between Producers, Consumers and the Government of a country, using real-world data.

The models show that they can accept the real-world data and produce a sensible result consistent with the wealth distribution, inflation and statistics described in previous sections.

Also, the models can be used to make predictions about distress in the economy. Distress is calculated as the percentage of people who cannot afford to buy the products they require. This output did not directly correspond with unemployment rates in Australia; however, it did correspond with the 1990 and 2008 recessions, which suggests that it may still be a useful metric for economic analysis.

These models show that Zero-sum Theory can be used with economic statistics to generate a sensible model of the money flow in an economy. Furthermore, measurements of 'distress' may be useful as an indicator of the economy; further work is required to determine what this metric actually represents.

5.1.8   *Properties of Zero-sum Economic Modelling*

As the previous sections have shown, Zero-sum Economic Models can produce explanations for several phenomena that have been largely unexplained by previous theories. These phenomena include business cycles, inflation, wealth distribution, Producer condensation, and globalisation preferences for labour, as well as outputs that resemble the world's economy over the last 100 years.

They will not, however, be able to predict when new industries will become available. Once these new industries are appropriately modelled, it may be possible to determine the effect of these industries on the existing system. New industries are created by people who can think beyond the current limitations of technology, and who are able to convince others enough to invest and actually purchase the new technology.

Zero-sum Modelling uses average functions to estimate spending habits. These can be described as 'voluntary' functions because the entities are not required to perform in any particular way. Zero-sum Economic Models cannot predict the behaviour of individuals. However, people have a tendency to behave consistently, and such behaviour can be reasonably accurately modelled mathematically.

The main functions in Zero-sum Theory that are voluntary are 'spending' habits. Neither people (Consumers) nor businesses (Producers) are required to spend money on any particular product or service. Sellers voluntarily set the price of a product, but buyers must still voluntarily purchase it. Income, on the other hand, is typically involuntary, people do not decide how much they get. They simply have to use what they get as efficiently as possible to achieve their goals. Thus there are voluntary purchases, voluntary employment and involuntary income.

The vast majority of current economic theories assume that wealth accumulation is a voluntary process; i.e. if people work hard enough, wealth will follow. Zero-sum Theory shows the opposite: even if you work hard, the only people who get wealthy are Producers. Zero-sum Theory reveals that the majority of economic phenomena are caused by involuntary functions. One of the main involuntary aspects from a Consumer's point of view is employment. The Consumer does not get to choose when they get employed or fired, Producers do. These behaviours ultimately shape the upper limits of economic productivity.

5.1.9   Unemployment and poverty

The main goal of microeconomics is to create highly efficient businesses. It is thought that more efficient businesses will out-evolve their competitors and dominate markets. The more efficient businesses are the fewer employees will be required in order to supply a particular product to an entire population. Business efficiency can be described as profit per employee:

$$\text{Business efficiency} = \frac{\text{Profit}}{\text{Number of employees}}.$$

This indicates the benefits of specialisation in an economy: it is more efficient to have particular people or businesses produce a product than to have everyone in an economy produce all of the goods they require themselves. The more efficient the business the less employees they have. Businesses always wat to be more efficient. The less employees they have the less money is being released into the rest of the economy.

The problem with this is that businesses will never employ the entire population:

1. The entire population is not required to produce all of the products they require.
2. Even if the entire population were employed, Producers would find a reduction in profits and would attempt to reduce costs i.e. reducing employment.

From this it can be concluded that, based on the way the economy is currently operated, we will never solve the unemployment problem.

Models using real data show that between 10% and 30% of the people in an economy may not always be able to afford their required products. In a lock-in state, it is possible Consumer distress would become consistent, but it would typically be at lower levels equivalent to the profit margin, which is typically 15–20% in real-world models.

The following is a summary from a report "*Poverty in Australia 2016*" from the Australian Council of Social Services and the Social Policy Research Centre, UNSW [142]:

Snapshot of poverty in Australia—in 2014:
- The poverty line (50% of median income) for a single adult was $426.30 a week. For a couple with 2 children, it was $895.22 a week.
- *2.99 million people (13.3% of the population), were living below the poverty line, after taking account of their housing costs.*
- 731,300 children under the age of 15 (17.4% of all children) were living below the poverty line.
- The proportion of people in poverty was slightly lower than in 2012 (a decrease of 0.6% from 13.9% in 2012). However, the 2014 headline poverty rate reflects persistent and entrenched poverty over the decade.
- Child poverty in Australia increased by 2 percentage points over the decade from 2003–04 to 2013–14.
- Of people receiving social security payments, 36.1% were living below the poverty line, including 55% of those receiving a Newstart Allowance, 51.5% receiving a Parenting Payment, 36.2% of those receiving a Disability Support Pension, 24.3% receiving a Carer Payment, and 13.9% of those on the Age Pension.
- Of people below the poverty line, 57.3% relied upon social security as their main income, and 32.1% relied upon wages as their main income.
- *From 2012 to 2014, poverty rates increased for: children in lone parent families (36.8 to 40.6%), those receiving Youth Allowance (50.6 to 51.8%) and those receiving Parenting Payment (47.2 to 51.5%). They remained very high (61.4% to 59.9%) from 2007 to 2014 for unemployed households.*
  The Australian Council of Social Services and the Social Policy Research Centre, UNSW, "Poverty in Australia 2016" *[142]*

This summary shows that, as at 2014, 2.99 million Australians (13.3%) were considered to be in poverty. This is close to the average profit margin in Australia (15.5%); it is possible to conclude that poverty is caused indirectly by the zero-sum nature of the economy and the fact that Producers make a profit—Consumers must make a corresponding loss. The simulations predict that, in a lock-in state, unemployment would be close to the profit margin. From Section 4.12, with a 65% participation rate and roughly 50% employment, the unemployment rate should be 15%. These values are all consistent with the values predicted by Zero-sum Theory.

The US Census Bureau reports on the state of poverty in the USA. An excerpt from their annual report is shown below.

The official poverty rate in 2015 was 13.5 percent, down 1.2 percentage points from 14.8 percent in 2014.

In 2015, there were 43.1 million people in poverty, 3.5 million less than in 2014.

The 2015 poverty rate was 1.0 percentage point higher than in 2007, the year before the most recent recession.

For most demographic groups, 2015 poverty rates and estimates of the number of people in poverty decreased from 2014.

Between 2014 and 2015, poverty rates decreased for all three major age groups. The poverty rate for children under age 18 dropped 1.4 percentage points, from 21.1 percent to 19.7 percent. Rates for people aged 18 to 64 dropped 1.1 percentage points, from 13.5 percent to 12.4 percent. Poverty rates for people aged 65 and older decreased 1.1 percentage points, from 10.0 percent to 8.8 percent.

B. D. Proctor, J. L. Semega, and M. A. Kollar, "Income and Poverty in the United States: 2015," US Census Bureau, Sep. 2016.[143]

The average corporate profit in the USA during 2014 was approximately 14.77% of the money supply; in 2015 it was approximately 13.8% of the money supply. As shown in the overview, the poverty rate was 14.8% in 2014 and 13.5% in 2015. This is also consistent with the theory that the profits made by companies are also reflected in the rate of poverty in a country.

Given the limitation in employment predicted by Zero-sum Models, and given that a significant proportion of these people will be left in poverty as a direct result of the nature of the economic system. From this, we can conclude that the current economic system will never solve poverty.

The difficulty is people who have money want to maintain their own security. The only way they can guarantee this is to buy "things" that maintain their own income as opposed to paying poor people. Consumers can only spend what Businesses pay them. Which creates a feedback loop where "The Rich get Richer and the Poor get Poorer".

Table 19 shows the money exists for everyone in the world and the selection of countries to be paid an "average" wage. The only reason people do not get paid is that the people who have the money do not want to pay the unemployed people. Ultimately, this shows that it is possible to solve the unemployment problem and hence any related poverty issues. It also gives some clues to how to solve the problem, which is a Universal Basic income.

Table 19: Wage Load for various Countries and the World

Country	Cash	Average Wage	Employed	Employed Wage Load	Unemployed	Full employment Wage load
Australia	2.5 Trillion	83,000	13 Million	1 Trillion	750,000	1.1 Trillion
US	20 Trillion	50000	157 Million	7.8 Trillion	9.3 Million	8.3 Trillion
UK	3.5 Trillion	32,000	31 Million	0.99 Trillion	1.6 Million	1.04 Trillion
World	100 Trillion	18,000	3.5 Billion	63 Trillion	186 Million	66.3 Trillion

5.1.10   Summary

The modelling and analysis of Zero-sum Economic Theory in this section aimed to examine and validate the theory to show that both the assumptions made for the theory and the actual models are consistent with existing macroeconomic observations.

The Zero-sum Models used have described the operation of business cycles consistent with observations made by economists. These models were flexible enough to account for the variation in the period of business cycles, as shown in Section 5.1.3.

Section 5.1.4 considered inflation and compared an analysis of the Zero-sum System Model with current research and observations of inflation. The mathematical analysis appears to be consistent with the main forms of inflation identified by current macroeconomic theory. These types of inflation include demand-pull, cost-push and the relationship between inflation and employment suggested by the Phillips curve.

It is possible to conclude that:

- Demand-pull inflation occurs when Consumers (or a subset of Consumers) receive more money and can therefore spend more on limited resources.
- Cost-push inflation occurs when the cost of labour increases. This cost increase is typically passed on to Consumers as an increase in price.
- The Phillips curve is an observed phenomenon that relates inflation to unemployment. The mathematical analysis of Zero-sum Economics shows that this phenomenon is inherent in the system model relating the cost of products to the employment rate.
- A model of wealth distribution has been developed that shows how money flow in the economy results in the existing cash distribution.
- The Global Labour Model demonstrates the preference of Producers for cheap labour and shows how cash is redistributed between countries when this occurs.

The Zero-sum Models have been adapted to use current measurements from real-world economies, including data from the USA and Australia. These models show that Zero-sum Economic Theory is consistent with the measurements taken from real economies.

Many of these phenomena are considered to be 'not well understood' in existing economic theory. Thus, the conclusion of this section is that the theory and modelling techniques used are consistent with existing economic theories and with existing measurements of real economies.

Finally, the analysis shows that under the current economic operation, the economy will never be able to employ the entire population consistently. The models show that between Producers and Consumers, Producers almost always end up with the majority of money. This, in combination with unemployment, means that a significant proportion of Consumers will always be in poverty. The models show that in some situations it is possible that unemployment would become constant; however, it will most likely be equivalent to the profit margin (typically around 15% in real-world models). The modelling outcomes were compared with actual statistics about poverty, which show that the real figure for poverty (approximately 13% of the Australian population living in poverty) is closely linked to the profit margin (approximately 15% profit in Australia). Given the limitation in employment predicted by Zero-sum models, and given that a significant proportion of these people will be left in poverty as a direct result of the nature of the economic system, it is possible to conclude that the current economic system will never solve either unemployment or poverty.

Chapter 6 will reveal that, with this modelling technique, it is possible to demonstrate how an economy can be stabilised to eliminate business cycles, minimise inflation and maximise employment.

PART III

Part III of this book is [finally!!!] about how an understanding of Zero-sum Economics can be used to stabilise an economy. The stabilisation is not about capital or the value of assets; it is simply about how to distribute money effectively to make sure everyone has enough money to get what they need. In doing this we ensure poor people have money—we could potentially eliminate poverty! It also allows the economy to operate to have a stable operation with zero growth.

6   Stabilising economies

Historically, no economic theory (Classical, Marxist, Keynesian, Monetarist, etc.) has been able to demonstrate a method for stabilising an economy. The typical economic view is that non-interventional 'laissez faire' strategies are the least costly to people economically, and hence the most effective strategies for operating an economy. Essentially, economists are suggesting that 'everything is fine', while wondering why we still have high levels of unemployment, poverty and wealth disparity. People's attitudes are often (or usually) blamed for the existence of these phenomena. As demonstrated in the previous chapter, using Zero-sum Theory can explain many of these phenomena in terms of 'mechanical' systemic behaviours, rather than 'psychological' economic decisions.

One of the most exciting aspects of Zero-sum Theory and the use of Control Theory is that it is possible to develop a system model that is stable and does not have economic business cycles, with minimal changes to the internal operation of businesses in general or the economy at large.

Economics (and especially money) is a human construct! Humans made money, and ultimately we control how money itself can operate. Thus, it *is* possible to change the way the system works in order to ensure a stable economy in which everyone can be both productive and able to purchase the goods they require to survive.

There are five things we need to do to stabilise the economy, minimise inflation and maximise employment:

1. Eliminate physical currencies and use digital money.
2. Pay all government expenses directly from the creation of money.
3. Create a universal income for Consumers, so everyone can afford to live.
4. Tax savings.
5. Subtract the universal income from the wages paid by Producers. This makes everyone cheaper to hire.

The outcomes from implementation of these actions can be demonstrated via numerical simulation (see Chapter 5). These simulations show that when the stabilisation actions are implemented, business cycles are eliminated, Consumer distress is eliminated, and inflation can be minimised or turned into deflation.

In the following chapters, I discuss these concepts and show the modelling that demonstrates how these changes can eliminate poverty and produce a stable economy.

6.1 Zero-sum Economic Stabilisation methodology

The third part of this research is a study of the Zero-sum Models, undertaken with the aim of designing a method for stabilising the economy. This design is then examined to determine the properties of the stabilised model, and comparisons are made with existing models of how economies should operate.

I employ the following guiding principles:

1. It is always good to spend money. Money always belongs to people, so the more that is being spent, the more people receive.
2. At some point, money is not going to be doing anything useful to keep the economy running. It will just be lying around in some rich person's savings account, not being spent. At that point it needs to be removed from the system.
3. The more of a product that exists, the cheaper it gets; so if something is expensive, make more of it.

6.1.1 Stabilised CPG Model

Technically, it is not possible to stabilise a basic CP system, as this requires controls on taxation and money releases, which require a Government.

Stabilisation has four main strategies:

- Ensure a universal income for Consumers.
- Create money to pay for everything.
- Tax savings.
- Pay all government expenses directly from the creation of money.

The wage offset allows inflation to be minimised.

A universal income for Consumers is a type of unconditional income paid by the Government, enabling Consumers to purchase the products they need. This concept has been investigated for quite some time [127–133], but the main problem is how to fund this concept. The solution is to create money directly. The difficulty is that this could lead to an oversupply of money.

To stabilise the money supply requires a 'money' tax. Money gets created to fulfil the needs of Consumers and of Government programs. The money is then given to Producers to develop and produce goods. After this redistribution, the money is taxed and deallocated. Deallocating means that the money is removed from circulation. The strategy for deallocation is the taxation of money. This method of stabilisation removes business cycles from the economy. It provides Consumers with enough cash to purchase the products required for them to survive. In turn, this provides Producers with a constant income. The CPG Model is used to demonstrate stabilisation. The system response is shown in Figure 80.

Stabilised CPG system response

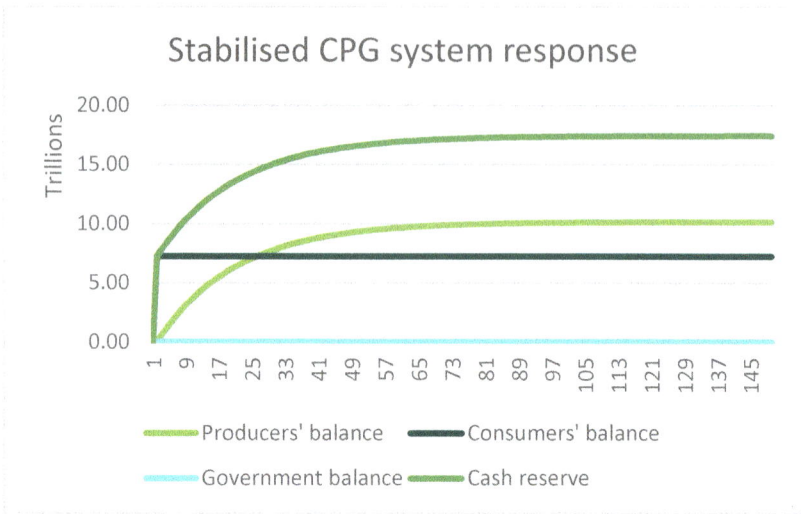

Figure 80: Stabilised CPG system response

The main feature of this solution is that the amount of money in the economy will approach a constant value. The tax on money (as a percentage of money in the economy) is the main method of controlling the final amount of money in the system, and in the case shown in Figure 80, the tax rate is 5%.

Consumer Distress

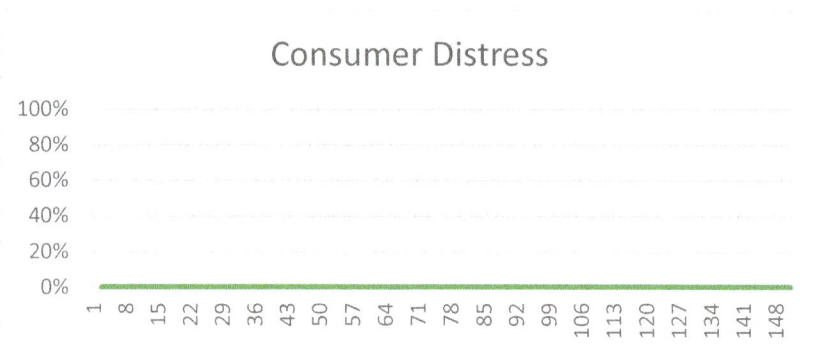

Figure 81: Stabilised CPG system response: Consumer distress

Notably, as Consumers always have 'enough' money in this stabilisation scenario, their distress is always 0%, as shown in Figure 81.

If any shortfall in taxes occurs, the expenses are paid by releasing more money. In the following cycle, the total tax will increase. Using the combination of money taxation and cash releases, the total amount of money in the system increases such that the taxation income equals the Government budget. If the Government budget increases or decreases due to war, famine, emergencies or other unknown or unexpected occurrences, the amount of money in the economy will increase to compensate for the changes. If the expenses of a Government decrease, the amount of money in the economy will also be decreased. Since the taxation of money will overcompensate for the expenses, this will reduce the amount of money in the system.

The major unknown in this system is the effect that the taxation of money will have on spending. In theory, it will increase spending, as any money remaining static in the economy will be taxed without compensation by assets. In theory, people would prefer to buy assets rather than leave wealth in cash that slowly disappears. Ultimately, this is a psychological issue, which (as stated previously) is not my specialty.

6.1.1.1   *Equilibrium*

If the demand curve is used with a supply cost line we can estimate an equilibrium point. The Henderson poverty line, put simply, is a measurement of the weekly income at which people are considered poor. For 2018 is reported as around $433 per week [151]. If this is used as the supply cost at maximum population of 17 Million people it results in an Equilibrium point of 14 Million people. This is consistent with the measurement 3.05 million people in poverty [151].

Existing Demand

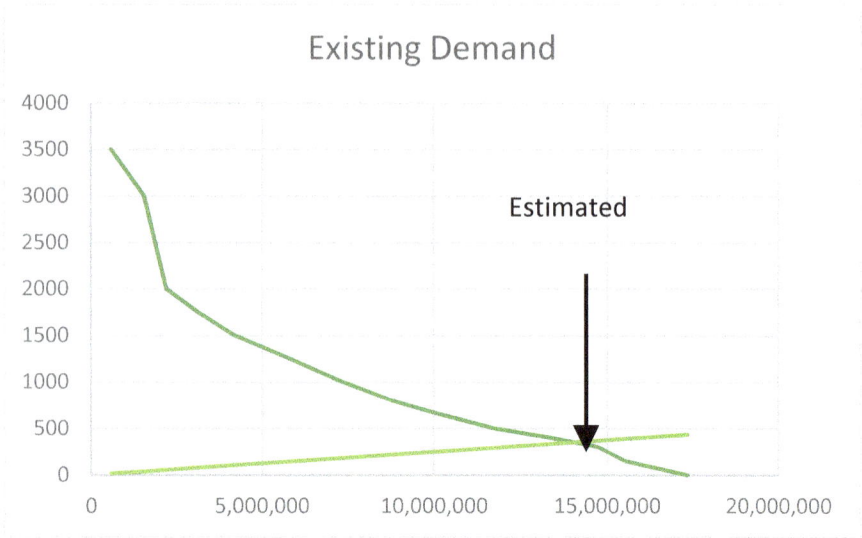

Figure 82 Australia Demand curve with Estimated Equilibrium 2019

If the UBI is implemented at $400 per week, using the same supply curve the equilibrium point moves up towards 16 million people. Also the next 1 million people have 90% of the money needed to avoid poverty.

UBI integrated Demand

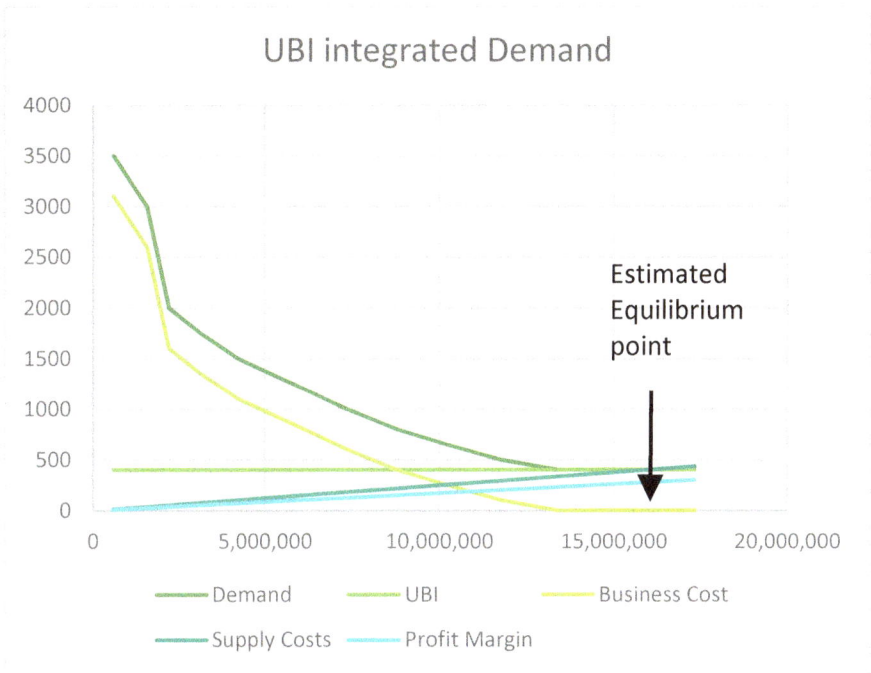

Figure 83 Australia UBI Integrated Demand curve with Estimated Equilibrium 2019

This shows that the effect of using an integrated Universal Basic income could be used to reduce poverty in Australia from 15% ideally to 0%, but in this diagram there may still be 1-5% who need extra support.

The advantage of reducing supply cost is that it makes products cheaper for everyone and ultimately reduces the cost of living. From this, countries would be better able to meet their own needs with their own people rather than having to outsource for cheaper labour.

This also makes it cheaper to start businesses and allows them to be operated potentially without making a profit. Larger businesses need to make a profit, as such it should be easier for smaller businesses to compete.

6.1.2   Stabilised Cash Distribution Model

The stabilisation method was applied to the Wealth Distribution Model. This model includes the use of ownership, which stabilises the wealth distribution. Figure 68 shows the distribution of the cash between the five groups of

Consumers over time. The oscillations in business cycles seen in the unstabilised system still occur, but with significantly reduced amplitude.

Figure 67 and Figure 68 show the cash distribution that results when each group of Consumers is fully supplemented by the stability payments. This means that each group of Consumers receives a different amount of support from the Government. In response to this, the final cash distribution remains the same as when applying the model from Section 5.1.5. Note that some oscillations do occur in the middle tier Consumers on occasion, but these are typically lower in amplitude than the unstabilised oscillations. Notably, the lowest level of Consumers are always stable, and in Consumer levels 2 and 3, the oscillations fade out after 40–50 years.

This might not be considered an optimal solution for moral reasons, because the Consumers are not being treated equally. When Consumers are given exactly the same level of support from stabilisation, as shown in Figure 84, the distribution of cash in the system equalises between the levels. The cash residing with the highest level of Consumers ('Consumers4') increased because they absorbed cash from the other Consumers, but eventually it stabilised to become fairly constant, with some oscillations. the cash distribution is dominated by the top-level Consumers and is stabilised. There are still oscillations internally in the cash distribution among the mid-level Consumers. This suggests that there may still be some distress within this group, even when the economy is stabilised. This may not be a problem, as the mid-level Consumers can still be owners of lower-level Producers and may be able to draw on funds from them. Second, the Consumers would always be able to purchase products from lower-level Producers.

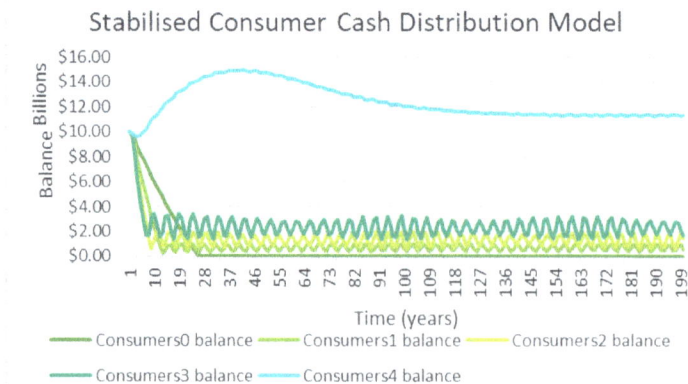

Stabilised Consumer Cash Distribution Model

212

Figure 84: Stabilised cash balances with investment

The Global Labour Model from Section 5.1.6 can be modified for stabilisation. In the case shown in Figure 85, again, the balances show that the total cash approaches a constant value. The limitation with this model is that all countries represented in the model use the same currency. This is mainly due to limitations in software development.

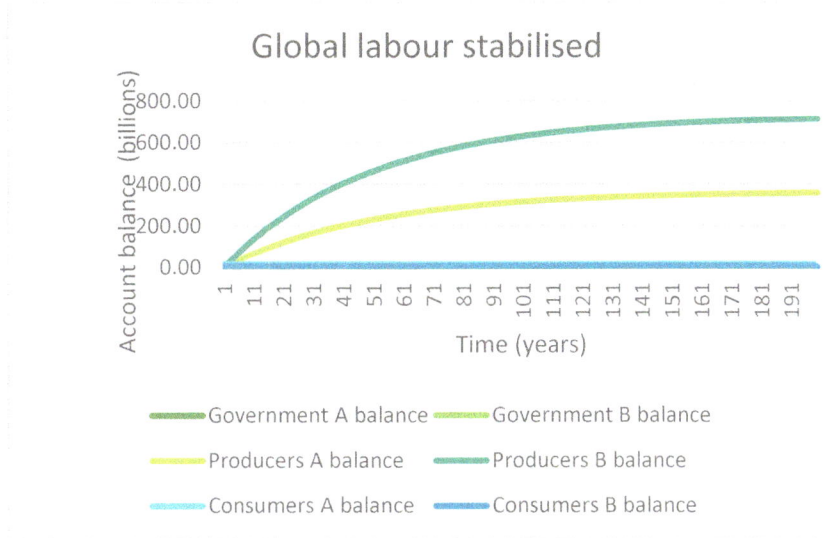

Figure 85: Stabilised global labour system response

The distress in the system is also constant at zero, as shown in Figure 86.

Consumer A + B Distress

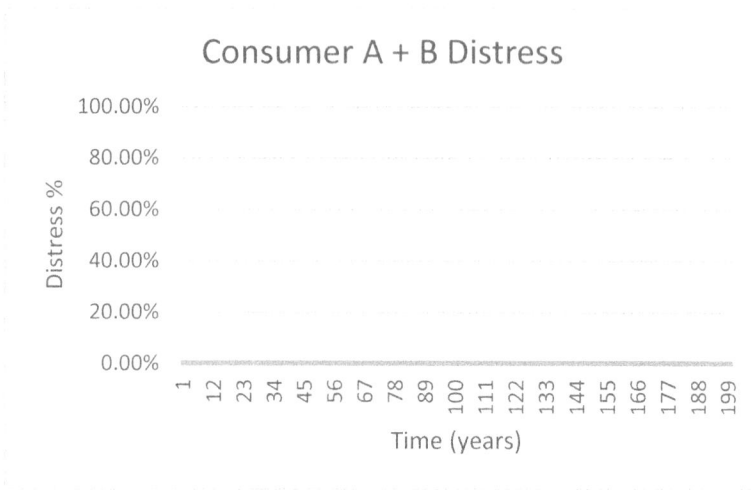

Figure 86: Stabilised global labour Consumer distress

This shows that even with multiple Governments, as long as all Governments perform the stabilisation, the system approaches a stable point (even if there is a disparity in purchasing between countries). One of the main limitations of the stabilisation process is that it will not solve the problems caused by excessive exchange rates. This may be the best argument for introducing a world Government that manages a world currency and money supply. If a single currency was used and taxed worldwide, that would guarantee that all of the economies involved would be stabilised. The difficulty with that, of course, is that all countries involved would have to agree to have the money supply taxed by a central organisation.

6.1.3   Supercharging an economy

Supercharging requires two further components:

- The universal income for Consumers needs to be larger than the minimum profit.
- The Consumers' universal income needs to be subtracted from the Producer-to-Consumer wages.

214

This allows the price of products to be reduced due to the lower cost of production, and introduces the possibility that Producers could increase the number of jobs and employ more people.

Supercharging the economy also enables rapid price deflation. Increased stability payments effectively decouples Producers from the cost of living and allows profits to be made, with a limited effect on the entire system. This also allows inflation to be negative, because Producers are only required to pay Consumers enough to motivate them to perform the tasks required for production. This also means that basic labour, or minimum wage labour, would be free from a business perspective. It would thus be possible for businesses and/or non-profit organisations to employ everyone in an economy, i.e. 100% employment, or 0% unemployment.

Most Producers operate at 10% profit margins; typically, their own employee wages make up 60–90% of costs. Consider a Producer who makes a total annual profit of $10 million, with their only expense being the employment of 1000 people at an average wage of, say, $50,000. Under the current economic conditions, this would mean the company income was $60 million per annum. Adding in the supercharging; if workers were paid say $20,000 by the Government, this would reduce the company expenses to $30,000 per employee. With 1000 employees, this adds up to a reduction in total Producer costs of $20 million. Notably, the employees do not see a change in their wages; however, Producers' 'profits' would in this case triple. The increase in profits would allow Producers to decrease the price of their products.

If the Producer's total income was $60 million and they were to maintain the $10 million profit with the $20 million reduced from costs, the Producer would be able to reduce the price of its products by as much as one-third ($1.0 - \frac{40\ \text{million}}{60\ \text{million}}$). Consumers would then be able to pay less for the products they need, allowing demand to increase and wages to be further reduced.

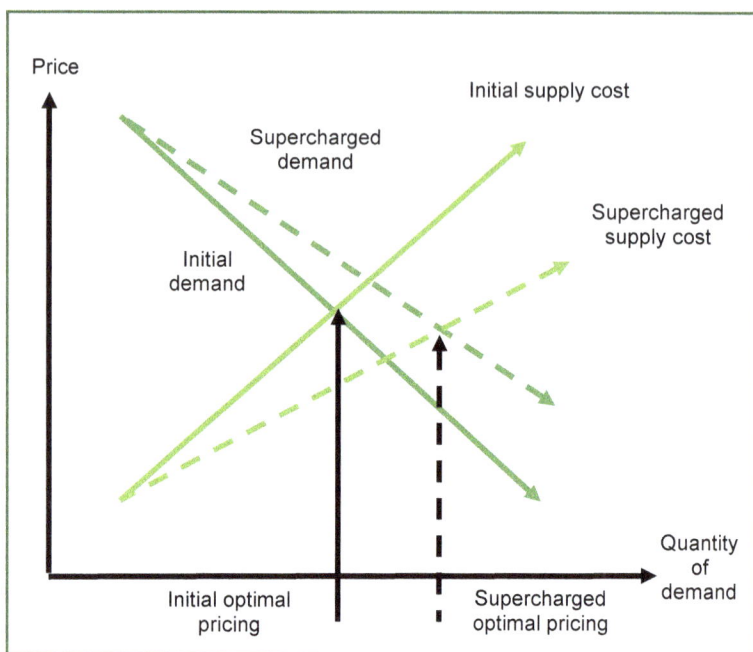

Figure 87: Effect of supercharging on supply and demand

As shown in Figure 87, when supercharging occurs, demand is increased, because more people have money to buy products; at the same time, supply costs are reduced, because Producers do not need to pay employees as much as they did before supercharging. In effect, this modifies both supply and demand curves such that the optimal price point moves towards a maximum quantity that supplies the entire population.

If Consumers always have more money than they are paid by Producers, this directly reduces pressure on inflation. As Producers are also paid, they require less profits, which again results in less pressure on inflation. Thus, if people are paid enough, it is possible to achieve a negative inflation or price deflation.

If Government payments could approach the average wage of Consumers, Producers would effectively not be paying employees anything, which means that it would be easier for Producers to employ more of the population. This creates the interesting situation in which non-profit organisations would also be able to employ more people, and thus to address the non-economic issues of our civilisation.

The rule is: if a Government wants to subsidise something, subsidise people, not a particular product.

6.1.4 Stabilised money flow

Stabilisation allows money to flow through the economy in a more linear fashion, as opposed to the Circular Flow of Money. It allows money to flow in a production–consumption cycle. Products are created from resources and traded to Consumers, who consume them, i.e. they effectively disappear. In an unstabilised economy, money is supposed to circulate, but it does not circulate evenly. The money in a stabilised system is allocated to Consumers and used on Government-approved projects. This money is spent and eventually finds its way into the hands of private enterprise (i.e. Producers). As it moves, the money is taxed and is continually removed from the economy. The stabilisation process deallocates money, at a slow rate. This allows the money to be used then removed from the system, much like the products that are consumed.

From the stabilisation, a money flow can be established, starting with money being allocated to Consumers or to any projects the Government has decided are necessary. The Government and Consumers can then use private enterprise, i.e. Producers, to meet their requirements.

This model, illustrated in Figure 88, has a predictable amount of money in the system. It is explained in more detail in Section 6.1.6.2. This economic structure allows a responsible Government to create funds that could then be used for many different tasks, and Consumers to receive money from a universal income so that they can buy the essentials for life—water, food and shelter.

Currently, money creation is performed by banks as an incidental consequence of the creation of debt. Banks are a private enterprise that do not act in the best interests of the people of the world. Governments are supposed to be organisations that represent their citizens. In theory, Governments should be better managers of the cash flow of an economy, because they are supposed to keep their citizens alive.

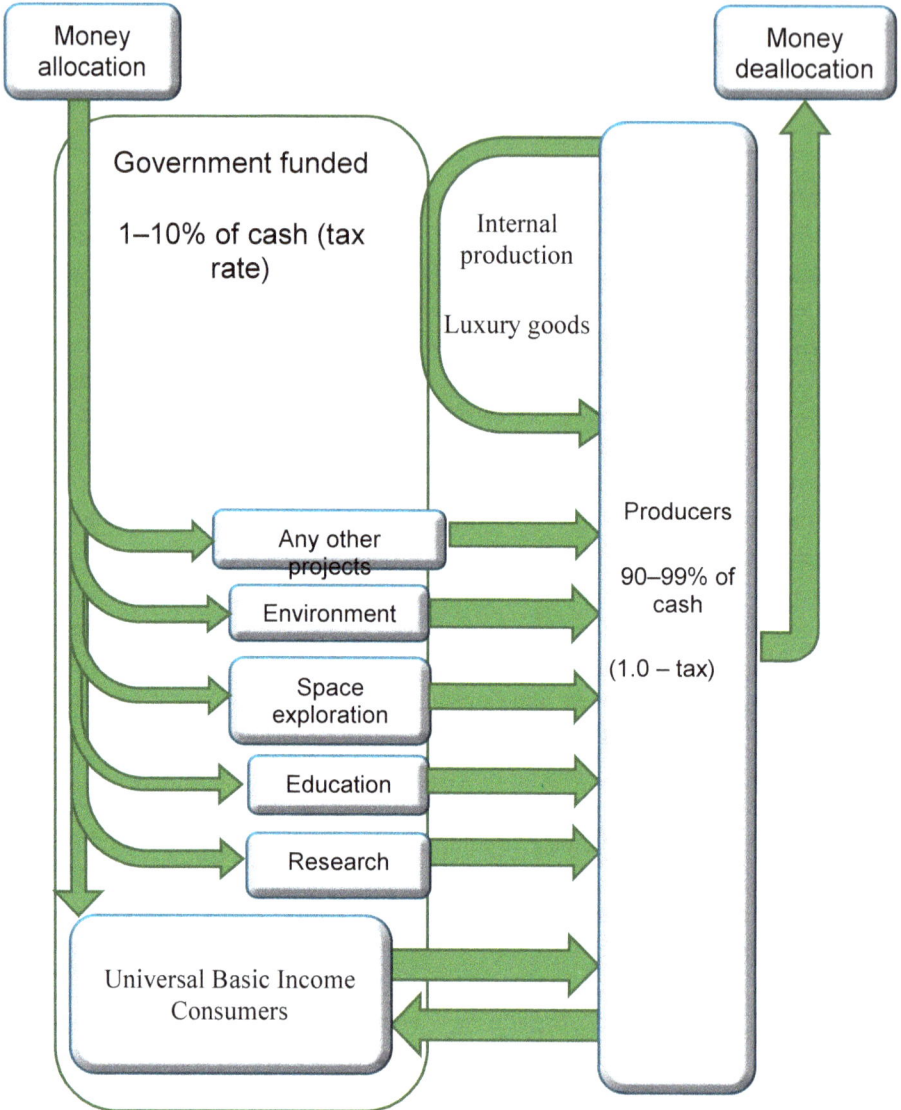

Figure 88: Proposed Government funding structure

This stabilisation strategy allows the Cash tax to run at various levels and it will still work. The only difference is the final amount of money in the system. The final value can be calculated from Total Government spending and the Cash tax.

$$\text{Total Currency} = \text{Total Spending} / \text{Cash Tax rate}$$

Table 20 Summary of Government Costs 4% Cash Tax

	Cash Allocated		Cash Deallocated
UBI	$400B	Cash Tax 4% ($2.5T)	$100B
Other Government Funding	$300B	Income Tax	$250B
		Company Tax	$100B
		GST	$80B
Total	$700B		$530B

Net Result Cash Released: $170B

Assuming no change in expenses, to balance this out the amount of Total Cash (Broad Money) would increase to $8.5T.

Table 21: Summary of Government Costs Balanced Cash Tax

	Cash Allocated		Cash Deallocated
UBI	$400B	Cash Tax 4% ($8.5T)	$350B
Other Government Funding	$300B	Income Tax	$250B
		Company Tax	$100B
Total	$700B		$700B

It is even possible to eliminate **all other taxes** and just use the cash tax.

Table 22 Summary of Government Costs

	Cash Allocated		Cash Deallocated
UBI	$400B	Cash Tax 4% ($17.5T)	$700B
Other Government Funding	$300B		
Total	$700B		$530B

This shows that between a 1% Cash tax and a 10% cash tax is there will be 10 times the amount of money in the economy for a 1% tax rate as shown in Figure 89.

Stabilised CPG with Multiple Cash Tax rates

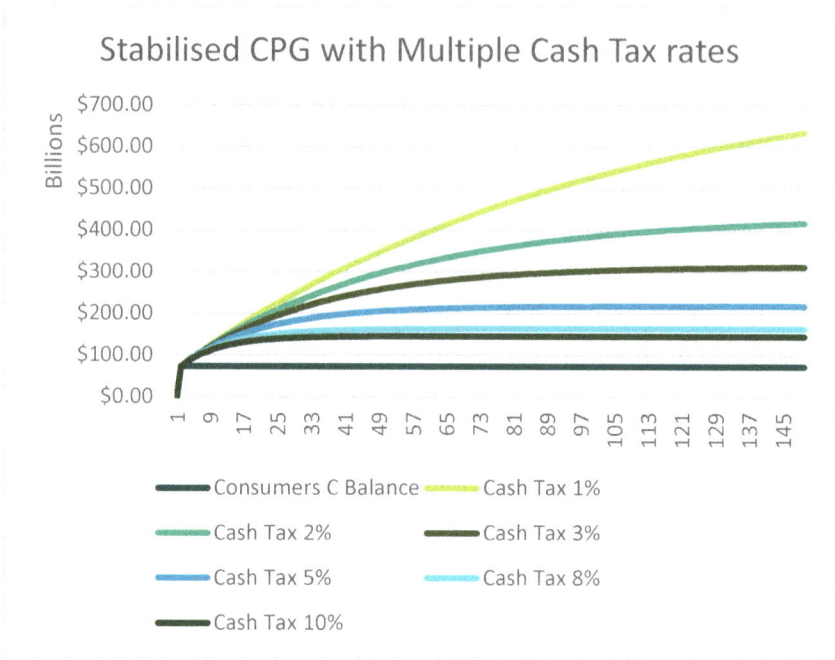

Figure 89: Stabilised CPG with Multiple Cash Tax rates

This means that the government can vary the tax rate depending on the situation. In years where there are many crises that need to be addressed, it is possible to increase the tax rate and encourage people to focus on government-funded projects.

The difficulty is if there is 10 times the money in the system the savings can be distributed unequally and may result in the same inequalities we are currently struggling against. As such, it is recommended to keep income tax at least which helps to minimise income disparity and minimise the cash required in the economy.

6.1.5   Flexible Government expenses

The stabilised CPG model was further tested using random Government expenses. The system response is shown in Figure 90. If government expenses are reduced and stabilised, the entire system also stabilises and returns to a stable and constant amount of cash.

With the stabilised models, one of the notable features is that over time, irrespective of whether the Government overspends or underspends, the amount of money in the economy approaches a constant value. So even if the government overspends, when their spending decreases the economy simply finds a new lower total cash level to stabilise at. The rate of stabilisation depends on the cash tax rate as shown previously.

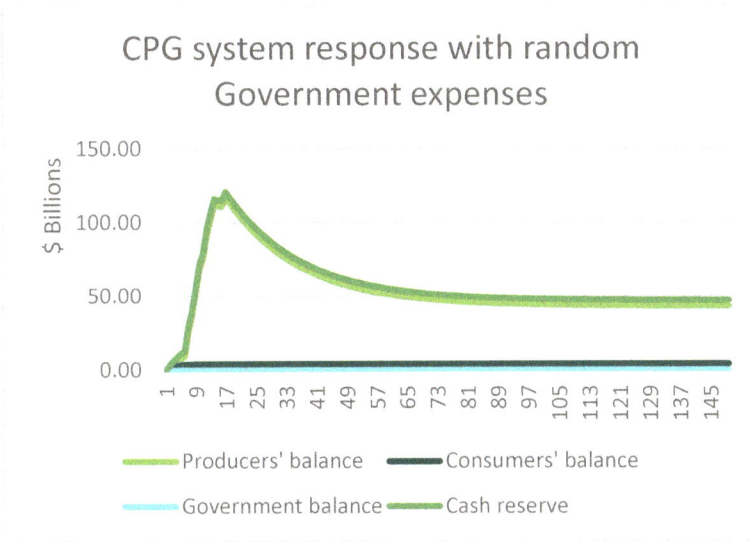

Figure 90: Stabilised CPG Model with random Government expenses

6.1.6 Properties of the Stabilised CPG Model

The stabilisation of the CPG Model has several distinct properties and requirements.

The requirements for both stabilising and supercharging the economy include:

- taxation of money
- stabilisation payments to Consumers
- stabilisation payments to Consumers larger than the minimum profit
- stabilisation payments to be removed from the Producer-to-Consumer wages
- reducing the price of products on the basis of the lower cost of production.

The outcomes of the stabilisation and supercharging include:

- no business cycles
- a finite amount of money
- maximum employment
- minimal inflation or deflation.

6.1.6.1   No business cycles

As shown in Figure 80, the primary feature of the stabilised models is that there are no oscillations. Business cycles have been eliminated completely. Thus, the economy should not experience any recessions directly from internal causes, although external factors (such as decrease in availability of resources, or excessive debt) may still cause recessions in an economy.

6.1.6.2   Finite money

As time continues, the system approaches a stable, but finite amount of money. This is in sharp contrast with the existing real economy, which shows money growing in the economy at an exponential rate.

The total amount of money in a stabilised system will be:

$$R = (P*W + G)/(1.0 - T)$$

where: R = reserve cash (total cash)

P = population

W = universal wage

G = Government expenses

T = money tax rate.

Notably, in this system a percentage of the money is still held by Producers.

The final limit will be: $R (1.0 - Tax)$.

Thus, if money is taxed at 2%, 98% of the money in the system will be held by Producers.

6.1.6.3   Money Tax

The design of the solution for the CPG Models requires savings to be taxed. If this tax is performed on a daily basis, a 2% annual tax rate would be 0.00553% per day. A person would pay 1 cent tax for every $180 in an account per day. This tax rate on $2 trillion would provide a constant tax income of approximately $110 million per day. If distributed over all the citizens of Australia (25,000,000 citizens), every person would be taxed $0.44 per day, This would represent an annual velocity of $4,015,000,000 per year; however, only the daily $11 billion needs to be transferred every day. Unfortunately, this amount of money is nowhere near enough to cover the daily requirements of living in Australia. The average income in Australia is around $80,000 per year as at 2017 (about $220 per day), so the money supply would need to increase significantly and/or prices would need to significantly reduce before every citizen could be funded appropriately through a 2% money tax. But this is exactly how such a system works. If extra money is required, it would simply be added to the economy through Government spending.

6.1.6.4   Deflation

In Section 5.1.4, a formula was derived that showed the relationship between profit and employment conditions.

The use of stabilisation payments and supercharging means that Consumers would be able to purchase more products, thus increasing demand. At the same time, Producers would not be required to pay the full cost of wages. Thus, Producers could make higher profits without affecting the final price of products; thus, they could potentially reduce prices.

6.1.7   Comparison with social values

As part of this research, the output and properties of the Stabilised CPG Model can be considered in terms of common social values. This should help determine how well people would accept this solution. In the following sections, we examine a few social values including:

- equality
- eliminating poverty
- motivation to work.

6.1.7.1   Equality

This strategy is consistent with the theories of Mill [26–28], who encouraged welfare and minimising of the effects of businesses on the environment. If production stopped, this system would spread money equally between all citizens involved in the economy. Equality is valued by many modern societies. This social value is not reflected in the current economy; however, using the CPG solution, it could be.

You may argue that some people work harder than others and as a result should be paid more. In private enterprise, people are often paid far more than in non-profit industries, despite the fact that private enterprise is often less essential than non-profit. For example, compare the pay rates of people involved in private enterprise toy-making or trading shares with those of people engaged in child care. This shows the current preference of private enterprise for rewarding profitable activity, rather than hard but less profitable activity. Child care is considered to be underfunded in many countries, despite it being arguably a more essential service.

One contender for justifying a payment advantage could be education level. People are generally not paid more just because they have a higher education; they are paid more when they get a job that requires the education. Someone who has a higher education has given up some of their potential earning time (typically at least 4 years for a degree, around 8 years for a PhD). This could be compensated for by a higher pay rate for addressing the more complicated problems of our world. Other possibilities include: people who attain a higher education could be paid more as part of a universal income, or they could be paid throughout their education.

The advantage of the economic stabilisation method is that almost any expense can be paid for by the Government; hence, if the Government (and hopefully the supporting population) decide that particular people should be paid more, it would be possible to do so. In most countries, people are given awards for public services or acts of heroism. These are people who the broader public may consider worthy of having higher support payments or an extra one-off payment.

The main function of these payments would be the rewarding of people for behaviours that the community wishes to promote. These behaviours could be as simple as starting a business, advancing one's education, completing some research, or contributing a benefit to the community. Ultimately, the stabilisation method gives us the capacity to reward beneficial behaviours and give everyone equal opportunities, not just equal payments.

6.1.7.2   Eliminating poverty

The stabilisation of the economy, if appropriately implemented, would ensure that all Consumers have access to enough funding to allow a stable lifestyle. The stabilisation modifications should eliminate poverty. They will not, however, necessarily create the opportunity for everyone to be employed.

6.1.7.3   Motivation to work

One of the main criticisms of welfare payments is that they reduce the motivation to work. However, if the economy was supercharged, it would be possible to employ everyone (but not necessarily by a profit-making business). Employment could be obtained from non-profit organisations that perform socially desirable tasks. More opportunities for people to be employed generally results in more people working.

For validation of these ideas, there are several sources of statistics. The World Bank has used a program of microloans in poverty-stricken countries , including in parts of Bangladesh [152], Eastern Europe, Russia and China [153]. These programs give small loans of as little as US$5 to people to buy tools and start small, simple businesses, such as a sewing business for the repair of garments or shoes. The results of these programs have been varied, with many people, but not everyone, fully repaying their loans. These programs have been shown to reduce poverty at a village level, especially for women [152]. This indicates that if people who live in poverty get even small amounts of funding, they are willing to work to improve their lives, i.e. the limitation in reducing poverty is not motivation, but funding.

Let us consider the situation of unemployed, underemployed and overqualified people in relation to the number of job vacancies. Unemployed people are people who do not have jobs and are actively searching for work. This group does not include people who are retired but who would still like to be employed, home-makers, or people who have simply given up looking for work. Underemployed people includes people who are employed but who would like to have more work, i.e. they have part-time employment, but would like more hours, or even full-time employment. Overqualified people are people who have higher qualifications than are required by their current job.

In Australia in 2013–2014, according to the ABS [129] there were approximately 12 million people who were employed. Approximately 800,000 people were considered unemployed, 1.1 million were considered underemployed and approximately 600,000 were deemed overqualified for the jobs they had. During this time, there were less than 180,000 job vacancies. Directly comparing the number of unemployed people with the number of job vacancies indicates that there are more than four times the number of people looking for work than there are jobs available. If the number of people looking for work included underemployed and overqualified people, there would be 2.5 million people attempting to fit into 180,000 job vacancies, nearly 14 people per vacancy. This suggests that 1.4 million jobs may be needed if we are to employ people at the level at which they wish to be employed. In addition, I suspect that many more people would enter the workforce, increasing the participation rate—if more jobs were available.

This suggests that the problem currently is not that people are unwilling to work, but that employers are not creating the jobs required for employing people. The idea that people are not willing to work is not supported by the existing statistics. The simple fact is that we can produce everything that people need without employing more people.

If the economic stabilisation method is employed, it is not likely to significantly change people's motivation to work, because it would only pay for basic necessities. People would still need to work to have a better-than-basic lifestyle.

6.1.8   Money Supply versus Velocity of Money argument

Previous economics researchers have suggested that an increase in the money supply would increase inflation. However, other researchers have shown that in most countries for which high inflation is a problem, the inflation is not directly caused by structural monetary issues.

Also, from a microeconomic perspective, Producers use local optimisation to attempt to maximise their own profits. Prices are set by considering the cost of production and the demand for products. In none of the economics textbooks reviewed has anyone referenced the total monetary supply or even considered inflation as a guide to setting prices.

A system has been presented here that is stable under many conditions. It is not claimed that this system is perfect, or that it will solve all of the problems encountered in an economic system, but hopefully it represents a significant improvement over existing strategies.

If enough money is provided to all Consumers, Producer income can become constant, avoiding welfare and decay states in the economy. Since Consumers are provided with enough money to purchase the goods they require, in theory it is possible to eliminate poverty. Consumers should be paid this money, even if they are employed, because this would reduce the burden on Producers paying employees, thus allowing more people to be employed.

It has often been argued that the average price of products in an economy will scale with the amount of money in the economy. Thus, the amount of money should be kept constant, because any increase in the money supply will cause prices to increase, and money will simply circulate more slowly. Frankly, this argument does not make sense. From the research presented here it can be shown that:

Total cash – Total income – Total savings = 0.

Thus:

Velocity of money = Total income / Time.

The velocity of money will vary depending on how much people actually spend and save in a given period of time. The more people save, the less money will be circulated, and this will produce a lower velocity of money.

Even if the previous argument is not accepted, one of the major effects of taxation and stabilisation of the economy is that the amount of money in the economy will approach a constant value.

6.2 Implementation of economic stabilisation in the real world

The implementation of a money tax is difficult with physical currencies, because it is generally not known how much of a physical currency any entity in the economy has (although 'money' in a bank account can be checked directly). The solution is to eliminate physical currency and to entirely rely on 'digital' currency. Digital currency can be tracked and measured at any time, so the tax that needs to be paid can be calculated simply by examining the balance of a digital account. If all of the accounts of a particular currency are held at banks that operate under the jurisdiction of a particular Government, the accounts can be taxed appropriately.

A digital implementation that taxes known accounts and pays Consumers can be created in hours. This implementation could be distributed to all banks and would be operational within days, or weeks at the longest. The main limitation of implementation would be the legal issues with international banking, and generally getting banks to implement the required policies. This is not to say that banks will resist the change, simply that there is always some corporate momentum to overcome when changing the way businesses and Governments operate.

6.2.1.1   Implementing a Universal basic income

This paper uses the current Australian population, budget and income distribution to demonstrate how a UBI could be funded and analyses the changes in income distribution and equilibrium in the Australian economy.

The funding strategy is to reallocate parts of the budget that are directly paid to people to account for a UBI. This includes a large proportion of social security and as much as 25% of other budgets. The second part of this strategy is to "print" any further money required and to tax the money supply (i.e. savings). This technique increases the amount of money in the economy (via printing) and at the same time removes money from circulation (from money supply taxation).

Table 23: Australian Government Budget 2019:

Social security and welfare	$180.1 billion
All other functions	$48.5 billion
General public services	$23.6 billion
Defence	$32.2 billion
Education	$36.4 billion
Health	$81.8 billion
Other purposes	$98.3 billion

Total $500.9 Billion

Table 24: UBI Comparison

	UBI $10,000 annual	UBI $20,000 annual
Total Cost (20 Million people)	$200 Billion	$400 Billion
Funding	(Billions)	(Billions)
Social Security& Welfare Offset	$46	$92
Wage Offset	$40	$80
Cash Tax 4%	$100	$100
Sovereign Currency Required	$14	$128

In Australia there are approximately 4.6 Million people on Government allowances including, Pensions and unemployment. Approximately 20 Million people in Australia over 15. If each is paid say $10,000, this means $200 Billion is needed to fund a basic income in Australia.

If we take the existing social security system, on Average Pensioners are paid about 26,000 per year, $51B to 1.95 Million people. The total social-security payments is approximately $120B which averages out to around $26,000 each supporting around 4.6 Million people.

If we pay a UBI in place of some of the pension all we are doing is reallocating money from the social security system to the UBI this would move $46 Billion from Social Security to UBI.

Average wage in Australia is around $80,000. A $10,000 UBI represents 12.5% of the average wage. The rest of the government budget is $320 Billion 12.5% of this is another $40B.

Simply using reallocation from the government budget $86 Billion of $200B has been found leaving $114B.

If we increase the UBI to $20,000 we require $400B. The reallocation in social security is then $92B. Reallocation in the rest of the budget 25% ($20,000 out of $80,000) is then $80B. This allocates $172B out of $400B required leaving $128B that needs to be funded.

The strategy I present to stabilize the economy is to create or "print" the money required and to tax the static money in the economy i.e. "savings". Not asking you to like it, but these two features in combination avoids the problem of hyper-inflation. The next feature we consider is the total amount of Australian money which is a bit over $2 Trillion. If we tax this at 2% per year this represents another $40B, 4% gives $80B, 5% gives $100B.

If the amount of money we need is more than what we tax out, this simply means that there will be more money created into the economy and therefor more tax would be received by taxing static money.

Depending on the tax rate and UBI amount leaves between $14B and $88B required. This final amount can be created directly from creating money. We can also consider the increase in demand by examining income distribution.

Income Distribution

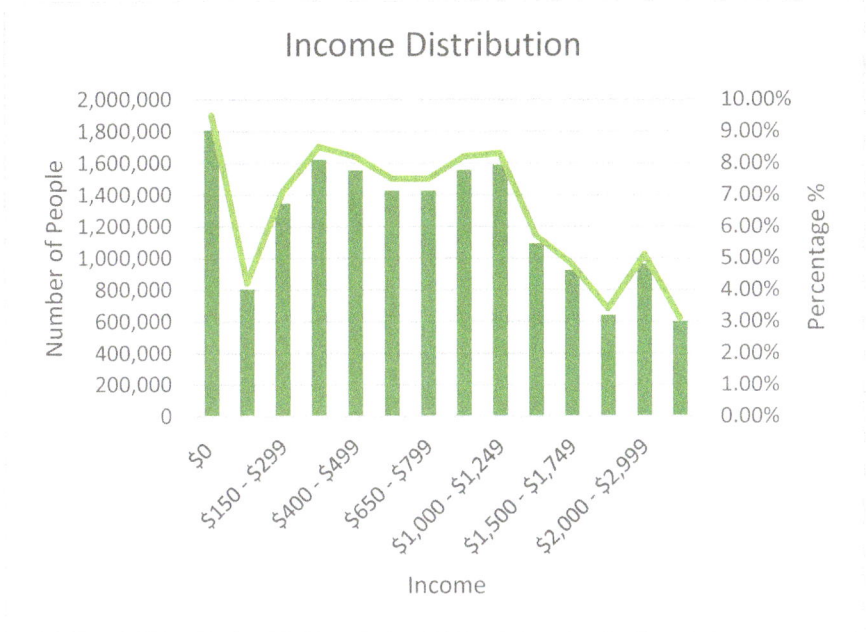

Figure 91 Income Distribution Australia 2019

Demand

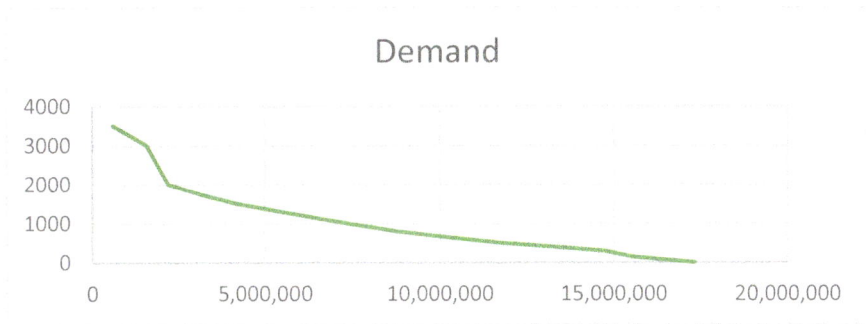

Figure 92 Australia Demand curve 2019

The existing demand can be calculated from income distribution and population as shown above. UBI can be added directly to incomes which results in the demand.

Income Distribution

Figure 93 Income Distribution with a Basic UBI

Demand with simple UBI

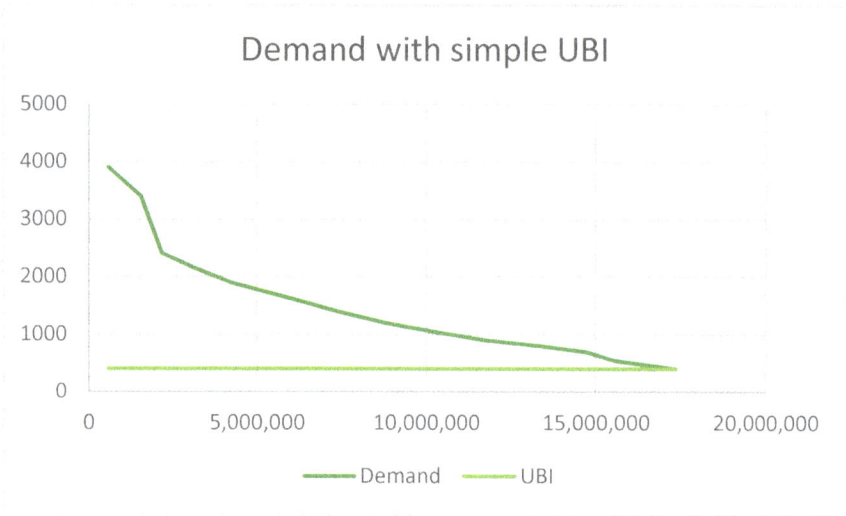

Figure 94 Australia Demand curve with simple UBI 2019

Using a UBI increases the amount of money the poorest 15% of the country receives. This represents approximately 3 Million people. A UBI of $20,000 represents an increase in their income of at least on average $10,000 to $15,000 per year. With 3 million people this represents an increase in demand at the low end of $30 to $45 Billion per year. If 30% of this comes back in tax on profits this also adds $10-$15B to the funding.

This either fully funds a Universal Basic Income or requires as much as $78 Billion with no increase in existing taxes, and 1 new tax.

The other potential benefit of this approach is that if we allow businesses to use the UBI as part of their responsibility to their employees' wages.

If we use a UBI of $20,000 and apply this against the wages paid by businesses. This means that businesses reduce their costs by $20,000 per person. With around 12,000,000 people employed this saves businesses $240 Billion per year. This means that businesses should be able to reduce costs by 20 to 25%. If costs can be reduced by 25% it means the government budget is effectively expanded as the cost of products are reduced.

This also eliminates inflation and, according to my research, recessions.

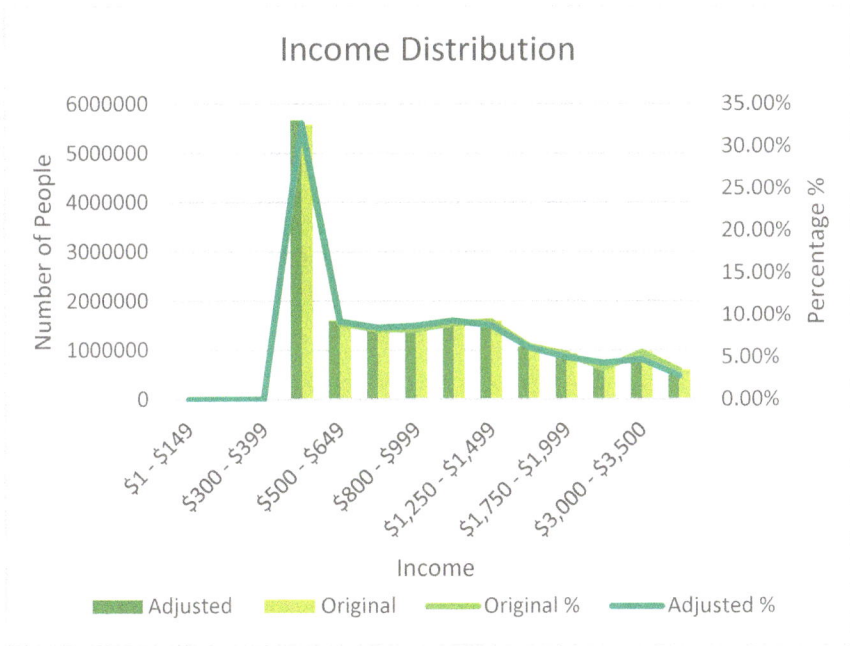

Income Distribution

Figure 95 Income Distribution with an Integrated UBI

UBI integrated Demand

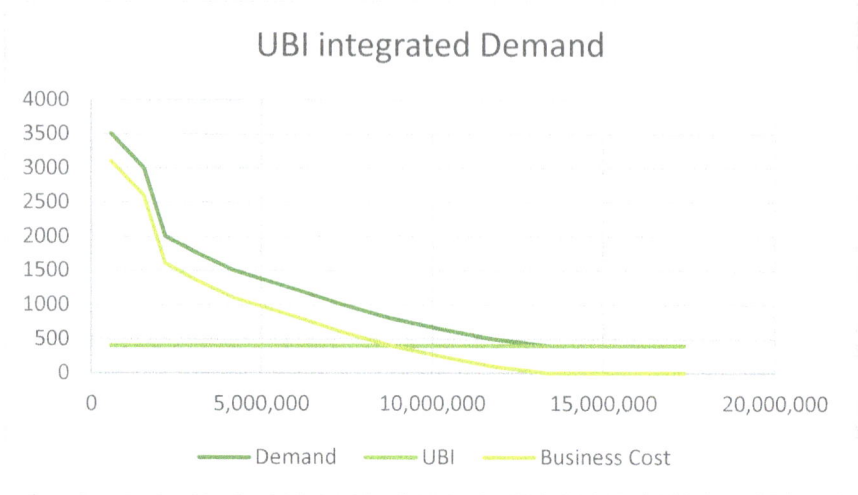

Figure 96 Australia Demand curve with Integrated UBI 2019

The other reason we want prices to decrease is to be able to compete better with other countries. The cost of living in China and India is almost 4 times lower than in Australia. This is why many jobs have been offshored to these countries. By decreasing prices we can begin to reduce the cost of living and hence shift jobs back to Australia (or any other country that implements a basic income).

This gives a summary of what we do know about how the economy runs. What we don't know is how much effect taxing saving would have on money flow. Essentially if money in savings disappears people and businesses are more likely to spend what they get. How much more is a good question and will only be answered by implementing these ideas.

6.3   Income Tax

The other major part of consumer income that disappears is due to income tax. This means Producers have to pay consumers more and consumers end up with less money to spend back on producers. With the use of Sovereign money, it is possible to eliminate income tax. However, there may be good reason to keep income it. As

6.4   Why will stabilisation work?

We can examine what happens at each stage of the cycle as shown in the image below. Producers spend money making a Product and add some extra cost to make a profit. The cost of making the product is the income the Consumers receive. After taking into account tax Consumers have some money left that they can spend on products. However, you can see with this that the Consumer budget is not enough to purchase the products.

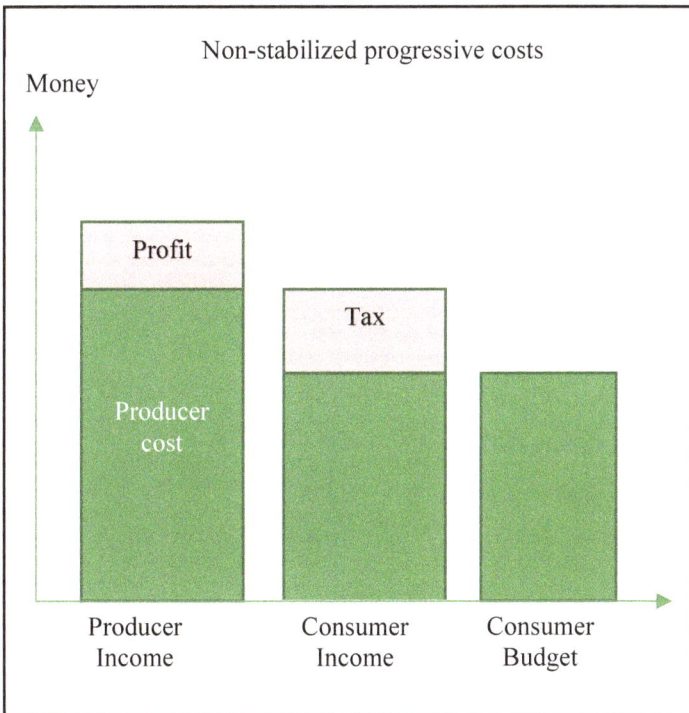

Figure 97: Non –Stabilised progressive costs

When we consider how stabilization works with the Universal income as shown below. The universal income puts the Consumer budget back up to the point where they can afford products. This means that all consumers can afford their products and thus Producers can maximise employment.

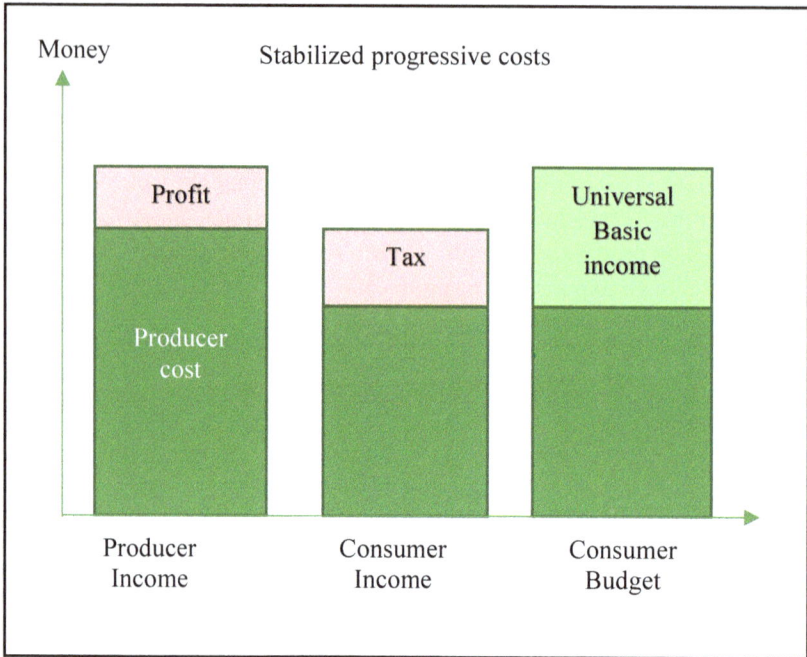

Figure 98: Stabilised progressive cost

The other rules of stabilisation ensure that there is not too much money in the system such that inflation kicks in again.

6.5   Why will supercharging work

Supercharging the economy takes stabilisation one-step further and reduces the cost of employment. This than allows producers to reduce prices and make as much profit as without supercharging. Further benefits can be made if producers are willing to make the same percentage profits and further reduce prices.

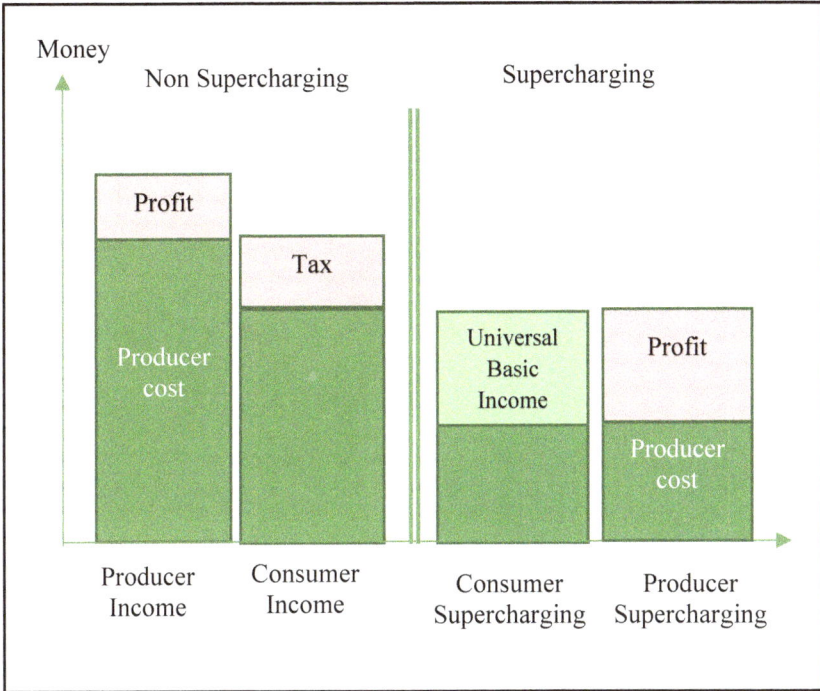

Figure 99: Non – Supercharged vs Supercharged progressive cost

This is evidence that even if there is "too much money in the economy" it will not cause significant inflation. This should satisfy the monetarist concern about having too much money in the economy.

6.6   Universal Income or Universal Jobs

From a few comments I have seen online many people say that they would prefer to have universal jobs as opposed to universal income. Universal jobs means that everyone gets to be employed. A universal income means that everyone gets paid regardless of whether they are employed or not.

One side note is that having a UBI does not preclude having a Universal Job Guarantee and vice versa, so there is no reason both cannot be implemented.

In principle, I totally agree with the idea of universal jobs. However, what I can say, based on the simulation work, is a universal guarantee of jobs to get to

100% employment will not work. The simulations show that on occasion the economy will be able to employ everyone, i.e. 100% employment. The problem is this situation is short lived.

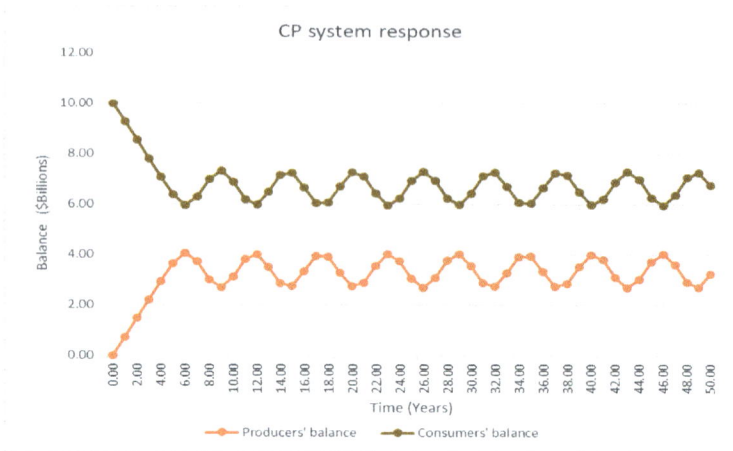

Figure 100: CP System Response

The consumer distress diagram below shows that distress varies between 0% and in the case shown below 18%.

Figure 101: Consumer distress

The point I am trying to show with universal income is that the result of implementing a universal income in an economy will be that of universal employment. The stabilised system shown below shows that if consumers

238

maintain a balance above a critical point they can spend what they have on the products they need, as a result businesses need to employ the maximum number of people to keep up with demand.

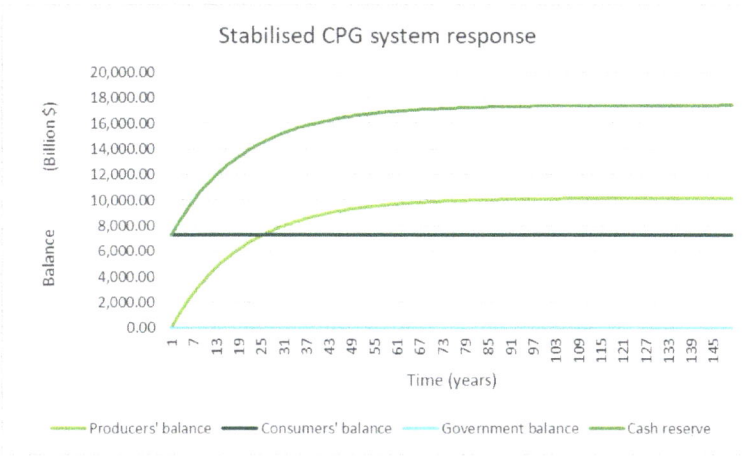

Figure 102:Stabilised CPG system response

As everyone can afford the products they need and everyone can be employed hence consumer distress is zero. 0% distress means 100% employment.

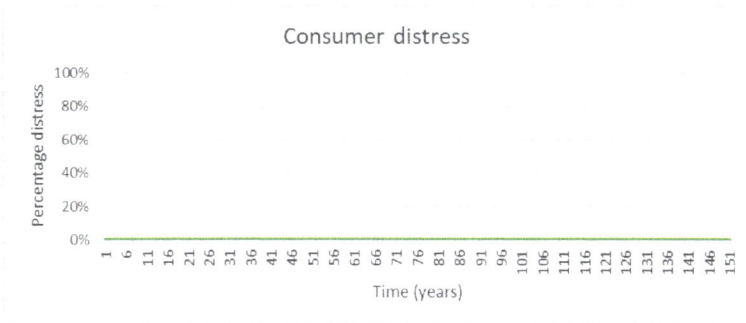

Figure 103:Stabilised Consumer Distress

This only occurs in a stabilised economy as the profits made by Producers in the economy are repaid by a third party with the universal income. Hence when the next cycle occurs consumers retain enough money to continue to buy their needed products.

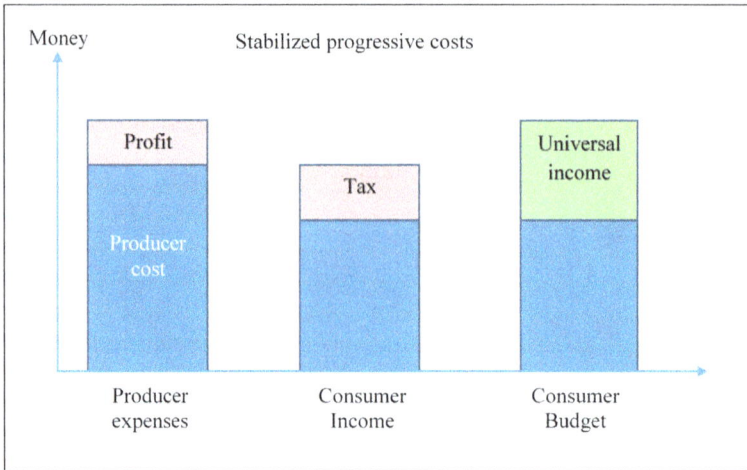

Figure 104:Stabilised progressive costs

The next big limitation of universal jobs is that it does not support Producers. A universal income can be used to offset the cost of keeping people employed as described in supercharging. Supercharging reduces the cost of employment so that employers can increase employment and keep prices down which allows inflation to be controlled.

To sum it all up: a universal income creates a situation where universal employment occurs, but <u>not</u> the other way around.

6.7 Limits of stabilisation

While the stabilisation and supercharging of an economy should significantly reduce poverty and increase productivity, it will not solve every problem that exists in the world.

6.7.1 Inflation

Can economic stabilisation eliminate inflation?

It should be possible to eliminate the vast majority of internal economic inflation and potentially create price deflation. Over the long term, it is theoretically possible to reduce prices to zero, but I am not certain whether this would work perfectly in practice.

Also, in terms of 'real' inflation, stabilising the economy would maximise the demand for resources. As the demand for resources increases, they become harder to find and harder to extract. Hence, it is expected that more labour will be required for extracting and refining resources. However, especially with space exploration, in my opinion we should always be able to find more resources, even if it takes more effort to utilise them, and we should always be able to find more space for people to live. Improvements in recycling may reduce the need for mining 'virgin' resources. With technological innovation it should be possible to minimise 'real inflation'; however, there is no guarantee that inflation could be eliminated completely.

6.7.2   Unemployment

Economic stabilisation, and especially economic supercharging, could significantly reduce the unemployment rate. However, can it guarantee 100% employment? Probably not. There will always be some people who are too young, too old or too disabled to be employed. Despite that, there should always be some way for everyone to be a part of society, even if it is through part-time or volunteer work.

Frictional unemployment is unemployment that occurs due to people changing jobs, or just taking time off between jobs. Typically, this is short-term unemployment. This is always going to exist. As long as people can get work when they need it and want it, unemployment should become less of a problem.

6.7.3   Limit of profits

Stabilising the economy does not mean that anyone makes more profit. It is more likely that more people would receive lower profits. However, the economy is still running as a zero-sum system. This means that not everyone can make a profit—some people will not make anything more than what is paid in the stabilisation payments. Some will probably refuse to work without significant compensation. In response, there may be more motivation for setting up profit sharing or other benefits to get people to work for particular businesses.

6.7.4   Market saturation

According to the employment records by industry (Section 4.12), you will notice that about 1.5% of the Australian population work in agriculture. This is due to the fact that those 1.5% of the population can produce enough food to feed the rest of the 98.5% of the population, and taking into account exports, probably more. Thus, even if more people want to become farmers, we do not need more farmers to produce enough food for everyone.

In many industries, once we have enough of a product—houses or cars, for example—production can be significantly reduced. This is something I call market saturation. Once everyone has a car to drive, we will only need to produce cars at the replacement rate at which cars wear out. This will be significantly below the maximum possible production rate for the economy as a whole. With houses, the problem becomes a bit more interesting. If we manage to achieve a stable population, i.e. the number of births per year equals the number of deaths per year, we will not need to make any more houses.

The up side is that everyone can still be productive (write books, do research, make movies, make YouTube videos), and as long as they can live off stability payments, everyone can survive and still be a part of the economy, i.e. buy stuff. The other big possibility is exploration, expanding the human race beyond earth.

6.7.5   Population growth

When applying the stabilisation strategy, the amount of money in the economy will grow with the population. This means the economy can be expanded further if and when we manage to colonise other planets.

6.8   Limitations of economic stabilisation

This 'solution' is exciting in itself and, hopefully, is a step towards eliminating poverty and creating a stable, balanced economy that allows people to live more fulfilling lives. However, it will not immediately create a utopia. Problems will remain. An economy deals with people, and people can be difficult if they feel they need to change things without good reason; occasionally, people just act like jerks. It is worth pausing to consider the limitations of this solution.

6.8.1   Employment

One difficulty is that when people are paid regardless of their employment status, there is less motivation to work. In response to this there are two main defences. First, there are already people called volunteers, who by definition do not get paid to perform the work they do.

Of course, people may not be motivated enough to perform certain necessary jobs. There are two alternatives: either automate the job, or pay people more to perform jobs that they don't want to do.

The 'stabilisation solution' presented here creates a different economic environment, and businesses will need to adapt to it. One difficulty is that it is impossible to predict which jobs will require more motivation than others.

6.8.2   Education

As previously mentioned, the main argument against paying people welfare is that there is then no motivation to 'work'. However, due to specialisation and business efficiency, we do not need everyone to work to provide the products we need, or (for the most part) to provide the products we want. There are good psychological reasons to "work" and be involved in a community. However this does not necessarily require earning a wage from work, it can simply be to volunteer in a community. Volunteering is more likely to occur if people have the resources to survive and know that their future is secure.

The process of stabilisation results all Government expenses being balanced by the direct taxation of money, eventually. Thus, it should be possible to expand the education system in any country, implementing this stabilisation method so as to retrain anyone who does not have a job.

Education is closely linked to jobs. If people are not going to work for profit-making enterprises, many can work for non-profit organisations for the betterment of the world. The best place for people who don't have anything to do is, arguably, the education system. If nothing else, it will encourage people to socialise and to learn something new.

There are at least three types of work that can be expanded indefinitely:

- research
- entertainment
- exploration.

Universities and research institutes are the primary performers of 'academic' research. Research has many benefits, including the discovery of new possibilities and the solving of society's problems. Grants could be established to assist talented people in creating new products. A research project could then be approved for funding through the education system.

Entertainment comes in many forms—live performances, music, dance, television, movies, computer games, and more. Everyone needs a break at times to enjoy themselves. Also, entertainment can be useful in providing common ground, linking the diverse peoples of this world. Sharing inspiration, humour and the human experience through the arts helps us to relate to one another.

Our world (Earth) is a big place, and space is even bigger. Exploring our world takes time and expertise. Such exploration offers (among other things) the possibility of a back-up plan, in the form of additional resources and alternative places to live.

While much of this 'work' may not be considered 'profitable', the benefits are obvious. If benefit becomes the test for receiving funding, many problems will be able to be addressed.

6.8.3   Inflation and deflation

If people are paid regardless of their employment status, it has been demonstrated that Producers can be encouraged to reduce prices as their costs are reduced. While it may be theoretically possible to reduce prices to zero by iteratively reducing wages and prices, this is not likely to happen, as doing so would remove much of the motivation to have profit-making businesses. As mentioned in the previous section, people may still need to be motivated (paid) to do particular jobs. If these jobs were an inherent part of a production process, deflation would not be able to reduce their wages to zero. In theory, if Producers are willing to accept lower profits, prices might continue to fall; however, when resources become limited, prices could rise. The good news is that as a general rule we know how to reduce prices: make more product or find more resources.

Inflation may still occur for particular products (the main one I can think of is housing). Owners will always be reluctant to sell products that are linked to a legacy of transactions for a loss. To avoid this problem, the Government will need to purchase any 'overpriced' product and allow it to be sold at a loss. That way the losses would be made by the entity in the system that can produce money without going into debt, i.e. the Government.

6.8.4   International Stabilisation

If individual countries enact their own management strategies (taxation and stabilisation payments) separately, there is still the possibility of currency collapses occurring. Currency collapse can occur when a country does not have a balanced trade portfolio. If a country consumes more than it produces, its currency can devalue.

There are two possible solutions for this situation. First, attempt to ensure that all countries can balance their trade portfolios. Each country has its own products, resources, requirements and limitations, and thus a unique set of import needs. With over 200 countries, thousands of products, and billions of people, this is a complicated and potentially impossible problem to solve.

A second strategy would be to use a single currency worldwide. Individual countries would then have less to worry about regarding trade deficits and exchange rates. A central authority would be required to implement the monetary distribution to stabilise the entire world economy and to perform monetary taxation worldwide. This is one of my wilder ideas, but it should work. Surprisingly, there are other researchers who have discussed such a solution for slightly different reason including Rogoff [154], Arestis et al. [155], Moore [156], Sajnoski and Madzova [157], and Haran [158].

There would be issues initially, due to differences in living standards between countries. However, with stabilisation and supercharging enacted worldwide, the differences in living standards could be normalised within a few decades. Most issues would be able to be resolved by appropriately funding projects to provide water, power, education and other infrastructure wherever required. Stabilisation gives governments the ability to operate without huge concerns about limited money.

Other benefits from this would be that Refugees would also be able to be paid a basic income. There are currently around 80 million refugees worldwide and with a say $10,000 basic income, these people would be worth $800 Billion for their origin countries. Hopefully, this would provide some incentive to repatriate people and have ensure that governments actually value their people.

6.8.5   Drugs and criminal organisations

Even if the stabilisation can be implemented, people will still be people. They will still want to relax and enjoy themselves, and (unfortunately) many will continue to do so to excess. Drugs will still be a problem, and may become more of a problem if the economy is stabilised, because more people will be able to afford drugs. In response, criminal organisations will likely keep supplying the demand.

6.9   Non-zero-sum Economics

Non-zero-sum Economics confers 'non-economic' benefits that can be shared by everyone in the economy. Thus, situations can be created where everyone wins—not just rich people, and not just workers.

Some examples of non-zero-sum activities include:

- learning
- research
- entertainment
- exploration
- production.

6.9.1   Knowledge

It is possible for everyone to benefit from the knowledge of previous generations and to contribute new ideas in areas such as history, art, culture, science, mathematics and engineering. In theory, it is possible for everyone to write a book or to complete a PhD thesis, to expand knowledge or to provide entertainment for others.

6.9.2   Research

Research can also be undertaken by everyone: reading reports of previous studies, performing experiments and collecting data.

6.9.3   Entertainment

Entertainment can now be found in many different forms: live musical and theatrical performances, movies, TV shows, Web shows, and written forms of entertainment (such as books, novels or comics). All of these activities can be performed by individuals at minimal cost to others.

6.9.4   Exploration

Everyone can increase their awareness of new places. Exploration makes possible the discovery of new resources and of new areas that can be colonised.

6.9.5   Production

It is possible for everyone to make, build or grow 'something'. Unfortunately, not everyone can make a profit from what they produce, at least not at the same time.

6.10 Pro-Con analysis of stabilisation

One of the disadvantages people have suggested with the stabilisation design is that there will be less motivation to work. We can further examine the benefits and disadvantages of stabilising economies in the Pro-Con table below.

Table 25 Pro-Con for Stabilisation

Pro Stabilisation	Con Stabilisation
Eliminate business cycles	
Stabilised pricing – Minimal inflation	
Eliminate poverty	
Eliminate poverty related crime	
Reduced stress as it would be less difficult for people to maintain their lifestyles	
Health benefits from reduced stress	
Government focus on solving problems rather than managing a budget	
Fully funded Police and emergency services	
Fully funded healthcare services	
Better cooperation between countries	
Maximised employment	
More people will be able to volunteer	People may be less motivated to work

Clearly, there are more positives than negatives here. In addition, the negatives still has some direct opposition from the explanations presented.

6.11 Summary

This chapter has presented a method for stabilising an entire economy through money generation, distribution and taxation. From the analyses of Zero-sum Economics Models, it has been demonstrated that this strategy can both solve poverty and minimise financial crises. It has been further demonstrated that mechanisms can be employed to create a situation that maximises production and allows price deflation to occur in an economy.

While these models are still only theoretical, they do give hope that the issues of poverty and financial crises can be addressed in the real world.

7 Summing up: Fixing economics

From the analysis demonstrated in the previous chapters, I have drawn a few conclusion about how economies operate.

This section is new in this edition. As I made a few realisations from writing and attempting to explain the first edition that I decided to add this new part in to go over some of them.

7.1 Supply vs Demand

One of the limitations with current economic theory is that it does not explain where demand comes from. Given the example I developed in chapter 4 to explain how the distribution of money can be used to explain demand. This combined with how profit changes the distribution of money demonstrates a feedback loop that occurs when money is in integral part of an economy. This feedback loop causes money to be reallocated towards people who are already rich, which is exactly what we see in the real world.

These effects when combined produce a reinforcing cycle. The more money you have the more wealth that can be accumulated. When the wealth is in the form of assets such as other businesses this allows more cash to be accumulated, reinforcing the cycle. This experiment demonstrates that the distribution of money and zero sum effects from profit are consistent with the "Marshallian Theory of Supply and Demand" discussed in Neoclassical Economics 2.2.

Furthermore, it is possible to explain various other of the Supply vs Demand phenomena such as "Consumer Surplus".

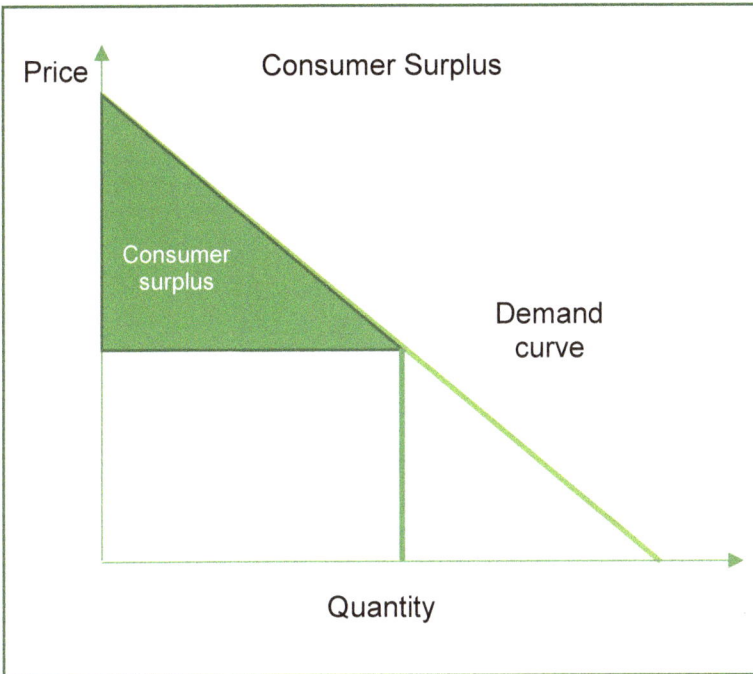

Figure 105: Consumer surplus

Consumer surplus is effectively the amount of money left over in an economy after products have been purchased.

From chapter 4.6, demand can be described using the distribution of money. So if we create a cash distribution as shown below.

Table 26: Cash distribution

Cash resources	$5k	$10k	$15k	$20k	$25k
%Population	20	20	20	20	20
Total % Population	100	80	60	40	20

A supply-versus-demand graph can be mapped from this data by graphing the total number of Consumers have a given level of resources or more.

251

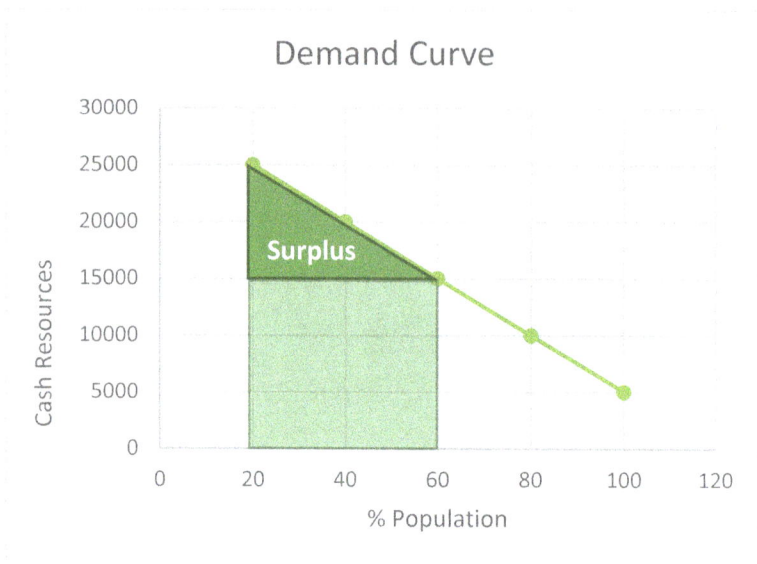

Figure 106: Demand curve

For a given price (for example the cost of living) the Surplus can be traced back through the distribution to the population that have the surplus. These people are the ones who have the most resources, i.e. rich people. Conversely by looking at the population that cannot afford "the cost of living" are the people who become poor.

7.2   Net Money Flow

One of the biggest flaws in current economic theory is about money. Current economic theory many economists interpret that money is not important and an economy should be able to operate without money.

Economics has established that money flows in the opposite direction to products. We also know that Consumers "consume" many products such as food, fuel etc. So as a result, we know that there is a net flow of products to Consumers.

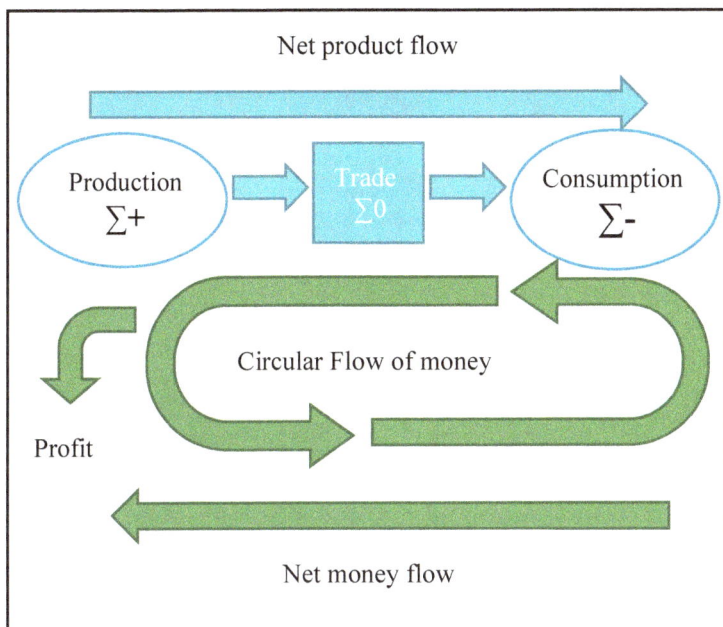

Figure 107: Net Product flow vs net Money flow

From the flow of money being in the opposite to the flow of products, if there is a net flow of money to Producers. As producers make a profit, they collect more money, which leaves less money in circulation. Invariably this leads to a recession, where less money is spent and values, especially of businesses, shares and regularly other assets decrease. This experiment demonstrates that the distribution of money and zero sum effects from profit cause.

Many economists do not seem to like the idea that money itself causes these problems. I suspect that they view money as less important than value in an economy. As such, this tends to lead them to dismiss the analysis of the money cycle in determining the causes of many of the problems with economics.

The US government shutdown in January 2019 showed that when people stopped being paid, they stopped working. When those people stopped being paid they stopped being able to afford rent and food. This in turn has catastrophic effects downstream in the economy.

It is possible to examine how the economy works by examining how products flow, but in a practical sense, in the real world: money is essential. When the money stops moving the economy stops moving.

8   Conclusions

Zero-sum Economic Theory is still very much in its infancy. Much work remains in terms of refining the existing components and shedding light on additional economic phenomena. The main goal of my research to this point has been to introduce the theory and assess it against existing theory and data. I hope that the research presented here is at least enough to generate some interest from academia and the general public.

In general terms, from the data modelling demonstrated in the previous chapters, it is possible to conclude that Zero-sum Economic Theory is consistent with much of the existing economic theory. I have demonstrated that Zero-sum Models can be used to examine the performance of an economy and make some accurate predictions.

This chapter presents some conclusions from my analysis.

8.1   Zero-sum Economics

From the arguments, evidence and experiments presented in the previous chapters, it can be concluded that many aspects of economies operate as zero-sum systems. This restricts the behaviour of economies, and specifically shows that where one entity or group of entities makes a profit, there must be a corresponding loss in another entity in the economy, even if there is no direct relationship between the entities.

This theory is directly in conflict with several current economic theories, including:

- the Velocity of Money Theory
- the Value of Money Theory
- the Trickle-down Theory
- the theory that money is exogenous to the economy.

For the most part, it is consistent with other mainstream economic theories. Theory and phenomena with which it is consistent include:

- the Phillips curve
- inflation (demand pull and cost push)
- unemployment
- most microeconomic theory.

Furthermore, Zero-sum Economic Modelling can explain several phenomena that are not well explained by current economic theory, including a derivation of inflation, taking into account the Phillips curve, business cycles, income distribution and the global labour market.

8.1.1   The Velocity of Money Theory

The Velocity of Money Theory suggests that everyone should be able to have enough money to buy everything they want. When there is less money, the money is supposed to move faster to allow access to money for everyone's needs. However, Zero-sum Theory shows that the *distribution* of money is very important in order for Consumers to be able to purchase the products they need. The speed at which the money is spent does not change the distribution of money, and thus will not meet the needs of all Consumers.

8.1.2   Value of Money Theory

A common practice in economics is to compare the prices of commodities at different dates. Due to inflation, the price of a product will typically increase over time. This has been thought to indicate the 'value' the same amount of money can have at different times, the assumption being that the money itself has increased or decreased in value to compensate for the change in a product's price. The Value of Money argument originated with the hyperinflation and currency dissolutions that occurred in Germany and Zimbabwe.

In Zero-sum Theory, the only real value of money is its face value. The value of money idea essentially becomes inverse inflation.

8.1.3   Trickle-down Theory

Money does not trickle down from wealthy people. Zero-sum Theory shows that, for the most part, money flows directly to Producers. However, for a business cycle to occur, money must be reinvested in Consumers for the economy to recover. A minimum amount of cash needs to be in Consumer hands for the economy to operate at all.

8.1.4   Money is exogenous to the economy

Exogenous means externally generated. This suggests that money is externally generated from the economy. This is not entirely true as banks generate money as part of creating loans.

This sometimes gives the impression that money is not important to the economy. Zero-sum Modelling shows that money is an inherent part of the economy. Its creation and supply is just as important as the internal operation of the economy.

The most important part of money is its distribution in the economy. The problem with zero sum systems is that when someone in the system makes a profit someone else must be making a loss. This is not to say that more money cannot be added to the economy, but it does mean that money is important to the internal operation of the economyThis leads to the profit making people in the economy absorbing any money that is added to the system.

8.2   Zero-sum Models

The Zero-sum Models are based on well-established models of the economy, systems analysis, and Control Theory. They demonstrate several phenomena observed in economics that are not well explained by mainstream economics, including:

- business cycles
- inflation
- wealth distribution
- global labour.

Conclusions

8.2.1   CP Model

The results of the Zero-sum CP Economic Model analysis show that the economic output of a profit-based system occurs in two stages. In the first stage, when Consumers have enough money to buy the Producers' products, both the Producers' and Consumers' incomes will be constant. However, if the Producers make a profit, the account balance of the Consumers will decrease linearly, until a critical point is reached at which not all of the Consumers will be able to afford everything they want, and there will be a reduction in spending. This will then reduce the Producers' income, leading to a general exponential decay in the entire system.

While this is the most basic model of an economy, it does not represent what actually occurs in the world. To achieve a more realistic model, the Zero-sum CP Economic Model incorporates a simple investment system. Once the model incorporates investment, it displays behaviour consistent with business cycles, which are an observed phenomenon in current economic theory, but which (according to many major economic textbooks) are not well understood.

The main reason for economic depressions or recessions is that Consumers run out of money and stop spending. Producers' profits are then reduced and they begin to lay off employees, resulting in an increase in unemployment. The economy only recovers when investments are made that go back to the Consumers, sufficient that the Consumers can afford to buy the Producers' products again.

There is a notable intermediate possibility referred to as a 'lock-in state', in which investment is enough to cover Consumer losses, but not enough to generate full productivity. In that case, there are no oscillations in the economy, but a significant proportion of the Consumers remain in distress. Models have shown Consumer distress to be present in anywhere between 10 and 80% of the population.

This demonstrates that the Zero-sum CP Model could be used as a basis for modelling economic phenomena. As this is the introduction of Zero-sum Economic Theory, focusing on four types of models, further research is required to take into account other concepts and to further extend and evaluate the Zero-sum Economic Theories. This model assumes that the production of food, water and shelter are included in the product purchased. This suggests that anyone who does not have the appropriate funding will be forced into either living off

257

the land at zero cost to Producers, or dying. Either way, they would no longer take part in the economy.

In summary, this research has demonstrated that (in theory) if money is fixed and finite, assets are transferred by zero-sum transactions, and the attempt of production companies to make a profit will cause any economy to become oscillatory.

The basis of Zero-sum Economics is that in a closed economic system with a fixed amount of cash, whenever a profit is made, it is balanced by an equal loss in another part of the system.

The solution to our economic problems is simple: *all Consumers need a constant input of funds in order to maintain a constant balance.*

8.2.2   CPG Model

The CPG Model shows that, even with Governments using income taxation and welfare, when Consumers are in distress, the system still results in behaviour consistent with business cycles.

8.2.3   Business cycles

An estimate of the frequency of business cycles can be calculated from (i) the profit Producers make and (ii) their investment rate. When this is symmetric, the frequency of business cycles is calculated at 2π years. It is noted that this estimate is based on a very simplistic model of investment, and that an improved investment model would allow more accurate predictions of economic performance.

8.2.4   Inflation

Analysis of the CP Model allows an equation for inflation to be derived that relates inflation to unemployment, consistent with the Phillips curve. This equation is also consistent with the current theories of inflation, including demand pull and cost push.

8.2.5   Wealth Distribution Model

The Wealth Distribution Model demonstrates that even when there are a set of Producers with a range of profit margins, the Producers with the highest profit margin tend to accumulate all of the money in the economy at the expense of everyone else.

8.2.6   Global Labour Model

The Global Labour Model demonstrates how cash flows to the Producers of the country with the lowest labour costs.

8.2.7   Real-world Data Model

The Zero-sum model can use data recorded from the real world (specifically, data for money supply, population and inflation). The outcomes generated are consistent with the data and can be used to determine the distress in an economy.

8.3   Zero-sum stabilisation

Zero-sum Theory has been shown in previous sections to be able to describe several phenomena that have not been well explained using existing economic theories. Zero-sum Theory can be extended to show how to stabilise an economy, and can explain why this theory actually works.

8.3.1   Stabilised CPG Model

The Stabilised CPG Model demonstrates that it is possible to stabilise an economy by releasing money into the economy (specifically, to its Consumers) and by taxing money to ensure that the total amount of money in the economy does not increase without bound.

8.3.2   Implementation of the CPG Model in the real world

The implementation of the stabilisation of an economy is shown here to be functionally quite simple: decommission physical currency, ensure that all the currency produced by a country is accessible in its banking system, and tax savings.

The main difficulty with implementing this strategy is people—more specifically, their unwillingness to have their savings taxed or to change banking regulations to support the strategy.

8.3.3   Worldwide implementation

One of the problems with the stabilisation solution when implemented on an individual countries basis is that there is still the possibility of an exchange rate failure. To solve this problem, a simple solution would be to have a single currency worldwide. This has the potential for eliminating poverty and economic instability worldwide, and is a good reason for having a unified world Government to help run the taxation and distribution of money.

While I am sure this would be fraught with diplomatic issues, it gives me a lot of hope that many of the conflicts in the world could be resolved. In the mathematical sense, "a solution exists". We just need to find a real-world method of implementing the solution.

8.3.4   Non-zero-sum Economics

In this research it has been demonstrated that many zero-sum systems exist inside an economy. Some of these systems are required by people for their survival and for the survival of our civilisation. However, there are several examples of zero-sum systems that provide a benefit to one group by disadvantaging another. If an internal system is shown to be a zero-sum system, there is no net benefit to the economy or civilisation as a whole. It will be up to Government policy to determine whether these systems are used, modified or replaced. Non-zero-sum systems are preferred, because everyone can benefit from their operation, and this allows everyone to be happy. Unfortunately, money in economics is a zero-sum system, which means we have a choice to make: do we keep this system that does not work properly or do we make the effort to change it?

It has been shown that happiness is related to wealth. Several studies [136–138] have shown that as wealth increases, people become happier, but only up to a point. These studies have also shown that once people have 'enough' money, further increases in wealth do not improve their happiness.

It is suggested in this research that other incentives exist that motivate people, but which are not directly economically justifiable. These incentives include the satisfaction of acquiring knowledge, of helping other people, and of helping the environment.

One goal of Governments should be to provide opportunities for accomplishing non-economic goals, especially if they believe that their citizens should be encouraged in 'the pursuit of happiness'.

This research has demonstrated that if Governments pay everyone enough to cover their living costs and some of their costs of social maintenance (transportation, power, etc.) and luxuries, whether they are employed or not, the cost of employing people will be significantly reduced. This could lead to deflation of prices and an increase in employment. It would also have the effect of changing the nature of the economy from a competitive system to one where cooperation is more rewarding. If Governments also recognise the benefits of people accomplishing non-economic goals, these other tasks can be performed as well as the economic tasks, and our entire civilisation will benefit and be happier.

8.4 Properties of Zero-sum Stabilisation

From analysing the properties of the Zero-sum CPG solution, it has been shown that the solution is inherently stable, once the payments to Consumers outweigh the profits made by Producers. The final amount of money in the economy would eventually stabilise out to a constant value, as opposed to the current economic situation, in which the amount of money in the economy increases exponentially.

By increasing payments to Consumers, so that an average living wage is received irrespective of the employment status of the Consumer, Producers would be enabled to reduce their expenses, make more profit, reduce prices and allow more Consumers to be employed.

Using this economic configuration, it would be possible to fund just about any activity desired. The major challenges in the world include environmental concerns, overpopulation, climate change and the expansion of humanity to other planets to avoid being wiped out by a planet-wide cataclysm.

It is important to remember is that ultimately money goes to people. It may be exchanged for goods or services, but a person always has the money. So, wherever the money is being spent, it is paying people to perform tasks. Hence, the Government should be able to spend money on any activity that accomplishes a task that is considered socially justified.

The main limitation to this design is that 'pumping' too much money into the system would require a higher taxation rate to ensure that inflation does not arise from a demand-pull situation. This problem will only be resolved with further research and experimentation.

8.5   Now what?

I'm the first to admit that this theory (Zero-sum Economics) is still a theory at this point, and it is quite possible (if not probable) that I have made mistakes. The good news is that it promises solutions to problems that existing economic theories have failed to solve. The theory indicates that the stabilisation strategy should work. Perhaps, I'm just being too optimistic. Further research is needed before implementation on a large scale. It looks like it will work, but to be sure, other people need to look at the work that has been done here.

This gets back to why I wrote this book. It doesn't hurt me to get the idea out. It definitely needs to be examined and investigated further. I encourage others to take this work and expand on it. Every step made to fix problems identified in the theory could take us closer to a stable economy and perhaps a stable world.

8.5.1   Visions of the future

Ultimately the question is: what do we want as a society? If we have the money problem addressed, what will we do with ourselves to keep everyone employed? I made a quick list of things we might or might not want in a future society. Have a quick look and decide which ones you want and which ones you don't.

Features of the future?	Funding Strategy
Nuclear explosions—radiation, etc.	Nuclear Weapons
'Zombies' (mutants)	Nuclear Weapons – Biological warfare
Roving bands of cannibalistic bandits	Nuclear Weapons – Biological warfare
Slums	Poverty
Disease	Medical research
People	Avoid Nuclear Weapons – Biological warfare Fund social civil developments
Cities	or Suburbs
Cars	Flying cars, Boats, Bicycles
Trees	Fund Reforestation
Animals	Fund Biodiversity programs
Drinkable water	Water Conservation
Space ships / space exploration	Space Exploration
Robots	Research
Exercise	Health
Boredom	Entertainment – Education
Overweight people	Health

Do we want these things in our future or not? We can choose what we want and what we don't want. Feel free to create your own list of ins and outs and figure out what is required to create the things you want and what is required to avoid the things you don't want. These lists can become the 'To do lists' for our society, especially if we find we share common aspirations.

8.6   Final thoughts

While I may be critical of economic theory and have shown that businesses making a profit cause problems, I am not intending to be critical of businesses or economists. For the most part, business people and economists undertake their work with good intentions to benefit everyone. Unfortunately, however, economic problems still occur. As they say, the road to hell is paved with good intentions. What I am attempting to do is to highlight the limitations of current economic practices that are causing problems, and to show how they can be resolved. What I am finding through this research is that it is not enough to have good intentions. People actually need to understand the systems they are dealing with in order to take the appropriate actions that will accomplish what people want and need to accomplish.

From the analysis undertaken here with Zero-sum Economics, we can see that there are many undesirable features in standard economic systems: uneven wealth distribution, inflation, business cycles. The analysis has shown that economics systems as they exist today do not reflect the values of the community. They will never reflect those values while the only reason we perform certain tasks is to 'make money'.

If economics is considered an active process, the question becomes: what do we want the economy to do? Do we want the world to be considered solely in economic terms? Or is economics another tool we can use to develop a society that we all want to live in. From the analysis of these economics concepts, we can see that the products that survive are the ones people buy; thus, if we want to have particular values in our world, those values will need to have money spent on them. This is achievable—by taking money from where it is not needed and putting it where 'we', as a society, want it. As a general rule, it is never a bad thing in economics to spend money. A better rule is to spend it on something we care about.

Zero-sum Economics is a new idea that has the potential to change the way the economy works. Unfortunately, this means we will need to change a few laws and taxes. The only way this will occur is if people are motivated enough to test the theory further and ultimately put it into practice. We have a choice to either stick with the same old practices that cause problems, or to take a chance and do something different. Ultimately, it's up to you.

Conclusions

So what do you want to do?

9 Bibliography

[1]   W. Collins, "Zero Sum Game," *Collins English Dictionary - Complete & Unabridged 2012 Digital Edition.* HarperCollins, 2012. [Online]. Available: http://www.dictionary.com/browse/zero-sum-game

[2]   C. Sagan and A. Druyan, *Pale Blue Dot: A Vision of the Human Future in Space.* Random House LLC, 2011.

[3]   C. Menger, *Principles of Economics.* Ludwig von Mises Institute, 1871.

[4]   N. G. Mankiw, *Principles of Macroeconomics : Australian Edition, 6th edn.* Cengage Learning, 2014.

[5]   A. W. Phillips, "The relation between unemployment and the rate of change of money wage rates in the United Kingdom, 1861–1957," *economica*, vol. 25, no. 100, pp. 283–299, 1958.

[6]   R. G. King and M. W. Watson, "The post-war US Phillips curve: a revisionist econometric history," in *Carnegie-Rochester Conference Series on Public Policy*, 1994, vol. 41, pp. 157–219.

[7]   G. A. Akerlof, W. T. Dickens, G. L. Perry, T. F. Bewley, and A. S. Blinder, "Near-rational wage and price setting and the long-run Phillips curve," *Brook. Pap. Econ. Act.*, vol. 2000, no. 1, pp. 1–60, 2000.

[8]   L. Ball and R. Moffitt, "Productivity growth and the Phillips curve," National Bureau of Economic Research, 2001.

[9]   T. Cogley and A. M. Sbordone, "Trend inflation, indexation, and inflation persistence in the New Keynesian Phillips curve," *Am. Econ. Rev.*, vol. 98, no. 5, pp. 2101–2126, 2008.

[10]   O. Coibion and Y. Gorodnichenko, "Is the Phillips curve alive and well after all? Inflation expectations and the missing disinflation," *Am. Econ. J. Macroecon.*, vol. 7, no. 1, pp. 197–232, 2015.

[11]   L. Benati, "The long-run Phillips curve: A structural VAR investigation," *J. Monet. Econ.*, vol. 76, pp. 15–28, 2015.

Bibliography

[12] O. Coibion, Y. Gorodnichenko, and R. Kamdar, "The Formation of Expectations, Inflation and the Phillips Curve," National Bureau of Economic Research, 2017.

[13] J. Davies, A. Koutsoukis, R. Lluberas, A. Shorrocks, and M. Stierli, "Global Wealth Report 2015," *Credit Suisse AG Zurich*, 2015.

[14] M. J. Flannery, S. H. Kwan, and M. Nimalendran, "The 2007–2009 financial crisis and bank opaqueness," *J. Financ. Intermediation*, vol. 22, no. 1, pp. 55–84, 2013.

[15] S. Dees, M. H. Pesaran, L. V. Smith, and R. P. Smith, "Identification of new Keynesian Phillips curves from a global perspective," *J. Money Credit Bank.*, vol. 41, no. 7, pp. 1481–1502, 2009.

[16] K. Knight, "AC Pigou's The Theory of Unemployment and its Corrigenda: The Letters of Maurice Allen, Arthur L. Bowley, Richard Kahn and Dennis Robertson," *BOOK OF*, p. 117, 2014.

[17] E. Yardeni and D. Johnson, "US Economic Indicators: Corporate Profits in GDP." Feb. 19, 2016.

[18] R. M. Goodwin, "A growth cycle," *Social. Capital. Econ. Growth*, vol. 5458, 1967.

[19] T. Piketty, "Capital in the 21st Century," *Camb. MA Belknap Press Harv. Univ.*, 2014.

[20] P. M. Romer, "Increasing returns and long-run growth," *J. Polit. Econ.*, pp. 1002–1037, 1986.

[21] O. Galor and J. Zeira, "Income distribution and macroeconomics," *Rev. Econ. Stud.*, vol. 60, no. 1, pp. 35–52, 1993.

[22] N. G. Mankiw, "Real business cycles: A new Keynesian perspective," *J. Econ. Perspect.*, vol. 3, no. 3 (Summer, 1989), pp. 79–90, 1989.

[23] A. Smith, *An Inquiry into the Nature and Causes of the Wealth of Nations*. London: W. Strahan: na, 1776.

[24] L. Walras, *Elements of Pure Economics*. London, UK: Routledge, 2013.

[25] K. Marx, *"Das Kapital" und Vorarbeiten: Ökonomische Manuskripte:*, vol. 1. Berlin: Akademie Verlag, 1887.

[26] J. A. Schumpeter, *Capitalism, Socialism and Democracy*. London, UK: Routledge, 2013.

[27] K. Verdery, *What Was Socialism, and What Comes Next?* Princeton: Princeton University Press, 1996.

[28] V. Bunce, *Subversive Institutions: the Design and the Destruction of Socialism and the State*. Cambridge University Press, 1999.

[29] F. A. Hayek, *The fatal conceit: The errors of socialism*, vol. 1. University of Chicago Press, 2011.

[30] J. M. Keynes, *The General Theory of Employment, Interest, and Money*, 7th edn. Palgrave Macmillan, 1936.

[31] A. Marshall, *Principles of Economics*. Digireads. com Publishing, 1890.

[32] J. G. Nellis and D. Parker, *Principles of Macroeconomics*. Pearson Education, 2004.

[33] A. B. Abel, B. S. Bernanke, and D. Croushore, *Macroeconomics 6th edn*. Boston: Pearson Education, 2008.

[34] K. Case, R. Fair, and S. Oster, *Principles of Economics, 10th Edn*. Prentice Hall Business Publishing, 2010.

[35] D. Romer, *Advanced Macroeconomics*, 4th edn. New York: McGraw-Hill, 2012.

[36] R. G. Hubbard, A. P. O'Brien, and M. Rafferty, *Macroeconomics*. Boston, MA: Prentice Hall, 2012.

[37] C. R. McConnell, S. L. Brue, and S. M. Flynn, *Macroeconomics: Principles, Problems, & Policies*. New York: McGraw-Hill Education, 2012. [Online]. Available: http://books.google.com.au/books?id=62gTngEACAAJ

[38] M. Parkin, *Macroeconomics*, 10th edn. Boston, MA: Addison Wesley, 2012.

[39]   D. Hume, *A Treatise of Human Nature... Reprinted from the original edition, in three volumes and edited, with an analytical index, by LA Selby-Bigge*. Clarendon Press, 1738.

[40]   D. Ricardo, *On the Principles of Political Economy and Taxation*. London: John Murray, 1817.

[41]   J. S. Mill, *Principles of Political Economy with some of their Applications to Social Philosophy*. London, UK: Longmans, Green and Co., 1848.

[42]   J. S. Mill, *On liberty*. London UK: Longmans, Green, Reader, and Dyer, 1859.

[43]   J. S. Mill, *Utilitarianism. Collected Works of John Stuart Mill, Vol. 10 Essays on Ethics, Religion, and Society*. Reprinted Toronto: University of Toronto Press., 1969, 1863.

[44]   K. Menger, "On the origin of money," *Econ. J.*, vol. 2, no. 6, pp. 239–255, 1892.

[45]   L. Walras, *Études d'économie politique appliquée:Théorie de la production de la richesse sociale*. Lausanne: F. Rouge, 1898.

[46]   L. Walras, *Études d'économie sociale: Théorie de la répartition de la richesse sociale.* Lausanne: F. rouge, 1896.

[47]   L. Walras, *Éléments d'économie politique pure; ou, Théorie de la richesse sociale*. F. Rouge, 1896.

[48]   A. C. Pigou, "The value of money," *Q. J. Econ.*, vol. 32, no. 1, pp. 38–65, 1917.

[49]   I. Fisher, *The Theory of Interest*. New York: The Macmillan Company, 1930.

[50]   J. Tobin, "A general equilibrium approach to monetary theory," *J. Money Credit Bank.*, vol. 1, no. 1, pp. 15–29, 1969.

[51]   W. J. Baumol, "The Transactions Demand for Cash: An Inventory Theoretic Approach," *Q. J. Econ.*, pp. 545–556, 1952.

[52]   M. Friedman, "The Demand for Money: Some Theoretical and Empirical Results," *J. Polit. Econ.*, vol. 67, no. 4, pp. 327–351, 1959.

[53]   E. R. Weintraub, *How Economics Became A Mathematical Science.* Durham and London: Duke University Press, 2002.

[54]   P. Mattick, "Economics, politics, and the age of inflation," *Int. J. Polit.*, vol. 8, no. 3, pp. i–143, 1978.

[55]   D. Gordon, *An Introduction to Economic Reasoning.* Auburn, AL: Ludwig von Mises Institute, 2000.

[56]   S. Keen, "Debunking macroeconomics," *Econ. Anal. Policy*, vol. 41, no. 3, pp. 147–167, 2011.

[57]   J. E. Stiglitz, "Information and the Change in the Paradigm in Economics," *Am. Econ. Rev.*, vol. 92, no. 3, pp. 460–501, 2002.

[58]   S. Bowles, "Post-Marxian economics: labour, learning and history," *Soc. Sci. Inf. SAGE Lond. Beverly Hills New Delhi*, vol. 24, no. 3, pp. 507–528, 1985.

[59]   J. Stiglitz, "Post Walrasian and post Marxian economics," *J. Econ. Perspect.*, vol. 7, no. 1, pp. 109–114, 1993.

[60]   T. Jefferson and J. E. King, "' Never Intended to be a Theory Of Everything': Domestic labor in Neoclassical and Marxian Economics," *Fem. Econ.*, vol. 7, no. 3, pp. 71–101, 2001.

[61]   R. Bellofiore and N. Taylor, "'The Constitution of Capital' Essays on Volume 1 of Marx's Capital," *R Bellofiore N Taylor Eds*, vol. 85, p. 80, 2003.

[62]   V. Nee, "A theory of market transition: From redistribution to markets in state socialism," *Am. Sociol. Rev.*, pp. 663–681, 1989.

[63]   P. H. Rubin, "Folk economics," *South. Econ. J.*, pp. 157–171, 2003.

[64]   R. S. Pindyck and D. Rubinfeld, *Microeconomics 6th edn.* Upper Saddle River, NJ: Pearson Prentice Hall, 2009.

[65]   R. Owen, *Observations on the Effect of the Manufacturing System: With Hints for the Improvement of Those Parts of it which are Most Injurious*

to Health and Morals... London: Longman, Hurst, Rees, Orme, and Brown, 1817.

[66]   R. Owen, "Report to the Committee of the Association for the Relief of the Manufacturing and Labouring Poor," *Life Robert Owen Bd IA Lond. Effingham Wilson*, pp. 53–64, 1817.

[67]   J. C. L. Sismondi, *Nouveaux Principes d'économie Politique, ou de la Richesse dans ses Rapports avec la Population.* Paris: Delaunay, 1827.

[68]   J. A. Schumpeter, *The Theory of Economic Development: An Inquiry into Profits, Capital, Credit, Interest, and the Business Cycle*, vol. 55 of Galaxy book. Transaction Publishers, 1934.

[69]   J. A. Schumpeter, *Business Cycles*, vol. 1. New York: McGraw-Hill, 1939.

[70]   R. Benkemoune, "Charles Dunoyer and the Emergence of the Idea of an Economic Cycle," *Hist. Polit. Econ.*, vol. 41, no. 2, pp. 271–295, 2009.

[71]   C. Cornélissen and J. K. Rodbertus, *Traité Général de Science Economique.* Marcel Giard, 1926.

[72]   H. George and J. L. Busey, *Progress and Poverty.* JM Dent, 1930.

[73]   M. Iacoviello, "Financial business cycles," *Rev. Econ. Dyn.*, vol. 18, no. 1, pp. 140–163, 2015.

[74]   F. Smets and R. Wouters, "Shocks and frictions in US business cycles: A Bayesian DSGE approach," *Am. Econ. Rev.*, vol. 97, no. 3, pp. 586–606, 2007.

[75]   R. G. King and S. T. Rebelo, "Resuscitating real business cycles," *Handb. Macroecon.*, vol. 1, pp. 927–1007, 1999.

[76]   P. A. Samuelson and R. M. Solow, "Analytical aspects of anti-inflation policy," *Am. Econ. Rev.*, pp. 177–194, 1960.

[77]   T. D. Willett and L. O. Laney, "Monetarism, budget deficits, and wage push inflation: The cases of Italy and the UK," *PSL Q. Rev.*, vol. 31, no. 127, 2014.

Bibliography

[78]   A. Kibritçioğlu, "Causes of inflation in Turkey: A literature survey with special reference to theories of inflation," *Econ. Bull.*, vol. 28, no. 21, p. A1, 2001.

[79]   R. Chand, "Understanding the nature and causes of food inflation," *Econ. Polit. Wkly.*, vol. 45, no. 9, pp. 10–13, 2010.

[80]   J. Ha, K. Fan, and C. Shu, "The causes of inflation and deflation in Mainland China," *Hong Kong Monet. Auth. Q. Bull.*, pp. 23–31, Sep. 2003.

[81]   A. J. Khan, M. Akram, S. Sajjad, and H. Sajjad, "Trends and Causes of Inflation: Reflections from Pakistan," *Bus. Manag. Rev.*, vol. 1, no. 3, pp. 58–69, 2011.

[82]   A. B. Mustapha and M. A. Khalid, "The Effects of Chronic Inflation on Resource Allocation: towards understanding non-neutrality of monetary inflation," *J. Econ. Sustain. Dev.*, vol. 4, no. 20, pp. 148–152, 2013.

[83]   S. K. Harvey and M. J. Cushing, "Separating Monetary and Structural Causes of Inflation," *J. Finance Econ.*, vol. 2, no. 3, pp. 16–30, 2014.

[84]   J. B. Davies, A. Shorrocks, S. Sandstrom, and E. N. Wolff, *The World Distribution of Household Wealth*. Center for Global, International and Regional Studies, 2007. [Online]. Available: escholarship.org/uc/item/3jv048hx

[85]   C. Lakner and B. Milanovic, *Global Income Distribution: From the Fall of the Berlin Wall to the Great Recession Policy Research Working Paper No. 6719*. Washington, DC: The World Bank, 2013. [Online]. Available: openknowledge.worldbank.org/handle/10986/16935

[86]   C. D. Carroll, J. Slacalek, and K. Tokuoka, "The Distribution of Wealth and the Mpc: Implications of New European Data," *Am. Econ. Rev.*, vol. 104, no. 5, pp. 107–111, 2014.

[87]   G. Corneo and O. Jeanne, "Status, the Distribution of Wealth, and Growth," *Scand. J. Econ.*, vol. 103, no. 2, pp. 283–293, 2001.

[88]   I. N. Hoch and S. Mohan-Neill, "Can Financial Literacy Help Alleviate Wealth and Income Inequality in the US?," *Acad. Mark. Stud.*, vol. 18, p. 31, 2013.

Bibliography

[89]   N. A. A. Razak, "Income Inequality and Economic Growth," PhD
         Dissertation, Louisiana State University, 2006. [Online]. Available:
         http://www.google.com.au/url?sa=t&rct=j&q=&esrc=s&source=web&cd
         =3&cad=rja&uact=8&ved=0CC4QFjAC&url=http%3A%2F%2Fetd.lsu.
         edu%2Fdocs%2Favailable%2Fetd-10272006-
         144739%2Funrestricted%2FAbdul_Razak_dis.pdf&ei=0o3NVJH_FYS7
         mQW52YLoCA&usg=AFQjCNEq1AP9N9cYPqdRovtz_zRT2c0r4w&b
         vm=bv.85076809,d.dGY

[90]   T. Ferguson and P. Temin, "Made in Germany: the German currency
         crisis of July 1931," in *research in Economic History*, Emerald Group
         Publishing Limited, 2003.

[91]   C. Dzingirai and B. Katuka, "Determinants of bank failures in multiple-
         currency regime in Zimbabwe (2009–2012)," *Int. J. Econ. Finance*, vol.
         6, no. 8, 2014.

[92]   A. S. Blinder, "Fear of offshoring," *Wash. Post*, p. A06, 2004.

[93]   D. L. Levy, "Offshoring in the new global political economy," *J. Manag.
         Stud.*, vol. 42, no. 3, pp. 685–693, 2005.

[94]   R. Baldwin, "Globalisation: the great unbundling (s)," *Econ. Counc.
         Finl.*, vol. 20, no. 2006, pp. 5–47, 2006.

[95]   W. Aspray, F. Mayadas, and M. Y. Vardi, *Globalization and Offshoring
         of Software Report of the ACM Job Migration Task Force, Association
         for Computing Machinery*. Report of the ACM Job Migration Task
         Force, Association for Computing Machinery, 2006.

[96]   R. Liu and D. Trefler, "A Sorted Tale of Globalization: White Collar
         Jobs and the Rise of Service Offshoring Working Paper No. 17559,"
         National Bureau of Economic Research, 2011.

[97]   M. Friedman, "The Counter-Revolution in Monetary Theory," in
         Explorations in Economic Liberalism, Springer, 1996, pp. 3–21.

[98]   A. Jones, "Inflation under the roman empire," *Econ. Hist. Rev.*, vol. 5,
         no. 3, pp. 293–318, 1953.

[99]   A. Ravetz, "The fourth-century inflation and Romano-British coin finds,"
         Numis. Chron. J. R. Numis. Soc., vol. 4, pp. 201–231, 1964.

Bibliography

[100] J. E. Lendon, "The face on the coins and inflation in Roman Egypt,"
Klio, vol. 72, no. 72, pp. 106–134, 1990.

[101] C. Katsari and others, *The concept of Inflation in the Roman Empire.*
University of Washington, 2002.

[102] P. Bernholz, *Monetary regimes and inflation: History, economic and
political relationships.* Edward Elgar Publishing, 2015.

[103] Brian Romanchuk, "Primer: Endogenous Versus Exogenous Money,"
Bond Economics, Sep. 25, 2016.
http://www.bondeconomics.com/2016/09/primer-endogenous-versus-
exogenous-money.html (accessed Oct. 30, 2021).

[104] Michael McLeay, Amar Radia, and Ryland Thomas, "Money creation in
the modern economy." Bank of England, 2014. [Online]. Available:
https://www.bankofengland.co.uk/-/media/boe/files/quarterly-
bulletin/2014/money-creation-in-the-modern-
economy.pdf?la=en&hash=9A8788FD44A62D8BB927123544205CE47
6E01654

[105] Christopher Kent, "How Is Money 'Created'?," *Reserve Bank of
Australia*, Sep. 19, 2018. https://www.rba.gov.au/speeches/2018/sp-ag-
2018-09-19.html

[106] Ben Dyson, Graham Hodgson, and Frank van Lerven, *SOVEREIGN
MONEY An Introduction.* Positive Money, 2016. [Online]. Available:
https://positivemoney.org/wp-content/uploads/2016/12/SovereignMoney-
AnIntroduction-20161214.pdf

[107] G. Flannigan, A. Staib, and others, "The Growing demand for cash,"
RBA Bull. Sept., pp. 63–74, 2017.

[108] G. Flannigan and S. Parsons, "High-denomination banknotes in
circulation: A cross-country analysis," *RBA Bull. March Viewed*, vol. 20,
2018, [Online]. Available:
https://www.rba.gov.au/publications/bulletin/2018/mar/high-
denomination-banknotes-in-circulation-a-cross-country-analysis.html

[109] S. Black, J. Kirkwood, T. Williams, and A. Rai, "A History of A
ustralian Corporate Bonds," *Aust. Econ. Hist. Rev.*, vol. 53, no. 3, pp.
292–317, 2013.

[110] Michele Bullock, "The Evolution of Household Sector Risks," presented at the Ai Group 2018, Albury, Sep. 10, 2018. [Online]. Available: https://www.rba.gov.au/speeches/2018/sp-ag-2018-09-10.html

[111] E. Doherty, B. Jackman, and E. Perry, "Money in the Australian Economy," *Reserve Bank Aust. Bull. Sept.*, 2018.

[112] J. Gustavsson and U. Sonesson, *Global food losses and food waste: FAO; 2011*. 2015.

[113] J. M. Sánchez and E. Yurdagul, "Why are corporations holding so much cash?," *Reg. Econ.*, vol. 21, no. 1, pp. 4–8, 2013.

[114] R. Rubin, "US companies are stashing $2.1 trillion overseas to avoid taxes," *Bloomberg*, Mar. 04, 2015. [Online]. Available: www. bloomberg. com/news/articles/2015-03-04/us-companies-are-stashing-2-1-trillionoverseas-to-avoid-taxes

[115] M. Zenner, E. Junek, and R. Chivukula, "Are US Companies Really Holding That Much Cash—And If So, Why?," *J. Appl. Corp. Finance*, vol. 28, no. 1, pp. 95–103, 2016.

[116] M. Fabrizi, E. Ipino, M. Magnan, and A. Parbonetti, "Do Foreign Cash Holdings Generate Uncertainty for Market Participants?," CIRANO, Montréal, Québec, 2016.

[117] J. Harford, C. Wang, and K. Zhang, "Foreign Cash: Taxes, Internal Capital Markets, and Agency Problems," *Rev. Financ. Stud.*, vol. 30, no. 5, pp. 1490–1538, 2017.

[118] S. K. Laplante and W. L. Nesbitt, "The relation among trapped cash, permanently reinvested earnings, and foreign cash," *J. Corp. Finance*, vol. 44, pp. 126–148, 2017.

[119] J. Wiseman, *SAS Survival Guide*. Glasgow, UK: HarperCollins, 2004.

[120] J. Wiseman, *SAS Survival Handbook: How to Survive in the Wild in Any Climate, on Land or at Sea*. Glasgow, UK: Harper Collins, 2004.

[121] P. D. Allison, *Survival Analysis Using Sas: A Practical Guide*. Sas Institute, 2010.

Bibliography

[122] E. Tiftik, M. Khadija, H. Tran, and S. Gibbs, "EM Debt Monitor MARCH 2016," Institute of International Finance, Washington, DC, Mar. 2016. [Online]. Available: www.iif.com/publications/global-debt-monitor

[123] Central Intelligence Agency, "The World Factbook," 2016. https://www.cia.gov/library/publications/the-world-factbook/geos/xx.html

[124] US Social Security, "National Average Wage Index." https://www.ssa.gov/oact/cola/AWI.html

[125] C. M. Reinhart and K. S. Rogoff, "Is the 2007 US sub-prime financial crisis so different? An international historical comparison," National Bureau of Economic Research, Working Paper No. 13761, 2008.

[126] V. Ivashina and D. Scharfstein, "Bank lending during the financial crisis of 2008," *J. Financ. Econ.*, vol. 97, no. 3, pp. 319–338, 2010.

[127] D. H. Erkens, M. Hung, and P. Matos, "Corporate governance in the 2007–2008 financial crisis: Evidence from financial institutions worldwide," *J. Corp. Finance*, vol. 18, no. 2, pp. 389–411, 2012.

[128] K. V. Lins, H. Servaes, and A. Tamayo, "Social Capital, Trust, and Firm Performance: The Value of Corporate Social Responsibility during the Financial Crisis," *J. Finance*, 2017.

[129] A. B. of S. (ABS), "Labour force Australia: June 2015," Australian Bureau of Statistics, Canberra Australia, 2015.

[130] National Bureau of Economic Research, Inc., "US Business Cycle Expansions and Contractions," May 19, 2017. http://www.nber.org/cycles.html

[131] World Bank, "World Bank Open Data." data.worldbank.org (accessed Mar. 01, 2017).

[132] Australian Bureau of Statistics, "6523.0 - Household Income and Wealth, Australia, 2013-14," Apr. 09, 2015. http://www.abs.gov.au/AUSSTATS/abs@.nsf/DetailsPage/6523.02013-14?OpenDocument (accessed Jan. 03, 2017).

[133] worldatlas.com, "Worldatlas," *What is the Gini Coefficient?*, Jun. 24, 2017. http://www.worldatlas.com/articles/what-is-the-gini-coefficient.html (accessed Jun. 24, 2017).

[134] H. Görg, "Globalization, offshoring and jobs," in *In: M. Bacchetta and M. Jansen (eds) Making Globalization Socially Sustainable*, Geneva: International Labour Organization–World Trade Organization, 2011, pp. 21–48.

[135] A. Mitchell, "Globalization: Managing Multinationals - a comparison of offshoring and outsourcing strategies in UK and German multinational corporations," HBS Working Paper, 2015.

[136] "Numbeo Cost of Living," *Numbeo*, Apr. 23, 2015. http://www.numbeo.com/cost-of-living/ (accessed Apr. 23, 2015).

[137] Australian Bureau of Statistics, "5676.0 - Business Indicators, Australia, Dec 2016," Feb. 27, 2017. http://www.abs.gov.au/AUSSTATS/abs@.nsf/DetailsPage/5676.0Dec%202016?OpenDocument (accessed Jan. 03, 2017).

[138] U.S. Department of the Treasury, "U.S. Department of the Treasury," Mar. 01, 2017. www.treasury.gov (accessed Mar. 01, 2017).

[139] US Census, "US Census," Mar. 01, 2017. www.census.gov (accessed Mar. 01, 2017).

[140] U.S. Bureau of Economic Analysis, "U.S. Bureau of Economic Analysis," Mar. 01, 2017. www.bea.gov (accessed Mar. 01, 2017).

[141] Australian Bureau of Statistics, "Australian Bureau of Statistics," Mar. 01, 2017. www.abs.gov.au (accessed Mar. 01, 2017).

[142] Australian Council of Social Services and Social Policy Research Centre, UNSW, "Poverty in Australia 2016," 2016. http://www.acoss.org.au/wp-content/uploads/2016/10/Poverty-in-Australia-2016.pdf

[143] B. D. Proctor, J. L. Semega, and M. A. Kollar, "Income and Poverty in the United States: 2015," US Census Bureau, Sep. 2016. [Online]. Available: https://www.census.gov/library/publications/2016/demo/p60-256.html

[144] H. Bhorat, "A Universal Income Grant Scheme for South Africa: An Empirical Assessment," 2002.

[145] P. Van Parijs, "Basic income: a simple and powerful idea for the twenty-first century," *Polit. Soc.*, vol. 32, no. 1, pp. 7–39, 2004.

[146] G. Standing, *Promoting Income Security as a Right: Europe and North America*. London: Anthem Press, 2005.

[147] L. Willmore, "Universal pensions for developing countries," *World Dev.*, vol. 35, no. 1, pp. 24–51, 2007.

[148] D. Tondani, "Universal Basic Income and Negative Income Tax: Two Different Ways of Thinking Redistribution," *J. Socio-Econ.*, vol. 38, no. 2, pp. 246–255, 2009.

[149] U. Colombino and E. Narazani, "Designing a universal income support mechanism for Italy. An exploratory tour," *Basic Income Stud.*, vol. 8, no. 1, pp. 1–17, 2013.

[150] J. M. Mays, "Countering disablism: An alternative universal income support system based on egalitarianism," *Scand. J. Disabil. Res.*, vol. 18, no. 2, pp. 106–117, 2016.

[151] Davidson M, Saunders, P, Bradbury, B, and Wong, M, *Poverty in Australia 2018*. Sydney: ACOSS/UNSW, 2018. [Online]. Available: https://www.acoss.org.au/wp-content/uploads/2018/10/ACOSS_Poverty-in-Australia-Report_Web-Final.pdf

[152] S. R. Khandker, "Microfinance and poverty: Evidence using panel data from Bangladesh," *World Bank Econ. Rev.*, vol. 19, no. 2, pp. 263–286, 2005.

[153] B. Armendáriz de Aghion and J. Morduch, "Microfinance beyond group lending," *Econ. Transit.*, vol. 8, no. 2, pp. 401–420, 2000.

[154] K. Rogoff, "Why not a global currency?," *Am. Econ. Rev.*, vol. 91, no. 2, pp. 243–247, 2001.

[155] P. Arestis, S. Basu, and S. Mallick, "Financial globalization: the need for a single currency and a global central bank," *J. Post Keynes. Econ.*, vol. 27, no. 3, pp. 507–531, 2005.

Bibliography

[156] B. J. Moore, "A Global Currency for a Global Economy," *J. Post Keynes. Econ.*, vol. 26, no. 4, pp. 631–653, 2004.

[157] K. Sajnoski and V. Madzova, "Globalization and global currency," pp. 395–403, 2013.

[158] J. Haran, "Globalization of Global Currency," *EconWorld2017*, no. The Sixth International Conference in Economics, Jul. 2017.

[159] R. A. Easterlin, "Income and Happiness: Towards a Unified Theory," *Econ. J.*, vol. 111, no. 473, pp. 465–484, 2001.

[160] R. Di Tella, J. Haisken-De New, and R. MacCulloch, "Happiness Adaptation to Income and to Status in an Individual Panel," *J. Econ. Behav. Organ.*, vol. 76, no. 3, pp. 834–852, 2010.

[161] K. Kushlev, E. W. Dunn, and R. E. Lucas, "Higher Income Is Associated with Less Daily Sadness but Not More Daily Happiness," *Soc. Psychol. Personal. Sci.*, vol. 6, no. 5, pp. 483–489, 2015.

* 9 7 8 0 6 4 8 1 8 6 1 6 8 *